Leisure Life

ONE WEEK LOAN

*Leisu[...]
the s[...]
class [...]
tiviti[...]
centr[...]
leisur[...]
its rel[...]
of th[...]

Th[...]
of th[...]
ticate[...]
theor[...]
new [...]

*Le[...]
appro[...]
maki[...]
studi[...]

Tony
Sheff[...]

Leisure Life

Myth, Masculinity and Modernity

Tony Blackshaw

Routledge
Taylor & Francis Group

LONDON AND NEW YORK

First published 2003
by Routledge
11 New Fetter Lane, London EC4P 4EE

Simultaneously published in the USA and Canada
by Routledge
29 West 35th Street, New York, NY 10001

Routledge is an imprint of the Taylor & Francis Group

Typeset in Times and Gill by BC Typesetting, Bristol
Printed and bound in Great Britain by
MPG Books Ltd, Bodmin

British Library Cataloguing in Publication Data
A catalogue record for this book is available from the British Library

Library of Congress Cataloging in Publication Data
Blackshaw, Tony, 1960–
    Leisure life: myth, masculinity, and modernity/Tony Blackshaw.
        p.   cm.
    Includes bibliographical references and index.
    ISBN 0–415–27072–3 – ISBN 0–415–27073–1 (pbk.)
    1. Men–England–Leeds–Social conditions.
    2. Men–England–Leeds–Social life and customs.
    3. Working class–England–Leeds–Social life and customs.
    4. Leisure–Social aspects–England–Leeds.
    5. Masculinity–England–Leeds. I. Title.

HQ1090.7.G7 B53 2003
305.31′09428′19–dc21   2002036786

ISBN 0–415–27073–1 (pbk)
ISBN 0–415–27072–3 (hbk)

Contents

Preface

This book is about the consequences of living in the individualised society (Bauman, 2001a). The theme that sets the backdrop against which this predicament is explored is leisure – specifically, the salience of leisure for working-class men. The book is about the distinctive leisure lifestyles and the sense of belonging associated with a particular group of working-class men that I am calling the leisure life-world of 'the lads'. Three aspects of this leisure life-world loom large in this analysis: myth, masculinity and modernity. In exploring these three themes, the book focuses on the extent to which these 'lads' collectively seek to preserve existing lifestyles and conceptions of self-identity and community. It shows that 'the lads'' leisure is key, as it provides them with the time and space for the making and the articulation of a spurious sense of belonging and certainty.

The book sews together ethnography, social history, personal history and autobiography to show that a particular form of working-class masculine behaviour is the key way of expressing the norms and values of the discourse of this life-world, which provides a form of ontological security for resisting the cultural and material practices of recent gender change. The central argument that runs as a thread throughout the book is that leisure is salient for 'the lads', because it provides the means by which they can challenge and undermine the vicissitudes of a contemporary liquid modernity (Bauman, 2000a) where it is no longer sufficient, socially, culturally, politically or economically, to be a 'traditional' working-class man.

Today we live in a world where working-class men, in particular, have been forced to renegotiate their conceptions of masculinity as socially constructed phenomena. However, it is the argument of this book that, contrary to this deconstruction of a particular form of hegemonic masculinity, when each of the men in this study makes his leisure with 'the lads' the centre of his attention, life *appears* still to be of a more 'solid' and certain kind. Given what each of 'the lads' wants – diversion, escape, excitement, combined with a sense of love, comradeship and community *without any harsh demands on their commitment* – I show that they are extremely well served by the vicissitudes of this leisure life-world. The conclusions emerging from this detailed analysis are, however, more wide-ranging. For it will be argued that the phenomenon of this leisure life-world is centrally important not only for those people involved but also for understanding one of the key roles of leisure in liquid modernity.

In embarking on the initial research project it never entered my head that I would be writing a book so ambitious in scope. My original intention was to represent as accurately as I possibly could the magic realism associated with this leisure life-world. Wanting to avoid charges of painting a picture of a leisure life-world sugared with succour, I set out to represent the 'lads' warts and all, with their demons, misdeeds and awfulness intact. I wanted to write a book that would enable the reader to see 'the lads'' Leeds as the living, breathing enigma that it is: on the one hand individualised, self-serving, avaricious, repulsive, violent, offensive, but on the other hand a contingent unity, a life-world of being-with and being-for which is both welcoming and affable, even compassionate. In stripping 'the lads' of their masks I wanted to open up their insecurities and the ambivalence associated with this leisure world to analytical scrutiny. I also wanted to make 'the lads' themselves less objects of inquiry than as human as I possibly could. Thus I employed a very particular approach to ethnographic writing, itself a product of my own interpretation of a range of contemporary theory, which sought to problematise conventional approaches to doing qualitative research.

This book is located in the realm of sociology, hermeneutics, ethnography and cultural studies, and one of its main challenges is of sketching a portrait of leisure, community, social identity formation and self-reflexivity which allows us to get beyond the protocols that divide the moderns (e.g. Roberts, 1999) and the postmoderns (e.g. Rojek, 1995) in leisure studies. In so doing the book also illustrates that the slide from concepts such as social class, community and homogeneity to difference, individualism and heterogeneity in the leisure studies literature has been too hurried, simplistic, inviting a skewing of both material and discursive practices as they are lived through and locally experienced in the quotidian of everyday life. The book argues that the figure of 'the lad' must be understood as a character in a plot, which is part of the wider story of modernity. The concept of 'the lad' and the discourse of the leisure life-world thus become of particular relevance for fleshing out one of the key aims of the book, which is to add to the ongoing debate on how we can think and understand modernity and post-modernity. The book suggests that the dichotomy of modern leisure and postmodern leisure is a spurious dichotomy that needs to be deconstructed to make visible in leisure studies the exemplification of an alternative approach with which to explicate contemporary leisure. By the means of drawing on a wealth of research evidence the book also shows that everyday life is much more complicated than library-based theorising in leisure studies (Rojek, 1995, 2000) is wont to acknowledge.

If Paul Willis's *Learning to Labour* (1977) showed how Anthony Giddens's abstract social theory could be applied to a counter-school culture, this book shows most evocatively how Zygmunt Bauman's sociology can be put to use, but in a more deliberately specific way which is both more rigorously and precisely applied and obviously more up to date. In this way the book combines an ethnographic research approach with a thoroughgoing commentary on Bauman's work with some exceptional insights to show the relevance of his sociology to questions of leisure and popular culture today by extending social theorising to issues grounded in the quotidian of leisure experience.

Bauman was one of the first major sociologists to write extensively and affirmingly on the topic of postmodernity. However, whereas he was once unhesitant about describing and theorising postmodernity in an open way, a certain reticence in this connection has appeared in his most recent writings (Bauman, 2000a, 2001a). Bauman (2000a, 2002) now prefers the terms 'solid' modernity and 'liquid' modernity as opposed to 'modernity' and 'postmodernity'. It should be stressed, however, that this change in focus merely marks a tactical shift in Bauman's work. Indeed, the ideas of freedom and equality remain as ever the cornerstones of his critical project. This shift in emphasis should really come as no surprise to us, however, given the irrepressible proliferation of discourses on the idea of the postmodern in recent years. Theoreticians – often diametrically opposed – have seemed determined to outbid each other in their zeal to reveal the 'truth' about the postmodern, rendering the term almost devoid of any critical use value.

Be that as it may, Bauman has always been very clear on this issue: his opinion has never been that there is a new condition of postmodernity, more that in the last twenty years or so it has become very apparent that sociology needed to develop an alternative sensibility with which to think and understand modernity. And it is Bauman himself who has shaped some of the most challenging ideas surrounding this emerging critical discourse. One of the key aims of this book is to elucidate, interpret and apply to the problematic of the leisure life-world a full range of the critical discussions that Bauman has initiated. Yet rather than drawing on the explicitly 'postmodern' focus associated with Bauman's writings in the 1990s, the book will draw much more on the discourse associated with his current 'liquid' perspective of modernity, which allows me to make better sense of the changes and continuities associated with the leisure life-world of 'the lads' while at the same time overcoming the semantic confusion generated by the idea of the postmodern.

This book shares another thing in common with Bauman's project. This is the way it develops through the analysis of the leisure life-world of 'the lads' a critical inquiry into the possibilities of the sociological imagination. What is offered in Bauman's sociology is a shift in the hermeneutics of inquiry. Bauman (2002) replaces orthodox sociology with a form of sociological hermeneutics, which quite properly endeavours to find the meaning of social phenomena in the conditions in which people conduct their lives. Drawing on this approach, I explore the connections between my research findings and extant theory, and I do so through readings of a number of theoretical positions, from classical sociology to anthropology, from cultural studies to hermeneutics and poststructuralism, from postmodernism back to contemporary sociology. In this way the book seeks to maintain the necessity of sociology at the same time as questioning sociology itself from a position which resists the endeavours of sociology to assign to it merely a sociological way of understanding the social world.

The book is also methodologically sophisticated and, contrary to most cultural studies work done during the 1980s and 1990s, it is not fixated on media or literary studies. It was the turn towards the textual and the discursive at the expense of researching the social that led me 'back forward' to the cultural studies tradition exemplified in Hoggart's *The Uses of Literacy* (1957) and Hobbs's *Doing the Business* (1988) which pays close attention to the lived experience of culture. It is imperative that cultural studies are able to refocus their critical gaze beyond media signification to once again perceive what should be their meat and drink: the quotidian of everyday life. McRobbie (1994) enters a plea for ethnography conducted through 'interactive research on groups and individuals who are more than just audiences for texts'. This book is a response to that plea.

In shifting back to go forward the book also moves away from traditional ethnographic approaches to provide a convincing conciliation of Foucault's (1980a) anti-realist methodological approach with ethnography. A more concretely grounded understanding of the work of Foucault here is recovered and a conversation with him here is continued. This involves a sort of reinterpretation and reconstruction of my own, in which the 'story' of 'the lads' is scripted as a response as much to the limits of ethnography and its associated methodologies as to the literary turn in cultural studies, addressing a course of events which both define and make real the historico-cultural constitution of this leisure life-world. This approach deals squarely with the poststructuralist challenge to ethnography. That is, ethnography's over-investment in the idea of the rational, thinking 'subject'. But if the poststructuralists, and Foucault in particular, rightly alert researchers to the efficacy of exploring discourse as 'social' practice, under this alternative schema the individual ultimately 'disappears' and there can only be interaction between pre-existing 'subject' positions in systems of discourse. I reasoned, however, that to deny the significance of individual agency would be to limit my understanding of the leisure life-world in a manner analogous to the restrictive focus on what individuals say and do, which Foucault's research agenda seeks to address. Thus I employ here an alternative approach to the ethnographic imagination, itself a product of my own interpretation of a range of contemporary theory, which seeks to problematise conventional ethnographic approaches to doing research.

From Foucault the book also shows that ethnographers are challenged to think far beyond the conventional reading and writing schemas that have become normative for anthropology, sociology and cultural studies. The process of narration, which involves character formation and the telling the stories of 'the lads', is achieved through 'thick description' (Geertz, 1973), which is best described as a form of 'tactics' for revealing the realism of both material and discursive events so as to absorb the reader into the leisure life-world. Specifically, a proper emphasis on the relation between discursive practices (Foucault) and material realism (ethnography) as an amalgam, without reduction of one to the other, provides the necessary corrective to the postmodern predilection for textuality, where 'signs' replace reality, and the form of academic reportage associated with traditional ethnographic accounts. This approach to writing allows the culture of the 'field' to 'reveal itself' to the reader, to represent the 'self-evidential reality' of the world it reflects. Essentially the way the book is written can be seen as an attempt to extend the reach of the leisure life-world of 'the lads' to readers who are not familiar with such a world in order to illuminate that world for them in all its ambivalent complexity.

As the reader will see, 'the lads' have their own version of the modern obsession with orderliness which in the leisure life-world is, to use one of Bauman's expressions, 'urgently undertaken and doggedly pursued'. What prompts them to pursue this utopia is the search for some order in a 'liquid' world of endemic disorder and it is in their leisure lives where 'the lads' perceive that utopia can be achieved. What the leisure life-world makes real is what Bauman (2001b) describes as the 'already existing reality', which is what 'the lads' strive for in their own version of the war against ambivalence (Bauman, 1991). The book attempts to capture this hybrid existence, balanced as it is between liquid torment and a solid modernity of leisure experience, to establish the idea of how a particular modern, masculine life-world can be perceived as a reality, to the extent that it becomes, albeit ephemerally, *the* whole world. In this sense it is shown that the leisure life-world can be understood as a metaphor for liquid modernity.

The book also explores what this implies for those who belong to that world (us) and those who do not (them). It explores too what 'the lads' tend to present as inherently natural, but which are in fact contingent and discursively rationalised interpretations of the Other. As the reader will soon become aware the leisure life-world is full of actions, images, language and gestures which once served in a more 'solid' modernity as a construct of a notion of a particular kind of working-class masculinity. Evidence will suggest that this leisure life-world offers its incumbents a sense of something rather bizarre: intimations of a working-class culture born of solid modernity, a phenomenon that, in liquid modernity, is alive and yet lifeless, real but illusory.

If this book is, then, first and foremost an ethnographic account of this leisure life-world, it can also be read as a kind of cultural lament on my own part. If you are born and brought up in a culture to which you are utterly devoted, as I was, and at some point you reach a point where what you once took for granted doesn't seem to be the same any more, you are bound to feel, particularly with the world fragmented and liquefied as it is today, as I do, that you have lost something very precious, safe. I don't really believe in the fantasy of the leisure life-world any more. Yet I must admit, the leisure life-world is a phenomenon which still occupies me today. I feel ambivalent towards it: I abhor some of it, but respect most of it. As the ethnographer I sometimes felt as if I was operating in a no-man's-land, neither with nor without 'the lads', simultaneously looking in and looking out, researching an incredulous world where my past and present coexisted. This revealed to me a sense of my distance from the academy, too. For I also appreciate 'the lads'' culture, which is also part of my culture. And I appreciate what 'the lads' attempt to sustain in such uncertain times as these. This book will not really be overly critical of 'the lads', then, it will merely attempt to put some flesh on the complex forces that both shaped and constrained the leisure lives of a group of working-class men during the period of the late 1990s.

Acknowledgements

The majority of the research for this book depended on and benefited from a PhD bursary at Leeds Metropolitan University between January 1996 and April 1999. At Leeds I received excellent support and advice from my supervisory team. I should like to thank Jonathan Long, John Spink and Mick Totten. To Sofian Omar Fauzee my thanks are due because he is a 'top man'. I also received support and encouragement from the other postgraduates in the School of Leisure and Sports Studies and I should like to thank, in particular, Jon Dart and Caroline Davies. Special thanks are also due to Tim Crabbe. I am grateful to him for his interest and support and the friendship I have gained through working with him at Sheffield Hallam University. For lots of reasons, I should like to thank Fiona, Siobhan and Nicky. Finally, a big thank-you must go to 'the lads', without whom none of this would have been possible.

T.B.

Chapter 1

Introduction

The leisure life-world of 'the lads'

It was eight o'clock on Friday night, in Leeds city centre. The pub was at the upper end of Eastgate, before it meets the Headrow. The architecture was Edwardian, like many of the other buildings around there. It looked oppressive, with its decades of Leeds subsistence, and it was dirty: stained with acid rain, welkin muck and starling shit. We entered the pub, not for any particular reason, but simply because it seemed to be the most natural place for us to be, the uncultivated house fittings and furbishing a part of our sense of belonging. The pub was very much part of our Leeds, 'town', an imaginary Leeds dislocated by time, ostensibly narrow, among parts of which we regularly meandered across well worn tracks. Like the atmosphere, everything in the pub seemed familiar to us: the sense of heady conviviality, the sort of women there, the gamut of working-class male strangers, more so the prospect of heavy alcohol consumption. You could say the barman was in some sense ours, too, for before we had so much got through the doors his fat, tattooed fingers were already fumbling in the cooler at the back of the bar. Even our choice of drinks was part of this communal ritual, for he knew which one we would choose before we said it.

'All right, lads. Carlsberg lager: only a £1 a bottle until ten o'clock,' he said, unfastening the first of six bottle tops.

As the evening progressed it seemed to collide with so many other evenings that the smallest actions were both burdened with the past and imbricated unconditionally with the future. And when one of 'the lads', Sean, a tall, powerfully built man, some four months past thirty-four years, returned from having his second piss explaining that he had swayed accidentally against some dickhead in the packed corridor leading back into the bar, we knew what was in prospect. The spastic had said something on the lines of 'Watch who you're pushin', y' fucker.' Sean said he laughed in his face and smiled at his bird, but had decided to leave it at that.

The whole situation became straight away for us all at once familiar, repetitive and new. It was like a video-recording often replayed, only this time it was once again real. We already knew that Sean was going to 'have' the cunt despite what he had said, because he had looked deadly when he returned from the toilet. He had immediately got in another round before sitting down with a fresh Carlsberg, with which he was still measuring the remainder of the fuckhead's life with large gulps from the bottle, when the silly twat came up to our table. We could sense that events would make a casualty of the spastic before very much longer.

The brave one, who might as well have had 'I am a stupid cunt' tattooed on his forehead, was staring at Sean, contemplating his opponent like a petulant football star, while his bird and spazwit mates looked on from a safe distance. In his mid-twenties, he was medium height, belligerent-looking and thin as a rake. He wore a checked Ben Sherman shirt outside a pair of white jeans. His thin blond hair was long and brushed back at the front and hung in a short mane down the back. His face was small and white, and blemished with the smallest of Borstal spots. The cunt wanted to be Ronan Keating, and although he was let down by the tattoo, it was mostly his eyes that wrecked his ambitions, because they each appeared to be looking in different directions.

'What's y' game, long bastard?' said the Boyzone wannabe.

It was still a startling image, even if Sean's response was expected and solicited. Moreover, it offered itself as a tantalising metaphor for the leisure life-world. With an understanding that comes from a wealth of experience of knowing what to do on such occasions, it was the way in which Sean made not so much a rational decision as a reflexive deliverance that did it. He said nothing before nutting the cunt between the eyes and punching him in the stomach. Ronan the Rake looked as if he wanted to be sick as he fell prostrate on to the ground.

As Sean's head did the strabotomy our collective past suffused us at once like over-the-top kitsch emptying into the present. Experiences common to us all geysered out of our minds, most of them not reaching our mouths. David 'D-ranged', however, was garrulous and he wanted to let the rest of the world know about 'the lads'; and he did. 'Anybody else want some of that?' he challenged the rest of the pub. Our body language suggested that the rest of 'the lads' concurred. The leisure life-world now was an exercise in technicolor, as it once again raced to its culmination. In it the whole world seemed much clearer. Incandescent, its incumbents glowed, as it was we who were now the stars of our own Friday-night show.

For a short while the pub was in a mild state of confusion. A couple of split-arses edged along the walls to avoid the *mêlée* as they made for the toilets, faces uninterested. A party of spoonhead bastards looked on nonchalantly at the headbutted one on the floor, who, without wasting any time, cowered back towards his bird and friends, two of whom berated him at once for his naive petulance. The bar staff were eventually heard shouting for the bouncers to intervene, but they need not have bothered, for it was quickly all over.

'Come on, let's go,' somebody said. And we did.

Ten months later. I was on the road, which has not been developed with pedestrians in mind, that leads the car driver towards the White Rose Centre, a shopping mall of barely one year, from where I could make out, in E. W. Burgess's terminology, the intermediate area of the city between the commuters' and the residential zones. But, at the point of that thought, and as if acting as an *aide-mémoire* to my crapulent brain, the sun peeped out from behind the wall of cumulonimbus to shine on the dilapidated estate of fifty or sixty council malsonettes, beyond the White Rose's moat (no doubt designed as if to keep out the estate's tenants), to remind me that Leeds is not at all characteristic of Burgess's early twentieth-century Chicago. The urban spatial structure of Leeds is postmodern, reflecting the ambivalences of a city dedifferentiated in a post-industrialising process.

On this Saturday the estate on the other side of the moat was punctuated with properties tinned up for security reasons, which stood out like black pegs in an already rapidly decaying set of teeth. Juxtaposed with the medieval Stank's Tithe Barn, the White Rose and the Arlington Business Centre, and the other steel and glass structures which compose the postmodern skyline in this part of south Leeds, the estate looked like an outsider in a world of avant-garde architecture, a flawed display at an exhibition to which it hadn't been invited.

Early Saturday morning's scrub of shoppers had swelled to a forest of regimental footsloggers. I was now walking through the busy department stores and eventually crossed the boundary which marks the starting point of what is ironically called Sainsbury's 'Savacentre', a massive supermarket sandwiched between the last remaining three-quarters of the White Rose and the car park. The windows of the supermarket were draped with logotype World Cup advertising, with the words 'Nestlé Nesquik: the Official Breakfast Cereal for France 98' repeated between the frames.

In the near distance I spotted a familiar frame walking towards the open-plan entrance. The tall, powerfully built man, now some six weeks past thirty-five years, was wearing a familiar neck of light brown hair: shaved to number one and tapered, not squared. Sean was walking determinedly, left hand sunk into the pocket of the rain-coat worn over his Levi jacket and matching jeans, his Kicker boots with tag displayed prominently: 'a lad's' uniform. He carefully drew on the last remnants of the cigarette he was holding in his right hand, before entering the main shopping area of the supermarket. Two young girls accompanied him down the aisle, chatting, oblivious to the crowds as they walked quickly past the electrical goods. They knew that their dad was in a hurry. I decided I would catch up with Sean after he had done his shopping.

In the meanwhile I saw another man I once knew. He was not one of 'the lads'. He was Jimmy Ronson and he was treading thin air as he endeavoured to get round the store on this day. Jimmy looked as if he had a few less teeth than he did the last time I saw him, which was when he was floating, intoxicated, around a Scandinavian super-market for flawed consumers, shoving 79p frozen dinners down his trousers. He had obviously moved up-market.

This time he looked as though he was in dire need of whatever shit he was pumping into his body at the time. His hair was wet, his face and body were twitching and his arms and left leg jerked about inces-santly. Seen as a whole, his klutzy performance reminded me of that one performed by the guitarist in the band Fine Young Cannibals when it played the song 'Johnny, why don't you come on home?' during the 1980s. What distinguished Jimmy from the man who played to Johnny, however, was that Jimmy looked as if he was about to burst. Could Jimmy stay still long enough to lift something? Would he risk trying to make it through the tills?

I looked at the other trolley pushers around me. Nobody else watched Jimmy. Surprising, this, for people who inhere these places usually stare at men such as Jimmy, who looks like one of those tattooed underclass white people often seen modelling for the covers of social housing organisation annual reports. I didn't want him to get caught thieving, but in my imagination I implored all the people there to watch him, and then perhaps they might have seen from Jimmy's face what hard work is involved in raising the money to buy a wrap of 'brown' heroin, which today in inner-city Leeds costs less than a two-litre bottle of White Lightning cider. As he went out of my view I thought to myself that Jimmy Ronson was much more a reminder of our present condition than was the architectural skyline I had earlier observed outside.

I heard Sean coming closer to his turn at the till – beep, beep, beep, as the cashier shoved through the mountains of shopping. I tried to catch his attention but I had to squeeze my eyes shut against the slight hangover that I could scarcely distinguish from the shriek of the myriad electronic scanners in the store.

'You look well rough. Too many beers last night?'

Sean walked towards me, his sharp blue eyes smiling warm-heartedly. He put his arm around my shoulders and squeezed.

'I've got some paracetamols in t' trolley. Do y' want some? (Laughing.)

He walked back towards his girls.

'Wait a minute, Tone. I'll be wi' yer in a tick.'

I watched as Sean took the two girls in his massive arms and held each of them for a few seconds: firmly, warmly, protectively. Safe. Then he bent down and kissed each gently on the lips, before giving them money to buy a magazine and sweets. He told them verbally not to talk to any strangers, and his eyes made it known to them that they would find him outside the main doors, in the car park, talking to me.

We stepped outside the front entrance. The intermittent rain had stopped and there was a mild breeze that felt good. Sean pulled a packet of Embassy Regal from the pocket of his denim jacket and took out a cigarette. He struck a match with the skill of a smoker of twenty-plus years and inhaled deeply, then ran his left hand through his slick-backed hair. I stared at him for a moment, at his handsome face and his almost outdated uniform, the sort that belonged more to a 1970s Weston than to the middle-class White Rose shopping centre.

'What you up to, cunty?' he said endearingly.

'Did you see Jimmy Ronson in there?'

'Yeah, I gave him a wide birth. The dirty robbin' cunt. He's never lifted a finger and he wa' always a robbin' cunt, even at school. He's fucked out on drugs. Even his family a' fuckin' wasters' have rock-all to do wi' him nowadays.'

'Long time, no see, anyway.'

'Yeah, I 'ant been out wi' t' lads for a couple a month, y' know. Have you?'

I ignored his question. 'Why?'

'Mi work, an' our lass's always workin'. Like today, I'm lookin' after t' young'ns. She's workin' till four o'clock. That's why I 'ave to do t' shoppin' an' that. I should be out at back end a' next month, though. Anyway, I've got to shoot off, mi old lady an' old man are comin' over from Ireland this weekend. I'll see y' soon, Tone. Hey, by the way, y' look a bit rough.'

'I'm out tonight. I saw Stout in t' Farmer's Arms last night and he said that him and Stevey are goin' in town for a few. I said I'd join 'em. Do you fancy it?'

'Can't make it, Tone. Sorry.'

Sean waved his right hand in the air, then turned towards the doors near to the magazine rack. As he did I saw an unfamiliar look on his face. He looked a forlorn figure as he stared into the shopping centre, looking for his girls. Those that were sharp blue only a few minutes ago were now large, sad eyes. I thought that I saw a tear trickling down his cheek, however, I definitely must have been wrong. Perhaps it was the hangover. I have never seen Sean cry when he is sober.

Starting points: the problem of 'synthetic' sociology

The course of events described in the opening episode at the pub are evidently contemporaneous, but I should like to argue that they have an immutable quality that has remained stable for decades, perhaps for centuries. I suggest this is so because pub brawls are old hat and so are men, such as Sean and Ronan, who are not happy unless they are making an enemy. There is also a consistency in the ways 'the lads' construct an imaginary sense of community in the first episode, as it is established through their shared symbols and participation in communal rituals within and without the pub. This historical continuity in local social relations is well documented in the community studies literature (Hoggart, 1957; Dennis *et al.*, 1969; Cohen, 1985).

Just the reverse, however, the events described in the second episode, observed in isolation, but understood also in the process of the juxtaposition, are purely contemporaneous. For as the representations of the cityscape of Leeds are revealed, and the features and actions of the characters come alive in the narratives, it becomes evidently clear that the second episode and the juxtaposition could have been located only in another time. Indeed, for even if the White Rose shopping mall wants to take itself seriously as the Meadowhall of Leeds, which it does, both the adjacent council estate and people like Jimmy Ronson serve only to subvert this seriousness with their own absurd inappropriateness. Seen in an analogous process, the men in the narratives represent an image of masculinity that is equally absurd and exhausted in the context of contemporary gender relations. Yet, at the very moment that we are led to believe that Sean is the epitome of the archetypal dinosaur and 'hard' man, the second episode reveals him to be the puritan, moralist 'new' man and intimate and receptive dad, rolled into one. This observation is an incongruity that undermines our initial understanding of Sean and disrupts the coherent order of things established in the first episode. I could go on. For as the juxtaposition unfolds, revealed are complex patterns and processes, both material and discursive in design, of de-differentiation, deconstruction (of hegemonic masculinity), decentredness, fragmentation and polarisation, uncertainty, risk, contingency, ambivalence and irony. The episodes are, to be sure, manifestations of a predicament created by recent structural transformations that would not have been the concern of sociology even, say, fifteen years ago.

This book is about the salience of leisure for working-class men in a sociality undergoing profound transformations. What I have set out below is the outcome of an in-depth study of leisure in liquid modernity (Bauman, 2000a). Given the subject matter, and the way I am positioned within the research process (I was brought up with 'the lads' in the study), the theoretical orientation of the book is distinguishable from the 'synthetic' tradition (Mestrovic, 1998) in contemporary sociological thought, based on agency and structure, subject and object, and so on.[1] I shall argue that this process of distinguishing between two types of sociology, and by implication two processes of 'methodology', is both relevant and necessary, because the ontological and epistemological orientation of this 'synthetic' tradition is not equipped to undertake the task of this book. To substantiate the argument, I shall, in the first instance, discuss this assertion.

The view that describes the individual and communal leisure experience of the type embraced by 'the lads', and discussed above in the episodes, as a 'separation' from 'normal' life, a liminal stage of margin (Shields, 1991; Rojek, 1995), a 'time-out' response (Moore, 1994) to 'paramount reality' (Cohen and Taylor, 1992) is one that is still authoritative in sociology. From this point of view, leisure is important in the sense that it provides liminoid situations (Turner and Turner, 1978) which contribute to the functional equilibrium of the social system (Parsons, 1951). For as Rojek (1995: 88) points out, when thought about in this sense, leisure thresholds of spontaneity and manumission cannot at any time be of any real facility, because although they may subvert 'reality', by giving rise to social conflict, challenging the *status quo* or even facilitating a spurious sense of belonging with participants, they remain 'inauthentic', or 'safe', because they do not survive the return to 'normality'. For Rojek, as for Turner (1973), inside the leisure liminoid both time and space become changed, but 'real' time and space remain out there, undisturbed.

There exists a similar problem in neo-Marxist accounts. Marcuse (1970: 179–80) pre-empts the postmodernists when he argues that, by the middle of the twentieth century, 'repressive reason gives way to a new *rationality of gratification* in which reason and happiness converge'. And in marked contrast to Featherstone (1991), who discusses the notion that in what he describes as postmodernity we are moving towards a classless mass society where 'everyone can be anyone' Marcuse is propagating what was to become one of the most celebrated interpretations of the ways in which the advanced capitalist economy was beginning to reduce the revolutionary potential of the working classes through the market place (Marcuse, 1972). Embodied in the process of *rationality of gratification* are new possibilities for the exploitation of the working classes.

For Marcuse, in high modernity, industrial capitalism is usurped by commodity capitalism, and within this process the mechanisms of the market transform workers into consumers. Whereas capitalism in early modernity required asceticism – 'the constraint on impulse, the limiting of self-expression' (Weber, 1930; Tawney, 1958), it now requires hedonism, or the 'will to happiness' (Bauman, 1997), through acts of leisure, pleasure and self-gratification. The logic of late capitalism now invades every sphere of our lives and *even* exploits the working classes through their leisure and pleasure pursuits. From this point of view, 'the lads'' actions can be interpreted as a form of labour that has a productive value, or surplus value, which is being exploited under capitalism. From this viewpoint 'the lads' can be seen to be alienated, in the sense that they have lost objective control over who they are, or who they are striving to be.

In a prodigious project, which to a large extent departs from earlier, and often crude, Marxian accounts, Habermas attempts to build on the earlier work of the Frankfurt school by giving recognition to communication and the media more readily than to the labour process. As Poster (1994) suggests, for Habermas, as for Baudrillard, the sign turns out to be of central significance. Yet Habermas's political objectives are far more ambitious than Baudrillard's. Indeed, where the latter locates the seeds of dissent in the nihilism of consumer culture – 'You want us to consume? OK, let's consume always more, and anything whatsoever; for any useless and absurd purpose' (Baudrillard, 1983: 46) – the former imagines political and spiritual emancipation in the 'ideal speech situation' (Habermas, 1979: 111–17). However, in embarking on this utopian adventure, Habermas's critical theory is confronted with the same quandary as Marcuse's sociology, that is, the problem of revealing structures of domination when no one is dominating, nothing is being dominated, and no ground exists for a principle of liberation from domination' (Poster, 1994: 81–2).

There also exists a different but related problem in the 'new wave' of writings on masculinities (see, for example, Connell, 1995; Horrocks, 1994; Mac An Ghaill, 1996; Seidler, 1994) which focus on the hegemony of masculinity to explore the multiplex of masculine behaviours and practices in a modern patriarchal society. These writings arguably oversimplify the masculinity debate in that they simply invert the logocentric modernist normalising principle by advancing theories which vilify men, such as 'the lads', instead of women (for a critique see Ryan, 1996). On top of that, masculinity theory carelessly advances the type of explanation it claims to be discordant with, in its own terms of reference, by promulgating a view that centres (rather than decentres) the shortcomings of inadequate modern men. The following quotation from Horrocks (1994: 67) elucidates the overall gist of this viewpoint: 'In becoming accomplices and agents of the patriarchal oppression of women, men are mutilated themselves psychologically . . . in hating women the male hates himself.'

Some ontological and epistemological questions

The structural functionalist account of Turner, the two respective neo-Marxian approaches adopted by Marcuse and Habermas and masculinity theory are very different at the level of their theoretical orientation. I mean this in the sense that, whereas Turner centres on flow-type experiences and societal co-operation, Marcuse and Habermas reckon with societal conflict, exploitation and false consciousness, and masculinity theory brings into focus the transformation of ideological formations away from women's domesticity to a more effectual and insidious form of hegemonic masculinity.

Despite these theoretical differences, however, each belongs to an Enlightenment tradition of thought which seeks to uncover the 'rational organisation of everyday social life' (Habermas, 1981), and that promulgates the idea of a *single* social system. Ontologically speaking, however, both essentialism and foundationalism remain a given to this type of social analysis. Consequently, each of the theories described above ends up elucidating an essentialist way of perceiving sociality, which comprehends *the* social world as a single coherent universe, or master narrative, identifying social reality as a reified structural entity, with a hierarchical 'order of things' (Foucault, 1973). Each perspective has a different priority in this 'order of things': Turner gives precedence to the 'needs' of the social system, Marcuse and Habermas to the class inequalities produced by advanced capitalism, and masculinity theory to the modern global gender order. However, in each case a reified conception of the 'world out there' is confirmed.

Alongside this ontological problem, and related to it, there remains another difficulty in understanding the sociology of 'the lads'' leisure experiences from each of these perspectives. This is their epistemological understanding of the organisational and social construction of time and space. Notwithstanding the impressive efforts of Anthony Giddens to transcend the normative tradition in mainstream sociological thought – which remains teleologically inspired – with his theory of time–space distanciation (Giddens, 1990), in most accounts space, but especially time, continues in the main to be under-theorised. As Jenks (1995: 144) points out, in the literature, more often than not, how space and time are known is considered with a 'categorical fixity and inviolability'. This is because the mainstream is dominated by a prevailing mind-set, which continues to promulgate a view of coherent, linear time that is oblivious to Natoli's (1997: 3) point that 'individuals can live in different reality frames although they *seem* to be sharing the same space at the same time' (my emphasis).

I am alluding to the quintessential point that it becomes unconvincing, epistemologically speaking, to think in terms which 'centre' reality, subjects, objects, experiences, desires, leisure, time, space or what have you. As Rojek (1995) shows, 'modernist' epistemological thinking no longer holds good – if it ever did – and there is much import in thinking about the sociology of leisure in ways that decentre the 'neatness' of modern theories, which tend to allude to centred, foundationalist and essentialist interpretations of the social world.

Assume that we tried to understand 'the lads' from a different epistemological position, adopted by poststructuralist theorists, such as Michel Foucault, which alerts us to the quintessential point that there are myriad ways in which people think about and know their own sense of reality; and that how the world is experienced is a matter for someone at some time and in some place. This is a view which supposes that every single way of knowing is situated ineluctably within the sense of reality or discourse that produces it. For example, in Foucault's (1979) own schema, the essentialist sense of reality is deferred to situate two senses of knowing about discipline and punishment within two – traditional and modern – reality frames, or discourses that produce them. Whereas actions and meanings tend to be 'centred' and taken for granted in orthodox sociological accounts, this alternative approach offers an interpretation that recognises their fragmentary grounds.

/This alternative position recognises also that time is fragmented into '*episodes*, each one cut from its past and its future, each one self-enclosed and self-contained. Time is no longer [thought of as] a river but a collection of ponds and pools' (Bauman, 1995: 91). Bauman is only partially right, of course, because although each episode of time is constructed and sanctioned within its own particular narrative, as it moves through time present, *en route* for time future, time past is inexorably wrapped up with it. For the past bears on all discourses and 'that means that temporal movement may not be progressive but regressive or may not move at all' (Natoli, 1997: 78). What Natoli makes explicit is the point that discourses are not without foundation, for 'habits cannot be changed at will' (Gitlin, 1995: 204).

In the selfsame way, to assume that social identities are today simply taken from 'secondary agencies and institutions, which stamp the biography of the individual and make that person dependent upon fashions, social policy, economic cycles and markets, contrary to the image of individual control which establishes itself in consciousness' (Beck, 1992: 131) is, as is Marcuse's Marxian account, not only an extremely questionable way of thinking about consumer choice but a patently limited way of understanding and describing the social world.

And, if in contrast to Beck, Giddens (1991) to some extent puts this anomaly right by identifying *re-embedding* mechanisms that take the form of new *habitats*, which 'unbind' time and weaken the coercive impact of the past (Bauman, 1992a), and with which the individual takes centre stage. He is guilty of marginalising the extent to which individuals, such as the working-class men in this study, for example, seek to preserve for themselves existing 'solidly' modern lifestyles and 'solidly' modern conceptions of self-identity. Conceptions which provide 'the lads' with a form of ontological security (Giddens, 1991) for resisting the cultural and material practices of rapidly transforming relations, where it is no longer enough to be a 'hard' man.

An alternative way of seeing the leisure life-world of 'the lads'

My position recognises that social actors can be embedded in multiple life-worlds and that any narrative of time and space is to a large extent contingent upon its own particular discourse. In this book I shall argue that, for 'the lads', the 'solidly' modern is required if their leisure lives are to proceed as 'normal'. Leisure provides the means by which they can challenge and undermine the 'irrationalities' of liquid modernity, where it is no longer sufficient, socially, culturally, politically or economically, to be a 'solid' modern man, and where modern men must renegotiate their conceptions of masculinity as socially constructed phenomena. The central argument of the book is that, contrary to the deconstruction of hegemonic masculinity, when each of them makes his leisure with 'the lads' the centre of his attention, life *appears* still to be of the more certain 'solid' modern world. I should like to argue that 'the lads' 'choose' to leisure alongside 'solid' modern versions of themselves of the kind that others have let pass them by.

The book follows a similar pattern to Foucault's work, in the sense that juxtaposition, as well as decentredness, is key to the analysis. The process of juxtaposition allows the thesis to be conceptualised and presented in a coherent and structured way by focusing on the dichotomy between Bauman's (2000a) idea of 'solid' modernity and 'liquid' modernity in relation to 'the lads'' leisure activities. This juxtaposing of the argument is made on the basis of the view that it is difficult to conceive a clear sense of the liquid modern 'disorder of things' without a concomitant understanding of the solid modern 'order of things'.

I am also proposing that 'the lads'' leisure experiences, and by definition their cultural resistance to the contemporary gender disorder, manifest themselves as hyperreal. However, I do not have in view a hyperreality in the sense that Baudrillard means – a depthless, 'hyperised' asociality. Postmodern social theory (Natoli, 1997) does not deny the existence of reality in Baudrillard's sense but suggests that we live in multiple representations of it. Time moves on but the leisure activities of 'the lads' remain fixed within a modern discourse. The past is key to 'the lads' because it institutes and maintains within the present what is absent. To be sure, 'the lads'' leisure lives are anything but simulation and are very real. Expressed in another way, the hyperreality of 'the lads'' leisure lives is best described as more modern than modern resistance to the material and discursive practices of liquid modernity. This understanding of the hyperreal presumes that 'solid' modern ideologies, perfectibilities, biases, prejudices, and the like, take on 'new' meanings in the 'liquid' leisure life-world of 'the lads'.

Leisure is the keystone of this predicament, as it provides the time and space for the making and the articulation of a spurious sense of certainty. Moreover, leisure is crucial to the maintenance of 'the lads'' sense of self and identity in liquid modernity. In their childhood, leisure provided the means by which those in working-class neighbourhoods were able to loosen the rigidity of a rationally ordered sociality. In their adulthood onwards, it provides the means to challenge and undermine what they perceive to be the 'irrationalities' of their current condition. In the leisure life-world, life appears still as a tightly structured working-class modernity.

The research approach enables the book to evince this leisure life-world as it is seen by 'the lads' and show how it is that the spatio-temporal configuration of their leisure activities needs a 'solidly' modernist past to enable it to go on in a particular way. For 'the lads' are of the time of the 'perfect world' conceived in 'solid' modernity, and 'one remaining forever identical with itself, a world in which the wisdom learnt today will remain wise tomorrow and the day after tomorrow, and in which the life skills acquired will retain their usefulness forever' (Bauman, 1997: 12). The significance of this approach is that it attempts to situate the narrative of this modernity of leisure experience in the sense of realism that constructs it (Hobbs, 1988).

To achieve this sense of realism, I explore the dialectical interplay between the material and discursive practices of 'the lads' and Others, most notably women, from the point of view of 'the lads'. In Foucault's (1973) sense, this means that I examine the masculine discourse of the leisure life-world of 'the lads' (what they know and say), their leisure practices (what they do and how they do it) and their institutional achievements (what conventions they carry out to know and do what they perceive they have to do) (Natoli, 1997: 6). *Pace* Moore (1994), this thesis remains nothing more than my own uncompromising attempt to describe the 'cultural imaginary' of the leisure life-world of 'the lads'. I will not be trying, in the ethnomethodological sense, to reconstruct the subjective reality of those in the field.

To summarise what this thesis entails, I should like to argue that it is the outcome of a cultural study of:

> the sort adumbrated, but not fully developed by, say Foucault . . . It [grounds] interpretive practices . . . ties morality and politics to local understandings, conditions, and resources. [It] is concretely situated in, and oriented to, local accountability structures, frameworks within which actors and actions are defined or define themselves in circumstantially relevant terms with reference to situated values. [It also elucidates] . . . the agonistic and resistive micropolitics . . . linked to local culture, [where individuals have to be] both responsive and

responsible to the practical contingencies and moralities of choice and action.

(Gubrium and Holstein, 1994: 699)

The 'lad' in me

This book, which undertakes to describe the 'cultural imaginary' (Castoriadis, 1987) of the leisure life-world of 'the lads', evolved from my initial idea that the starting points of research would be at selected locations and through contacts with individuals through community and friendships contacts in the Weston area of south Leeds. These were selected to provide access to different social networks. The key question underpinning the initial research proposal was the argument that, if (formerly) industrial urban communities are no longer sustained by work, to what extent (and how) are they supported by community leisure? Put simply, the project would seek to investigate the extent to which leisure is capable of creating its own 'communities'. However, growing theoretical contradictions were to throw into doubt and challenge this line of thinking, to such an extent that the thesis had to confront the not insubstantial problem of 'community' head-on.

As the research developed, it continued to concentrate on the leisure sites and wide-ranging social networks of Weston, but it came to focus on the particular social network of a group of working-class men with whom I had grown up. From this point onwards, I realised that the research would not just be about community leisure in Weston, it would be about the leisure life-world of 'the lads': my lifelong friends and acquaintances, with whom I had shared so much. This also meant that the study would be about their leisure life-world, my leisure life-world, our leisure life-world.

My introduction and admission to 'the lads' came about in a circuitous way. When I was eight my expanding family moved to south Leeds. The 'corporation' had refused my mam and dad a transfer to a bigger property and they were forced into owner occupation. What later came to be known as inner-city Weston was their upper limit. About a year later, during my early (and lonely) boyhood wanderings in Weston, I came across a tall, light brown-haired boy named Sean whose family had several months earlier moved into the locality from Ireland, via Glasgow. I quickly developed a friendship with Sean and his brothers Michael and Thomas. This also meant that I was no longer thought of as the 'new boy' by Scott, Colin and Stephen and the other lads in the area. I was elated at the prospect of being accepted into the fold, which was finally endorsed when the other children stopped singing to me that well honed Beatles song 'Get back' (to where you once belonged).

Time rolled on, and we found ourselves growing apart from Sean in the field of education. Being a 'left footer', he was forced to travel to a Roman Catholic high school in north Leeds. The rest of us either followed Richard

Hoggart by attending the grammar school in Hunslet or accompanied most
of the older lads in the area to the local boys' comprehensive. I went to the
grammar school in Hunslet, the local apogee of an ostensibly divisive education system. But going to school was no different from the local community
life of Weston, where we were also segregated residentially from the growing
number of Asian settlers in the area.

In the same manner that we loathed the 'Pakis' for taking over 'our' area,
we loathed school for curtailing our freedom and attempting to inculcate us
with its middle-class values, and we couldn't wait to leave. The only reason
we attended was to assert our masculinities – there were fights and more
fights – and to penetrate as many young women as possible. I left school
at sixteen and trained as a frozen food packer and fork lift truck driver in
Hunslet. The other 'lads' trained variously as bricklayers, painters, joiners,
electricians and labourers.

Work meant we had money to spend, and leisure meant the pub, the club
and the night club. Like the rest of 'the lads', I longed each working week for
Friday night and dreaded each end-of-the-weekend Monday morning. For,
as any 'lad' knows, Friday night is a 'real' night and Monday morning is
a 'post-real' morning, tinged with sadness, the loneliness of work and the
inevitable hangover. When the central goal in life is the weekend, everything
else in life is shaped around this purpose. But life moves on. Each of 'the lads'
has moved on.

Sean has moved on. However, he remains the personification of 'the lad' in
the late 1990s. While on a pragmatic level, and in conjunction with most of
his contemporaries, he is forced, through family, work and other commitments, for long periods, to reject 'the lads'' version of a legitimate lifestyle,
with its membership of a leisure life-world and weekends spent drinking,
pubbing and clubbing, deep down he misses with a vengeance this narrative that he only intermittently buys into, but always with a great deal of
enthusiasm. For underneath the facade of 'new' man Sean believes that
any 'lad' worth his salt should, in an ideal world, get down to the real
work of denuding his 'true' masculine self, with the other 'lads', of course.
These days, as we saw from the episodes, it is more difficult for Sean to
light upon his favourite transformative challenge. But if, for Sean, the hegemony of the pragmatic life is a powerful one, his 'will to leisure' with 'the
lads' can at times be stronger. This book is an attempt to both describe
and understand that 'cultural imaginary' (Castoriadis, 1987) as it manifests
itself in the current leisure life-world of Sean and the rest of 'the lads'.

Elucidating the reflexive project of the leisure life-world of 'the lads'

As the work of Bauman (1997: 87) continues to show, our past experience of
the modern world, 'as we tend to reconstruct it now, retrospectively, [is]

known to us [only] through its disappearance'./Accordingly, 'the lads'' cultural resistance to liquid modern transformations should be properly understood, not as a form of collective modern stubbornness, but as the coming together of a group of individuals who share a common reflexive narrative. For, in liquid modernity, men and women are above all else, at the same time, both rational and self-determined individuals (reflexive selves). And the concepts of rationality and self-determination have two vital things in common: each puts the emphasis on the will of the *individual* rather than on the will of others. This combination of rationality and self-determination is essentially what makes modern men and women autonomous individuals. And being autonomous/means that agents are only partly, if at all, constrained in their pursuit of whatever they have institutionialized as their purpose' (Bauman, 1992a: 192)./

In Giddens's (1991: 244) scheme of things, the reflexive project of the self is a cognitive process, 'whereby self-identity is constituted by the reflexive ordering of self-narratives'. Each reflexive-self cognitively understands the accomplishment of encountering and knowing the social world through his or her everyday knowledgeability as a contingently positioned individual. The existential contradiction that marks off individuals in late modernity – as opposed to traditional and modern men and women – is that they reflexively understand themselves as being both part of and yet detached from the social world of others. For Giddens, the fusion between the knower and the known is never complete and in every epistemological relation, there is always some element of detachment. This is because the late modern individual perceives that s/he is the centre of the social world and that external subjects and objects are taken into the self to be constituted reflexively in terms of that individual's cognitive understanding.

Yet, for Foucault, this Anglo-Saxon grasping of the rational, cognitive individual at the centre of the social world represents an acute epistemological misreading, which leads to a simplistic and inadequate understanding of the complex discursive processes that connect human beings and shape individual 'choices'. Foucault (1981) arrived at a form of social analysis that focused on systems of discourse and discourse as practice, not on understanding cognitive processes, which place exclusive emphasis on people and what they say. While this gave Foucault (1981, 1986, 1987) no reason to reject the idea of reflexive selfhood,[2] it gave him a good reason to dig *less* deeply into explanations for individual agency. Thus Foucault came to place the emphasis of reflexive selfhood, not on cognitive reason, individual controlling knowledge, rationality and calculable logic, but on events which can be grasped only through a form of knowing that relates to that which we belong and which belongs to us and that which is invariably local and is both materially and discursively situated.

Accordingly, we must try to understand 'the lads'' collective leisure experiences as a life-world that each of them reflexively buys into with varying degrees of enthusiasm. But what is meant by the concept of the life-world? Before the study of 'the lads' can begin, some kind of an answer must be given to this question. The idea of the life-world (*Lebenswelt*) is difficult to conceptualise, and a detailed discussion is beyond the scope of this book. However, in following analysis I draw on the work of hermeneuticians as different as Heidegger, Ricoeur, Foucault, Derrida, Rorty and Bauman to develop a sociological approach that is best understood as a phenomenological hermeneutics[3] to the idea of a particular life-world – what I describe as a leisure life-world – as a 'realm of lived life and experience' (Bech, 1997: 6). The analysis developed charts the ways in which the incumbents of this leisure life-world live, experience, understand and recognise this world *Erlebnis* as both a 'real' and a meaningful already existing reality. And in representing 'the lads'' shared leisure experiences as a life-world this analysis seeks to capture the central importance of the social in the study of this culture.

In recognising the limitations of phenomenological approaches to life-world studies (Schutz and Luckman, 1973) the analysis also recognises that this already existing reality is always articulated in stories previously told and consequently that discourse is fundamental to understanding the leisure life-world of 'the lads'. In light of this second aspect, I make use of Foucault's idea of the discourse formation, which enables me to provide a more discursive understanding of the idea of this particular life-world, which tells its own story, has its own discourse. This hermeneutic approach, which draws on both deep and surface phenomena, follows Ricoeur (1991) in assuming that because the events, actions and contingencies – both material and discursive – constitutive of this leisure life-world are reflexive, it makes sense to interpret them in similar ways as theorists such as Foucault and Derrida interpret discourse as text or writing.

With Dreyfus (1991: 204) this approach also assumes that 'an interpreter, if he is to understand what is going on, must share the general human background understanding of the individual or group being studied'. Indeed, uncovering the leisure life-world of 'the lads' for analytical scrutiny necessitated the identification of the ontology that underpins that world. Consequently my phenomenological hermeneutics rests on the tacit assumption that myself as the researcher *had* to belong to the leisure life-world to understand that world because myself as researcher and the world he was exploring co-determined that being-in-the-world *Dasein* (Heidegger, 1962). And it was presupposed by me that knowing *Dasein* and life-world knowing are both at the same time constituting and constitutive of one another. In a nutshell, my research approach assumed that, because the leisure life-world existed, for myself as researcher to exist it also followed that it took myself as researcher to recognise, experience and reflect that world in its worldliness. To this end the book provides the reader with an admission ticket to an alternative life-world of leisure with its own set of protocols, convention-alities and patterns of collective behaviour.

In this sense, the book can be seen as a critical response to Bauman's classic sociology of intellectuals *Legislators and Interpreters*, which calls for the extension of communication between autonomous communities. Indeed, one of my key aims in this book is to develop a deep understanding of the leisure life-world of 'the lads' and to communicate the meaning of that world. To paraphrase Bauman (1987: 5), the book has two key intents in this regard: it seeks to establish a conversing tradition between the leisure life-world of 'the lads' and the academic community and at the same time it attempts to make sure that the message from the former to the latter is undistorted (regarding the meaning of the leisure life-world) and clearly understood.

In getting to know 'the lads', however, the reader needs to grasp the point that each of them is implicated in a host of other life-worlds, which some-times intersect, but which also hold experiences and antecedents that are private, exclusive to those individuals involved. In the selfsame way, the guid-ing discourse of the leisure life-world of 'the lads' has its own private ways of making meaning, to which myself and each of 'the lads' are affiliated. It is both a private and public life-world that is about to be brought out into the open in this book. But how will this problematic be achieved, and is the decision to uncover this life-world an ethical one?

I have moved on. The way that I attend to the world has become different. Today I am a profoundly different person from the Weston 'lad' of, say, fifteen years ago. During this period I have become a partner and a father. I have been to college and university and have made new friends. How I see my world has changed. My values and thoughts about issues such as masculinity, gender and sexuality, race and ethnicity, class, culture, politics, 'the lads' and what have you have altered.

The upshot of these processes of reflexivity and self-realisation meant that, at the beginning of the research process, I was positioned to carry out a cultural study of 'the lads' in a particular way. In Pike's (1967) sense, I was obviously positioned to elucidate an emic account, from an 'insider' per-spective, but was very much aware also that the findings would be contingent on my own subjective explanations. One of the most important questions I had to ask myself at the outset of the research was: what understanding of who I am is best equipped to evince the social 'reality' of this leisure life-world? For one of the undoubted strengths of the book would lie in my ability to elucidate the world as it is seen by 'the lads'. Yet there was a pressing ethical problem at the back of my mind, that related to the issue of drawing the leisure practices of 'the lads' into the open. From the perspec-tive of my 'new' world-view, I now found many of the leisure practices of 'the lads' unsettling and offensive. And, as the ensuing analysis will show,

I observed that the most contemptible of these often interfered with the accomplished leisure practices of others, notably women. In part this justified my decision to both uncover and deconstruct this leisure life-world.

However, I should also like to point out that the book does not seriously try to make clear how an overarching ideal of 'right' behaviour, or 'leisure practice', should be connected with 'the lads' and their relations with the Other. It strives instead to avoid a reified conception of morality in attempting to situate what 'the lads' perceive to be just within the meaning of the 'cultural imaginary' (Castoriadis, 1987) that produces it. In this sense, the book is not an exercise in 'lad' bashing, rather it makes an attempt to describe and understand this life-world inasmuch as it has a particular significance for sociology, leisure studies, cultural studies and for 'the lads' themselves. For the central basis of this book is that it is leisure which allows 'the lads' to imagine life as being 'solid' and 'perfectly' ordered, concentric and harmonious, and that this forms a marked contrast to their wider liquid realm of futile, fragmentary and chaotic existence.

Into the bargain, there was the critical point that both the research and my own reflexive sense of selfhood were inevitably going to be transformed as the work progressed. However, the rationale remained more or less consistent once these issues became clearer in my mind. The key questions underpinning the research would attempt to ask:

1 What is it about this leisure life-world that makes it worthwhile for 'the lads'?
2 What are the shared meanings and values that shape this spatio-temporal configuration? What is the significance of these for 'the lads'?
3 How does this life-world intersect with the leisure practices of the Other?
4 What does all this tell us about working-class men's leisure in liquid modernity?

I reasoned that if I could put some flesh on these questions by the end of the book, it would have all been worth while.

The framework of the book

The next chapter is concerned with the metaphysical and 'methodological' dimensions of the study. The point of this chapter is both the philosophy and the pragmatics of the research enterprise. Drawing on my research experiences with 'the lads', I first of all question the ontological and epistemological premises of the orthodox sociological approaches to research and critically discuss the limitations of conventional ethnography and cultural studies. This discussion explains by example, drawing on the fieldwork and the author's critical engagement with the literature, to illustrate the biography of the research project. In so doing this chapter argues that the phenomenon of the leisure life-world of 'the lads' is not understood through a process of 'involvement and detachment' (Elias, 1987), which draws on library-based theorising and consults a registry of methodological tools. Instead, it demonstrates that there is no epistemological split in the research process and that the author is already infiltrated with what is to be reached 'objectively'. Drawing on a theoretical amalgam which encompasses the philosophy of Henri Bergson, the sociology of Mafessoli, the anthropology of Clifford Geertz and the hermeneutics of Raymond Williams, Richard Rorty, Michel Foucault, Jacques Derrida and Zygmunt Bauman, the chapter begins to elucidate a disciplined, rigorous and intuitive exploration of the struggles of a group of embodied agents seeking freedom, autonomy and recognition in a concrete life-world of mutual participation.

Chapter 3 begins to elucidate the convergence of the ethnography with the theory by placing the spatio-temporal configuration of the leisure life-world of 'the lads' into a historico-sociological setting. The reader will quickly see that 'the lads' move in a parallel universe where everyday events take back seat to a fantastical world of leisure. However, if this chapter offers the reader a sense of the verisimilitude of the leisure life-world to show how that world is both lived and understood by 'the lads', it also demonstrates, by drawing conjointly on the hermeneutics of Heidegger and Ricoeur, how the discourse surrounding this life-world constructs the identities of its protagonists in constructing its own stories told. As the reader will quickly discern, the allure, fascination and desire to perform as one of 'the lads' are entwined with the need to be part of this leisure life-world. Ricoeur's hermeneutics also suggest a dialectic of self and Other and it becomes clear in this chapter that, if 'the lads' are subjects in their own stories, the Other is a subject in their stories too, and the analysis begins to elucidate a sense of how the Other is constituted through the discourse of the leisure life-world, a topic which is explored in greater detail in Chapter 4.

As the discussion in this chapter unfolds the reader will also begin to see that the leisure life-world is established through exclusions and divisions that also hem 'the lads' themselves in: they cannot leisure in ways that are not sanctioned by the strictures of the discourse surrounding this world of leisure. Moreover, in this chapter it becomes clear that, paradoxically, it is individual autonomy and reflexivity that centralise this life-world and occasion its unity and continuity, however fragile that unity and continuity are, given the ambivalence that is inherent in living in liquid modernity. The figure of 'the lad', it is argued, is best understood as a self-constancy (Heidegger, 1962) achieved in response to the protocols characteristic of and demanded by liquid living.

It is 'the lads'' encounters with the Other which set the focus of Chapter 4, which is about gender relations, leisure lifestyles, masculinities and the ambivalence of the discursive construction of the black Other. The strength of the analysis in this chapter lies in its ability to critically elucidate the meanings associated with the radical exteriority of the Other as constituted by the discourse of the leisure life-world. The first part of the chapter analyses especially the masculine lifestyle practices of 'the lads' in relation to the interplay of discourse and action. Specifically, I bring masculinities into focus by articulating what 'the lads' know, say and do in their leisure time and space and how they do it. I move from masculinities to men and examine 'the lads' practices, social relations, assumptions, and beliefs about 'the lads' and Others. In this sense I analyse agency and the material and discursive practices of 'the lads' in terms of the extent to which and the ways in which they are masculinised. Although this analysis makes the lifestyle practices of 'the lads' the primary focus of attention, it does recognise, however, that women's practices, and men's and women's relations, are of crucial importance, too. As we shall see, these themes enter into and become pivotal to the analysis. The associated works of Derrida, Foucault, Irigaray and Cixous provide the intellectual reference point for the analysis. This poststructuralist amalgam is used to develop our understanding of working-class masculinities using evidence to question gendered binary oppositions. In the context of this analysis I also explore, not only the importance of power to these dichotomies, but the contingency rather than the fixity of gendered relations. This chapter also focuses on the 'consumption' of the black Other in the leisure life-world. I use Derrida's concept of the trace to show how the black Other influences and facilitates the leisure life-styles of 'the lads', but is radically absent from that time–space, in the sense that it is perennially erased and denied a presence. For 'the lads', the black Other is always kept at a distance because it remains an indirect and local threat to their status and the material and discursive aspects of their lives.

In Chapter 5 I formulate an analysis of the concept of community, which enables me to describe the quotidian of 'the lads'' putative sense of belonging. I suggest that this postulated community is 'a work of imagination spurred on by [the fear of] *homesickness*' (Bauman, 1995: 47) and that 'the lads' live, perceiving that their task is now to find that point – in their leisure time and space – where they can feel at 'home' to assert that monosemic identity of the 'true' and 'solid' modern man. Drawing on the research, I argue that this longing for 'home' is intensified all the more as liquid modern conditions makes the reflexive individual 'lad' ever more aware of his insecurity. Moreover I argue that this turn to the postulated community evinces the seriousness of 'the lads'' leisure, as they seek to experience the ultimate in being and meaning through their collective identities.

It is stressed at the outset, however, that the discussion in this chapter is not concerned so much with an endeavour to retheorise community as with reflexivity and the need for belonging inherent in this life-world. To this end the analysis contemplates why 'the lads' carry on with this leisure existence and suggests that it is because they have a special camaraderie, a

perfect relationship that can be acquired only between those who understand. This discussion also shows that if 'the lads' are given to contemplation,
they actually wallow in it. In this regard it is suggested that, rather than being
healthily durable, in its latter-day incarnation the leisure life-world has
fossilised and that 'the lads' themselves are unable to accommodate themselves to the present or the future because they are busily maintaining
extant pleasures. As the reader will see, the leisure life-world is always a
procession of contingent events leading tidily from the present to the past.

Chapter 6 carries on with this theme to explore the continuum between the
mundane and the spectacular aspects of the leisure life-world, paying particular attention to the cultural geographies of 'the lads'' leisure exploits.
Within this analysis, the roles of myth and memory are revealed to play a
vital role in shaping the collective identities of 'the lads', transforming
actual events into recollections and, thereafter, 'new' leisure experiences.
These processes, which involve 'the lads' having recourse to powerful oral
histories, become the myths, the 'true fictions' (Denzin, 1989) of this leisure
life-world, the stories 'the lads' continue to leisure by. As the reader will see,
the truth of the success of the leisure life-world lies in its ability to balance the
unending spinning of a familiar tale – the story of themselves is the one 'the
lads' never tire of – with the most satisfying of leisure experiences.

The evolution of the myth of the leisure life-world of 'the lads' is traced
through an extant body of theory in this chapter, but the work of Baudrillard
emerges as particularly important. His discussion of the disappearance of the
'real' is taken up and critically developed, as it helps me to elucidate the
significance of the leisure life-world as it is experienced retrospectively.
I use Baudrillard's work to argue that, for 'the lads', the transition to
liquid modernity has meant that, regardless of the unmitigated inculcation
their *habitus* – in Bourdieu's meaning – has inscribed and bequeathed
them, liquid modernity has forced each of them, individually, to radically
reconstruct his sense of self-identity. In some cases this has resulted in leaving
the individual with a fractured sense of ontological security (Giddens, 1991).
I develop these arguments to show that, in 'the lads'' meaning, liquid
modernity is experienced as a hyperreality, and it is only in the leisure life-
world that life carries on as 'real', in the 'normal' solid modern sense.

The theme of hyperreality re-emerges in Chapter 7, where the analysis continues to focus on the reflexivity which undergirds the leisure life-world, but
also community relations in liquid modernity more generally. In this respect
the chapter provides the reader with the possibility of glimpsing a further
dimension to the sense of togetherness associated with the leisure life-
world of 'the lads', which features the holiday world of Rose Dale – 'the
lads'' second 'home' – to explore the absurdity that, even when they are
apart, elsewhere, 'the lads' can still be together in their leisure time.

The concluding chapter brings together the key themes of the study in
order to contemplate the research problematic. I suggest that there is an

importance to the leisure life-world of 'the lads' that can be understood only in the context of working-class men's lived experience of the condition of liquid modernity. In a time that has witnessed both the collapse of the 'solid' modernist order of things and the re-enchantment of the social world, the ultimate appeal of the leisure life-world of 'the lads' is that it will fulfil the longing for home and security and the desire for the quotidian of the non-rational (leisure, play and pleasure). For 'the lads', the leisure life-world is *the* pivotal point in a fragmented life, which allows them to fashion a sense of order out of the disorder of the everyday. However, in their leisure 'the lads' experience only intimations of a return to a deeper, more certain world that has in reality disappeared: solid modernity 'has come to be known to us mainly through its disappearance. What we think the past had – is what we know we do not have' (Bauman, 1997: 87). On top of that, I suggest that the appeal of the leisure life-world is ultimately double-edged, in the sense that it is also experienced as self-defeating. This is because, in common with other men and women, each of 'the lads' is guided by the wider discourse of individualism, and he is a reflexive individual, who is guided by the will of himself, rather than by the will of others.

The book closes with an episode which traces the ambivalent endurance-cum-fragility of the leisure life-world to explore how 'the lads' have come to accept that their imminent exit from 'paradise' cannot be avoided. The epilogue concludes by suggesting that the leisure life-world never loses its potency because with it there is never any form of culmination or ending.

Notes

1 As Mestrovic (1998) shows, this 'synthetic' tradition reveals itself across a broad spectrum in modern sociology, from structural functionalism to the contemporary writings of Anthony Giddens.
2 As Ritzer (1997: 75) points out, 'Instead of a genealogy of power, [the later Foucault] sought to do a genealogy of self-awareness, self-practices, and self-control in the realm of sexuality'.
3 Following Bauman, I assume that sociology and hermeneutics presuppose one another.

Chapter 2

Deliberation

Some questions of methodological approach

A one-off Thursday evening at Kingston Working Men's Club

As we entered the club it was almost surreal to see the most treasured dreams of ours coming true on either side of the room: wall-to-wall fanny – albeit the local variety and some of it a bit rough, too – and fuckloads of beer, gratis. It was a mate of Scott's thirtieth birthday party. Sean was standing at the bar, already well pissed. He had a big grin on his face when he shouted, 'Let's get up' (on the dance floor). It's 'Come on, Eileen' (a song by Dexy's Midnight Runners). And we did, approximately twelve of us. We danced – if that is the right word for it – for most of the rest of the evening. I joined in, but I also observed it all. To the casual observer, the scenes that took place that evening probably resembled a series of snapshots from a slapstick comedy. As the DJ flipped through his repertoire 'the lads' could be seen, at different points, pushing and shoving, holding hands, holding each other, lying on the dance floor; generally 'having a good time'. Yet what I felt and observed was something more than that. It is difficult to describe exactly what it was, but it was like a Maffesolian 'eruption' of a communal 'will to live' and it was masculine, exciting, mystical, erotic, aesthetic and magical, all at the same time. And it was about us; just us.

While the rest of 'the lads' focused their collective gaze on D-ranged, going for it, 'mental' on the dance floor, I watched, and laughed, at all of us moving there, hermetically sealed in 1982, doing our own modest trade in social pasts. You could tell that each of us wanted this night out to go on *ad infinitum*. The motto of 'the lads' prevailed: 'Please God, make it go slow tonight. Make it not be in ordinary time at all. Make it last for ever more, *tout à fait.*'

You see our leisure in a time not adjacent to the now. It is together, back then, when we were experts on lads' time, which is a different time zone from the Greenwich version. In lads' time the weeks are short, the weekends are long and these mirror each other. For most people there is time past, time present and time future. With the leisure life-world, though, there is also a sense of time immortal; a continuous time that exists in our conscience collective. The spirituality of the leisure life-world is understood and felt as something very different from everyday consciousness, and lads' time plays games with time and with reality. Time, that should be linear, becomes structured by another type of rationality, which is not only more reliable but also marvellous.

All week we had longed to be with each other, to get away from the outside world and return to the particular time and space which is the 'warm' seclusion of the leisure life-world. Here we knew we would be able to concentrate on the more important tasks which life has to offer – tonight it was beer and fanny – which would open themselves up to us and which would facilitate our entry once more to this our very own realm of ultimate truth.

As if celebrating Baudrillard's mantra we extinguished rationality with feeling. The club was lively with the transient elixir of togetherness we collectively oozed, exaggeratedly present; it was unrelenting. We were happy, at peace with ourselves – the coolness of our collective nostalgia came from the dazzling disco lights flickering across the dance floor, and seemed to affect everyone. As we continued to dance we endeavoured to knit through our clumsy actions the diaphanous threads that connect us with each other and with the imagined certitudes of our past. And we were prevented from spinning out of this fantasy of community because both the music and the alcohol were incredibly good. Tonight was four hours of travel through a past teeming with our mutual encounters and experiences both together and together apart.

Yet if we had cared to look more closely at each other we might have seen the flame of ephemeral unity lit in each other's eyes. For we all knew that this excitement would very soon evaporate, even though we felt that we did not want it to end, this night away from ourselves, at 'home' together. The great thing about lads' time is that it loses all sense of chronology; but the unfortunate thing about it is that its tangled fragments come and go. Nevertheless this didn't undermine the significance of what, in Sean's words, was a 'top' night out.

Introduction

The initial idea underpinning this chapter was that it should simply chart for the reader the biography of the research project to elucidate how the author entered into the lived experience of the leisure life-world of 'the lads' in order to elaborate that world. However, what is scripted below also encompasses a critical discussion of the limits of conventional ethnography and cultural studies. The chapter begins with a discussion of my initial attempt to 'apply' qualitative 'methods' of social inquiry 'to' the 'field'. It then describes the deconstruction of those 'methods' before providing a critical discussion of conventional ethnography and cultural studies. In Rorty's (1986) sense, this critique 'changes the subject' about doing qualitative social research. In an attempt to build on conventional ethnography I offer an approach to social inquiry which draws and builds on the work of poststructuralist authors, and particularly Foucault's (1980a) genealogical approach, in order to develop the sociological imagination. The aim of this discussion is to show, by drawing on the research with 'the lads', that important insights connected with doing qualitative sociology can begin to emerge from a conversation between Foucault and extant approaches in ethnography. Finally, I discuss the writing of the ethnography and the analytical strategies adopted in the later chapters. I hope the reader will countenance the rather dense argument developed here, but in elucidating the complexity of this research project I aim to establish a radical approach to ethnography hitherto not cultivated in mainstream sociology. If this critique posits the 'end of ethnography' as we have come to know it, it also insists that we must not lose sight of what the Chicago school did for ethnographic work, by insisting on the centrality of lived culture being at the heart of the sociological project.

The research journey

In the beginning, and as the project initially evolved, I tended to describe the research as a phenomenological analysis involving extensive observation and participant observation. In one particular working paper, I paraphrased Hammersley and Atkinson (1995: 1) to argue that I was participating overtly and covertly in people's lives for extended periods of time, watching what was happening, listening to what was said, asking questions – in fact collecting whatever 'data' were available to throw light on the issues that were the focus of the research. I argued further that this ethnographic approach, in turn, facilitated both observations and unstructured interviews with key respondents in the field. That these unstructured interviews allowed me to confirm my observations of these events and to place the respondents in a situation where they could be more open with their responses. I suggested that the unstructured interviews were necessary, as the respondents, I found, in the main, disliked the formality of standard interview techniques.

In the initial research process I also undertook a number of semi-structured interviews which, I argued, would make the research more 'quantifiable' than was allowed through the ethnography. I targeted a key body of eight informants, each of whom I interviewed on at least three occasions.

Moreover, I made over 150 pages of field notes in my notebook and kept computer records. During the times when the ethnography was central, I spent between one and thee days (mainly evenings), for up to eight hours each, in the field.

As the research advanced, in a later working paper, I argued that in order to give the ethnography some structure, so to speak, I would need to organise the research process to give more prominence to the shared and individual, social and cultural characteristics of 'the lads'. In Goffman's (1969) sense, I argued that I would need to give more attention to the 'face-work' and 'teamwork' involved in (re)producing the leisure life-world. Specifically, I decided that I would focus on ethnographic work at six pubs and clubs in the locality and join in trips with 'the lads' into 'town'. I subsequently suggested that this work allowed me to engineer the ethnography to explore in greater depth the leisure life-world and that this shift elucidated a wealth of 'data' pertaining to 'the lads', such as notions of belonging and together-ness, divisiveness, masculinity, ethnic and gender inequalities, and class. I also suggested that I was now using the field as a grounding for theory, in Glaser and Strauss's (1968) meaning, and that I had begun to analyse the 'data'.

It was argued in the initial 'methodology' that my insider status would allow me to study the field in an emic sense, providing an account of the community dimensions of leisure through thick descriptions (Geertz, 1973). I suggested that ethnomethodology would enhance this process in that it would enable the research to become more responsive to the 'methods' by which those in the field made sense of the situations in which they found themselves and how they managed to 'sustain an orderliness in their dealings with others' (Layder, 1994: 81). I argued that, as a member, I was familiar with the appropriate 'identities' or 'categories' (Sacks, 1974) associated with the leisure life-world. Subsequently I suggested that ethnomethodology had enabled me to identify 'categories' which were constitutive of this leisure life-world: masculinity, hard drinking, 'hardness', 'whiteness', a particular dress sense, loyalty and more.

As the research model later emerged, I suggested that it had become apparent that it would be appropriate to elaborate a historical method that facilitated and focused on the micro-sociological aspects of the 'field'. Therefore I developed a life history method (Denzin, 1989), which invited respondents to recount and elucidate their individual and shared historical leisure experiences as interpreted and defined in their own terms. I suggested that the essence of this method was concerned with the subjects' definition of the situation and that this method would enable the research to balance its 'objectivism' 'with the internal, covert, and reflective elements of social behaviour and experience' (Denzin, 1989: 209). I argued, in the event, that my use of the life history method allowed me to focus on past leisure experi-ences and leisure events situated in the context of the leisure life-world and that the research would make plain how such historical events throw light on the present, just as present events supplied 'the lads' with some sense of historical events. What Garfinkel terms members' 'retrospective–prospective sense of occurrence' (Cuff and Payne, 1979: 133).

Considerably down the research path by now, I argued that it was perhaps more appropriate to suggest that the project was making possible the incorporation of a number of distinct, but related, methodologies into an overall scheme of work. Thus achieving a 'multimethod triangulation' of the 'data' (Denzin, 1989) increasing both the 'reliability' and the 'validity' of the research.

The research project was moving along swimmingly. Yet something seemed wrong. Something ethical. There was a pressing problem at the back of my mind, which involved a question that I was continually asking myself. What was I doing pretending that I was following what most other sociologists would no doubt describe as rigorous and scientifically grounded methodology, when the theoretical insights that I was developing had not been simply 'found' or 'grounded' in any 'data', but had been constructed by myself, as a present-minded and discursively positioned sociologist, who was operating with his own unique degree of reflexivity? In response to this anxiety, I made the decision to abandon the pretence of using a methodology in the conventional sociological meaning. When I made this decision in favour of using an alternative ethnographic approach, it produced a serious degree of worry for myself. For I saw myself as I imagined my peers would see me: as a 'postmodern' madman whose 'stories' amounted to nothing. Was my 'new' way 'wrong'? Was it 'right'? Was it just being trendy? Was it daring? Or was it a 'new' way of opening up sociological research to enable it to fulfil its latent potential?

In the end I reasoned that, quite simply, what I had decided to do by abandoning a conventional methodology and adopting an alternative approach was developing a way of researching which did not entail me having recourse to dubious and vague rules of a methodology to arrive at the 'truth' about what I was doing. In Pike's (1967) sense, I was obviously positioned to elucidate an emic account, from an 'insider' perspective, but was very much aware also that this account would be contingent on my own subjective explanations. One of the most important questions I had to ask myself at this decisive point in the research process was this: what understanding of who I am is best equipped to evince the social reality of this leisure life-world? For I reasoned that one of the undoubted strengths of the thesis would lie in my ability to elucidate the world as 'the lads' see it.

I was aware that in abandoning a conventional approach I could not justify my position in the rationalist sense, by spelling out beforehand the criteria (a methodology) by which the study would be assessed. I reasoned that the thesis underpinning the book would have to work on the basis of its own merits; it would have to have relevance for the reader. It would work for different people and in different ways. Yet I still had a nagging doubt in my mind. Would my decision to 'change the subject' be accepted by the academy? Would the research be treated differently, less favourably, given its alternative approach?

An opposing research strategy

In contemporary sociological research and writing it is still the case that, for most of us, our justification for questions surrounding the 'knowledge' about 'doing' research *has* to be couched in the terms of a rational scientific argument, that is, around issues of epistemology, ontology, ethics, validity, objectivity, method and the like. In terms of 'good' social science research practice, a rigorous methodology is seen as a necessary requisite that enables the reader to evaluate critically the empirical and theoretical validation of a research project (Scatzman and Strauss, 1973). It would seem that 'good' researchers *must* justify their methodologies in terms of the strict rules of foundational philosophical reason, even if this means marrying ideas which are radically incompatible (see Hughes, 1990).

True to form, then, my approach demands a critical discussion of methodology as the philosophical justification for adopting particular investigative principles and techniques in social research. However, the way I go about this is not the usual approach that uses the techniques of science to argue against the 'straw targets' who advance positivistic methodology (in the manner of Lincoln and Guba, 1985; Thomas, 1992; Guba and Lincoln, 1994, for example). My approach undertakes to follow the pragmatic philosophy of Richard Rorty by reframing the debate about doing social research, thereby 'changing the subject', to deprive the promulgator of modernist scientific method *his* 'choice of weapons' (Rorty, 1986). In the course of the discussion I will demonstrate what I actually did to elucidate how an 'alternative' qualitative research approach emerged.

The reader will see that this discussion deconstructs the 'privileged description' (Rorty, 1979) of scientific methodology in sociology to argue that it is a waste of time constructing and defending elaborate analytical methodologies when there is 'no way to prove that what we say about the world or ourselves corresponds to what the world is or we are' (Natoli, 1997: 181). Instead, the discussion 'changes the subject' to an alternative vocabulary, that is, an 'abnormal discourse', which does not oblige me to have to make my work take on the 'normal discourse' of science. My approach does not follow a 'method', in the conventional sense, but seeks to undermine the 'epistemologically centred philosophy' (Rorty, 1979) of science, which tends to preclude alternative ways of social inquiry. For mine is an interpretive hermeneutic position, which recognises that there is always something more to be said and that there are infinite ways to inquire into the social world. For the position underpinning this book is that 'reality is one, but descriptions of it are many. They ought to be many, for human beings have, and ought to have, many different purposes' (Rorty, 1998: 9.4). In relation to the aims of the book, this approach enables me to get on with the task of representing the leisure life-world of 'the lads'.

This discussion leads me on to another crucial issue that pertains to Rorty's point about 'changing the subject'. How does one go about moving from an empirical and systematic study approach of all there is out there to a hermeneutic ethnographic approach, which, rather than rationalizing its methodological 'strengths', advances its inherent deficiencies? I should like to suggest that this can be achieved through the 'alternative vocabulary' of pragmatic discourse (Rorty, 1979), which emerged when it dawned on me that the dominant vocabularies of sociology were not sufficiently developed to express what I wanted to express about the leisure life-world of 'the lads'.

The view that I develop throughout the book suggests that, if we are properly to understand 'the lads', we must be able to see the 'world as it is' from their point of view. My approach follows Rorty in insisting that 'there are people out there whom society has failed to notice' and the aim of this book is to make 'the lads' visible by showing how to explain the nature of their already existing reality in terms of a coherent, if unfamiliar, 'emic' framework, but one which elucidates the 'world as it is' from their point of view. This approach recognises that we 'live in mediated realities, each reality believing and arguing that there is no mediated reality but the reality in itself' (Natoli, 1997: 198). Moreover, it recognises my role as the subjective researcher to the project and that I am an active participant in the inception, the production and the maintenance of the leisure life-world of 'the lads'. For I made a decision, that was contingent upon my own subjective way of seeing the world, about which slice of the incredibly complex reality of the leisure life-world of 'the lads' to research.

The work of Rorty is fundamental to the position of this 'abnormal discourse', which I adopt in preference to a disciplinary methodology. Rorty recognises that the dichotomy between the natural and the social sciences collapses. Whereas philosophy traditionally thinks that 'uncovering' social reality converges around complex theories, Rorty thinks that inquiry, or 'making' culture, converges around using the tools that are contingent upon our own frames of reference. Rorty wants to know what is really going on in the social world, but in his schema there is no essential means of reporting sociological research. Rorty's approach allows sociology to ask somewhat different questions of ethnography. For Rorty, it is 'genres such as ethnography, the journalist's report, the comic book, the docudrama, and, especially, the novel' (Rorty, 1989: xvi) rather than philosophy (and, one could argue, social science more generally) that provide the best means of 'seeing' the social world. Whereas social science traditionally thinks that 'uncovering' social reality converges around complex theories and method-ologies, Rorty imagines that social inquiry should be a creative way of 'making' culture, which should converge around using tools that are contingent upon particular frames of reference, recognising the performative and rhetorical aspects of ethnography.

It perhaps seems incongruous to encounter such an eminent philosopher encouraging scholars to abandon tried and trusted theories and methods. Some readers will no doubt find Rorty's call philosophically or sociologically unsound, anti-intellectual even. We are not used to hearing respected academics comparing ethnography with comic books and novels. We are even less used to them explicitly privileging 'fiction' over 'facts'. In response no doubt some readers will choose to write off Rorty's appeal. Others might reason that the actual task of doing empirical research – as opposed to philosophical inquiry – is in all probability peripheral to Rorty's project and it is pointless to focus obsessively on details of wording in his occasional allusions to the topic. Yet this chapter will demonstrate that Rorty's approach demands a more thoroughgoing revision of the essential concepts and tools of ethnography than sociology up to now has ever demanded.

If what is scripted below is implicative of an abnormal discourse it also encompasses a critical discussion of the limits of ethnography. In evoking Mills's (1959) concept of the sociological imagination – 'that realm which creatively might connect the self and the other, private worries and social issues, individual identity and the public good' (Beilharz, 2000: 159–60) – the following discussion illustrates that just as 'the lads'' leisure is 'real life' driven by an energising imagination, so should be sociology. This approach recognises that the liquid world in which sociologists today operate has changed and that the usefulness of some of the still dominant ways and means of doing sociology have deteriorated to such an extent they no longer work as well as they once did. Indeed, when aesthetic, surface and liquid conditions replaced ethical, deep and solid ones the essential concepts, tools and epistemological and ontological frameworks analogous with classical sociology and its associated qualitative methodologies, such as ethnography, if not becoming redundant, lost much of their explanatory power. Yet most empirically minded sociologists themselves have in the main been oblivious to these changing circumstances. This chapter does not merely constitute the beginnings of an ethnography of the leisure life-world of 'the lads', then, it also involves a critical discussion about the possibilities of ethnography – the difficulties, contradictions and problems involved, as well as the risk and excitement of capturing in a monograph the lived experience of culture. To paraphrase Clifford Geertz (1973),[1] it is to the cutting of the ethnography concept down to size, therefore actually ensuring its continued importance rather than undermining it, that this chapter is in the main dedicated.

The limitations of ethnography (and cultural studies) in sociology

During the last twenty years or so we have witnessed unprecedented developments in social theory across the body of the entire social sciences, including sociology, leisure studies and cultural studies. However, in relation to qualitative empirical work it has been very much a more uncertain story. In sociology and leisure studies empirically minded qualitative researchers seem to have become enclosed in the confinements of the ethnographic methods developed by the Chicago school in the 1920s. The more recent developments in ethnographic work, such as Geertz (1995) and Clifford and Marcus (1986) in social anthropology,[2] are conspicuous by their absence in sociology and leisure studies. Dick Hobbs's (1988) ethnography *Doing the Business* is a case study which illustrates this point. The key strength of Hobbs's book is its close attention to the lived experience of culture. However, the major problem with this account is that although the author recognises that ethnography is always a form of self-indulgence on the part of the researcher, he never questions the tacit assumptions underpinning the ethnographic enterprise as it has been understood since its evolution in the work of the Chicago school. As Bauman (2000a) points out, 'solids are cast once and for all' and as such they inevitably keep their shape. Cast in 'solid' modernity, ethnography is a case in point. Hobbs (p. 15) simply suggests that:

> The Chicago School and its associated methodologies have endured sufficiently to have been an influence on a good many criminologists, ethnographers, and urban sociologists, and I make no apology for working in this tradition. Better writers than I have gone the way of the buffalo, leaving behind a body of work whose principal contribution has been to improve our understanding of social phenomena.

More recently, in their important discussion of ethnographic work in leisure and sport studies, Sugden and Tomlinson (1999) have also been keen to make the case for the type of ethnography developed by the Chicago school, by reiterating the significance of the sort of depth ethnography practised by Douglas (1976). I want to go as far as to suggest that the tried and tested model of ethnography celebrated by these authors has become responsible for undermining the very potential of the ethnographic imagination itself.

If ethnographers in sociology have been busy maintaining the legacy of the Chicago school in their fieldwork, cultural studies seem to have been reduced to a sophisticated form of 'textual' analysis, giving the impression that their chief protagonists rarely get beyond the gates of the academy. McRobbie (1994: 58–9) elucidates:

> the problem with cultural studies today is the absence of reference to
> real existing identities in the ethnographic sense. The identities being dis-
> cussed . . . are textual or discursive identities. The site of identity forma-
> tion in cultural studies remains implicitly in and through cultural
> commodities and texts rather than in and through the cultural practices
> of everyday life.

Echoing McRobbie's response to this bifurcation, Whannel (1998: 231) has
also suggested that there is a definite 'need to bridge the gulf between textual
analysis and ethnographic work'. In the course of this chapter I also try to
furnish elements of a response to this challenge. This will be achieved
through addressing the course of events which both define and make real
the historico-cultural constitution of the already existing reality, which I
have already described as the leisure life-world of 'the lads'.

The way I go about this is as follows. I offer a critique, based on the
research with 'the lads', which takes three things for granted: First, the
need for ethnography to engage with, though not necessarily wholly
embrace, developments in sociology and cultural studies in the light of the
poststructuralist challenge. These developments are used here as a way of
opening up the debate surrounding the tacit assumptions underpinning
ethnography, as it is generally understood. The key aim of this discussion
will be to show that important insights connected with 'doing' research can
begin to emerge from a conversation between poststructuralism and extant
approaches in ethnography. Second, this argument assumes that ethnographers must more readily acknowledge that they have got to come to terms
with the ways in which the world has changed around them and that this
awareness should be a prime concern of ethnography. Third, and perhaps
most importantly, it recognises that empirical findings will always remain
partial and in the light of this assumption that it is important to recognise
that it is the explanatory power and potential of ethnographic writing, not
the establishment of methodological frameworks, which should be recognised as the key strength of an ethnographic imagination, as Bauman
might say, that is 'made to the measure of liquid modernity'.

Ethnography post-poststructuralism

I should like to make it very clear at the outset that what I am offering here is
most unequivocally not a poststructuralist approach to social research. The
poststructuralist research agenda is anti-humanist in orientation, dealing
with antisocial signs, language and writing (Harland, 1987) and on the face
of it has no direct filiations with ethnography. Foucault's project in particular has been criticised for being 'anti-realist' and too remote to be of any
practical use for ethnographic work (Hammersley and Atkinson, 1995).
However, I want to challenge this perception and further illustrate my

arguments by making reference to my own research, which is a practical attempt to 'ground' poststructuralism.

Poststructuralist theory itself has also been criticised for reaching a level of abstraction which is unsurpassed in the literature. However, the themes and issues with which we are concerned here suggest possibilities for engaging poststructuralism on a less abstract level, bringing it down to a more concrete level to engage with issues regarding ethnography. What I will be doing hereafter is drawing on some of the critical insights of post-structuralism in order to show how they can help us deal with a network of issues concerning ethnographic research. I also demonstrate how I employed an alternative approach to the ethnographic imagination, itself a product of my own interpretation of poststructuralist theory, which sought to problematise conventional approaches to doing research. To begin with, though, there is a need to outline some poststructuralist assumptions, as these enable me to set out the backcloth against which I offer my critique of ethnography. It is to these that I now turn.

As I have said already this critique moves away from traditional ethno-graphic approaches to provide a conciliation of Foucault's (1980a) anti-realist methodological approach with ethnography. In this regard the critique deals squarely with ethnography's over-investment in the idea of the rational, thinking 'subject'. But if the poststructuralists, and Foucault in particular, rightly alert researchers to the efficacy of exploring discourse as 'social' practice, under this alternative schema the individual ultimately 'disappears'; and there can only be interaction between pre-existing 'subject' positions in systems of discourse. I must stress at the offset that I expressly reject this aspect of Foucault's 'model', because to have denied the signifi-cance of individual agency would have clearly limited my understanding of the leisure life-world in a manner analogous to the restrictive focus on what individuals say and do, which Foucault's research agenda seeks to address. Moreover, in precluding a Foucauldian anti-realism that sees the world only through the lenses of textuality the research approach identified in this chapter shows too that the discursive is best read as a 'social' affair, implicating 'the lads' at once as speaking and acting 'subjects', texturing the genealogy of the leisure life-world as an adventure in discourse and action.

The poststructuralist argument has an underlying metaphysic which suggests that 'subject' positions or individuality and difference are ephemeral surface phenomena, destined to disappear as people move between dis-courses. This is why Foucault (1981) arrived at a point in the research process where he focused on systems of discourse and discourse as practice, not on understanding cognitive processes which place exclusive emphasis on people and what they say. For Foucault, the Anglo-Saxon grasping of the rational, cognitive individual at the centre of the social world represents an acute epistemological misreading, which leads to a simplistic and inadequate understanding of the complex discursive processes that connect human beings (Harland, 1987). Foucault re-presents the concept of agency in the sense that he theorises the agent as being both at the same time constituting of and constituted by discourse. However, for Foucault, being constituted is not the same thing as saying that the individual is determined in the structuralist meaning. Quite the opposite, for Foucault, as for Butler (1991: 13), 'the constituted character of the subject is the very precondition of its agency'.

Another tacit assumption of the poststructuralist approach to social inquiry is that there is no epistemological split, or subject–object relation, in the research process and that the researcher is 'already infiltrated with what is to be reached "objectively"' (Natoli, 1997: 182). Foucault breaks the distinction between involvement and detachment (Elias, 1987) in the research process to show the illusory nature of the assertion that we as researchers have the ability to mark our independence, or disengage ourselves, from others through detachment. Foucault has perhaps an overly complex view of epistemology, but the issues he identifies cannot be denied. Epistemologically speaking, the research process as it is understood as a convergence between the 'subject' and 'object' or the knower and the known cannot be reduced to such a simplistic mechanical process, which leads to an inadequate understanding of the complex relationships that connect human beings.

I do not wish, however, to press this epistemological argument and I am aware that it is one thing to reject something on epistemological grounds and quite another to suggest that no practical guidelines can be identified for researchers. On a day-to-day basis researchers are confronted with a range of practical issues and they require practical guidelines in order to forge an adequate basis for 'doing' empirical work. But the best that researchers can do in attempting to detach themselves practically is to try to contemplate the field of research from an *ironic* distance, in the Rortyan (1989) sense. After all, an *ironic* distance is the best researchers can achieve, because, as Foucault shows us, in reality there is no magical 'buffer zone' between the knower and the known. There is no way of keeping one aspect of 'reality' from another. As Natoli (1997: 182) points out: 'We cannot isolate any part of the world from any other part, just as we cannot isolate ourselves from the world.'

Now that I have provided a thumbnail sketch of some of the central assumptions of poststructuralism, with an appropriate critique, I want to demonstrate how I applied these ideas in the research process. In the subsequent discussion I first of all deal with the idea of the ethnographic self and the perennial problem of involvement and detachment. The reader will see that these two issues raise some important points of discussion in themselves, but also that they become even more significant when we consider the implications of the type of knowledge which is generated through ethnography post-poststructuralism. Two further concepts are identified in relation to this critical discussion: Raymond Williams's (1970) idea of the 'knowable community' and Henri Bergson's argument that it is intuition (Deleuze, 1988), not analysis in the scientific meaning, which is better suited for revealing the truth about the social world. In the final part of the critique I draw on poststructuralism to discuss two problems: conventional ethnography's fixation with depth and deep meaning and the issue of the writing of ethnographic accounts. With regard to the former the reader will see that in the main it is Derrida's poststructuralist approach which enables us to see that much conventional ethnography results in a situation where one form of social analysis is put to use largely at the expense of another. Drawing on Derrida's work on binary oppositions, there are two key points to be brought out here. In relation to the latter problem the author argues that the strength of ethnography post-poststructuralism is its conviction of the explanatory power and potential of ethnographic writing.

As an overture to the application of the ideas outlined above the author asks the reader to first of all consider the episode at the beginning of this chapter, which illustrates a number of the key arguments to be put forward in the final part of this chapter. In the first instance the reader should use the episode to reflect on poststructuralism's critique of involvement and detachment in the research process to consider the following argument: that is, that the relationship between myself as the researcher and the rest of 'the lads' was not detached but, on the contrary, irrevocably discursive and passionately involved.

Researching the leisure life-world of 'the lads'

In an attempt to respond to the idea of the 'self as ethnographer' and the problem of involvement and detachment, the research approach developed with 'the lads' arrived at another way of recognising not only how ethnographers carry out their craft, but how they also generate sociological knowledge. The reader should recognise that what is written in this book is to some extent constituted of knowledge generated by empirical research, but it is also constituted of an other sort of knowledge that is involved and passionate and is derived of an intimate and intuitive 'seeing', which is representative and reflects the communion between the knower (myself) and the known (the rest of 'the lads'). The knowledge generated by this field relationship is marked not by 'involvement and detachment' (Elias, 1987), 'semi-detachment' (Sugden and Tomlinson, 1999) or 'engaged detachment' (Rojek and Turner, 2000) but by mutual intimacy and its nearness to everyday life. The knowledge created through this relationship is also an intimate and self-reflexive sort of 'seeing' rooted in a constancy which extends across time, revisiting and reliving past moments, without congealing into any one given moment. Interpreting the social world in this way involves a much more thoroughgoing project than generating empirical 'data'; it is formative of a critique that recognises that there is a plurality of ways to interpret, explain and theorise the cultural positions, values and everyday ways of being, to explore the multifaceted texture of the world that we live in.

In relation to the research, I understood that there were essential aspects of the 'reality' of this life-world I was dealing with that I 'knew' to be 'true' as a knowledgeable and reflexive actor. I was convinced at times that I 'knew' the reality in question better than some of those in the field. The fact is that more often than not I felt that I did not need 'empirical' data to tell me certain things, because I perceived that I already understood the language of the life-world, intuitively. This approach not only recognises and celebrates the subjectivity of the research process, but also understands that what we know intuitively remains beyond what we can possibly 'discover' empirically. It recognises too that the life-world knowledge it makes is also intuitively created through a 'knowable community' (Williams, 1970).[3] For Williams, any knowable community has got to be approached in terms of its authors' viewpoints and consciousness. The knowable community of the leisure life-world of 'the lads' is characterised by a mutually engaged responsiveness to historical tasks and challenges and active participation in, with and for the others with whom we (myself and the rest of 'the lads') are united through our shared knowledge. The intimacy involved in this knowable community is reminiscent of Giddens's (1992) pure relationship, which is maintained simply for its own sake.

The discourse of the leisure life-world has its own lexicon and we, 'the lads', read from our mutual discourse. When we are together conversation moves from subject to subject, moving one way and then the other. We can finish each other's sentences, and communicate, more remarkably, without speaking at all. With a real affinity, and in the spirit of the communion that exists between each of us, we also use gestures known only to ourselves. For when we are at our leisure, we are one. I know 'the lads' and they know me: the relationship between the knower and the known in the research process is therefore an intimate one. It follows that since this particular 'home' of the knowable community is not merely a 'particular building, street, landscape or company of people', it is 'stripped of all material features' and it is 'not even *imaginary*' (Bauman, 1995: 97) that the knowledge about this 'home' can be interpreted by the reader *only* through the author's way of seeing. What is required for exploring a feeling of the sort of 'home' 'stripped of all material features' is a sociology appropriate for the task in hand. To recognise the full significance of the knowable community, readers will have to make adjustments in important aspects of their understanding of what constitutes social research.

This book deals with the problem of confronting the already existing reality of this particular knowable community head-on, by exposing the limitations of conventional ethnography. It suggests that it is not enough to research a social phenomenon such as the leisure life-world *directly*; the way to both approach and 'reveal' the leisure life-world of 'the lads' is also through a tactics of *indirection*, of intimations in the form of a mimesis for representing this already existing reality, but which does so uncompromisingly through a dialectics of conventional ethnographic research techniques and intuition, invoked through pragmatism.

As Bech (1997: 6) puts it, this interpretive approach 'snuggle[d] up to what [was] quotidian and recognizable, even trivial, for the inhabitants of the life-world', but obviously it did not remain within the boundaries of that 'reality'. This is because it 'went academic' in much the same way as Hobbs's (1988: 15) ethnographic approach and it avoided 'going native' by doing so. This approach enabled me, to quote Henning Bech (*ibid.*) once more, to shift 'advantageously between insider and outsider perspectives, going into and out of the life-world; as well as a tack between levels of concrete experience and abstract theory'.

In anticipation of my critics I am very much aware that conventional ethnography maintains that the interpretation of culture should never be allowed to drift into intuition, 'no matter how elegantly the intuitions are expressed' (Geertz, 1973). In response to Geertz, I should like to stress that if this study celebrates the idea of a 'method of intuition', this does not imply that that intuition is understood merely as some sort of 'gut feeling'. In this work it is rather interpreted as what Bauman (1999: 9) describes as the sociological sixth sense. That is, it is understood as a critical way of knowing the social world, which implies an expansion of the sociological imagination through empathetic insight. The research approach developed here, then, follows Henri Bergson's argument that it is intuition (Deleuze, 1988), not analysis in the scientific meaning, which is better suited to carrying out qualitative research.

I know of no commentary or application of Bergson's ideas in ethnography.[4] However, in the realm of sociology theorizing Michel Maffesoli (1996) has alluded to a Bergsonian research agenda. In the preface to *The Time of the Tribes,* Shields (1996: x) points out that, contrary 'to the lifeless groupings imposed by sociologists, Maffesoli exploits Bergson's vitalism to argue for the power of the basic sociality – the "being-together" – of everyday life'. For Shields, Bergson's concept of the *élan vital* – the 'creative impulse' or 'living energy' – is explicitly taken up by Maffesoli in *The Time of the Tribes.* For Maffesoli, as for Bergson, science and the intellect cannot ever really grasp the meaning of the *élan vital,* which is the basis of all life.

The problem is that in *The Time of the Tribes* the central tenets of what this approach might involve are never articulated in any detail. This is because what is lacking in Maffesoli's sociology is the rudiments of an empirically informed study that successfully links his theoretical insights with research evidence. Deleuze's (1988) book *Bergsonism* is no more empirically applied than *The Time of the Tribes,* but it deals more thoroughly with what Bergson has to offer empirically minded social theorists. Indeed, Deleuze shows how Bergson's philosophy contributes in no uncertain terms to methodological issues, establishing 'intuition' as the critical concept in Bergson's metaphysics to be used in a methodological form. As importantly, however, Deleuze also identifies Bergson's related concepts of 'duration', 'becoming' and 'memory' as being crucial to ontological questions. In relation to these Deleuze draws, from Bergson, the themes of 'duration' and 'becoming' and he links both of these with the concepts of time and space.

Where conventional ethnographic accounts tend to represent reality as a set of empirical 'facts', spatialising time as if it were still (Deleuze, 1988: 104), thinking about issues of 'duration' and 'becoming' enabled me not only to think about the leisure life-world in terms of the period when 'the lads' were together, but also to articulate the *élan vital* of this spatio-temporal configuration to understand the *circumstances* of its duration and becoming rather than simply what it appeared to be. This approach provided the means for me to challenge the frameworks provided by traditional ontological thinking in ethnography to recognise that time and space are not merely 'real' in the everyday understanding of the words but that they are contingent to time and context. From reading the episode at the beginning this section of the chapter the reader will have seen that inherent in the spatio-temporal configuration of the leisure life-world of 'the lads' is a particular quality that involves its members in such a way that duration and becoming are invoked in a way which challenges commonsense conceptions.

Surface and depth in ethnographic work

If conventional ethnographic accounts have tended to be unimaginative in their understandings of ontological questions they have also been largely uncritical in their interpretation of what constitutes the 'proper' way of doing ethnographic work. Sugden and Tomlinson (1999) provide the back-cloth against which I offer the critique. Right the way through 'Digging the Dirt and Staying Clean' Sugden and Tomlinson present an interpretation of ethnographic work which leads to the conclusion that ethnography can legitimately be characterised as a particular form of depth analysis for exploring culture. In shaping this quite specific vision of ethnography, Sugden and Tomlinson, like Hobbs (1988), draw heavily on the vocabulary of the Chicago school of urban sociology, which, as we have already seen, originated from early social anthropology. I want to argue here that under-standing ethnography in this way is not arbitrary but subsumed by a very specific discourse emanating from the Chicago school, which utilises very specific modes of making sense of social reality, and the metaphor of *depth*, in particular, which is perceived to be more adequate for revealing 'reality' than any other. From my experience it would seem that all ethnographers rely to some extent on this imbalance, and they all consider depth indispensable to their craft.

This critique utilises what Foucault (1980a, b) in his metaphysical language terms his genealogical tactics, which set out to explore what is absent in discourse as a consequence of the institutionalisation of power-knowledge. In relation to this particular discussion of Sugden and Tomlinson's interpretation of what constitutes 'good' ethnographic work, Foucault's genealogical inquiry requires us to ask how these authors come to accept certain things about ethnography as authoritative; and how they came to consent to them, to regard them as legitimate, and to value them as such.

It becomes manifestly clear when you read Sugden and Tomlinson that these authors pursue ethnography in a way that gives preferential treatment to the concept of depth. Consider the following quotations from the article. The authors argue that to be effective ethnographic researchers we must get 'at *deep* insider information' (p. 386), use '*deeply* grounded, free-standing commentaries' (p. 388), 'providing detailed and *deeply* situated comparative data' (p. 388), 'using methods which get 'beyond gazing at the surface' (p. 389) and which 'penetrate far beneath the surface and rhetoric of international sport' (p. 389). For Sugden and Tomlinson, *deep* meaning is taken to be 'true', whereas *surface* meaning is considered as inadequate or misleading, if not altogether false.

However, this all-embracing concern with depth suggests a genuine problem not only for ethnography but also for sociology more generally and raises two key questions. To what extent does the research process become classified by its capacity to seek deep meaning? Why is it by depth that ethnography here gets defined? I neither underestimate the efficacy of deeply grounded ethnographic work nor reject the contribution of depth immersion studies to sociology. However, I want to briefly consider why, and under what discursive conditions, in the Foucauldian sense, depth and surface become the salient defining features of good and bad ethnographic research practice.

Following Derrida (1973), I want to make two key points here. First, there is always inequity in binary oppositions, such as depth and surface. Second, in every understood binary opposition, one part of the relationship is always seen as 'inferior' to the other part; but despite this the 'inferior' part always remains part of the 'superior' element. An understanding of these political dimensions is a guiding thread that runs through all Derrida's work. Here, I want to relate Derrida's two points about binary oppositions to what Sugden and Tomlinson (1999) (and most other ethnographers) do when they are dealing with the concepts of surface and depth in relation to the research process. Following Foucault, I want to argue that this proclivity of giving precedence to depth over surface in the research process is motivated, not by sound argumentation, but by the values of researchers themselves, which reflect a particular discourse of ethnography in sociology, to deny the actual in the name of 'universal' reason.

In an attempt to undermine conventional wisdom, Foucault (1980a, b, 1981), in his genealogical period, set out to undermine this binary opposition by giving precedence to surface over depth in the research process. Foucault's genealogical period marks a clear shift from, but 'follows on where his "archaeology" left off, extending into new areas of discourse the campaign against science and humanism' (Harland, 1987: 155). The published treatment of this methodological shift in Foucault's work is thorough enough that a major discussion is not required here (see Harland, 1987; Ritzer, 1997). However, several important consequences follow from this turn.

First, and as I have said already, Foucault (1981, 1986, 1987) is determined to develop an epistemological and ontological understanding which allows for the 'individual' and a 'culture of individuality', but which also shows that it is ultimately discursive practices, not cognitive selves, that determine what individuals do. It is crucial to note also that Foucault's poststructuralist project concerns itself with signs, not concepts (Harland, 1987). It is signifiers and signifieds, then, not cognitive forms, which form cultural meanings. In the appendices to *The Archaeology of Knowledge*, Foucault (1972) emphasises this poststructuralist point when he argues that discourses should be interpreted in terms of their 'exteriority'; meaning that it is appropriate for the genealogist to analyse discourses on the basis of their 'surface values'. For Foucault, it is erroneous to attempt to interpret discourses in any 'deep' sense. This is why Foucault focused on discourse as practice, instead of on people and what people say, because everyone is discursively positioned. There could be no other way in the Foucauldian scheme of things.

Foucault (1980a, b) made it clear that, for him, power-knowledge is the force that transforms the cultural world and genealogy is the 'tactics' by which the researcher attempts to unearth 'local discursivities' and 'subjected knowledges', to reveal the connections, practices and institutions that comprise discourses. The research activity of genealogy suggests the possibility of an alternative approach to social research, which focuses on discourse as practice rather than trying to get beneath the surface in any deep sense.

It would have been easy for me to conclude that what in essence the figure of 'the lad' is about is something that is 'deep' inside him, but my approach developed a way of doing ethnography which held that what we find *in* 'deep' meaning and *on* the 'surface' is in tension. In carrying out the ethnographic research I relied on the concepts of surface and depth simultaneously.[5] Henning Bech (1997), in his book *When Men Meet*, recognises that 'surfaces' have become crucial to understanding the social world in liquid modernity. I also have developed an approach to ethnography that takes account of 'surfaces' as seriously as it does interviews and theories: one that listened not only to what 'the lads' said and did, but took account of what was unsaid, the symbolism involved and their relationships and encounters.

Following Foucault, I also both looked for and avoided the sense of a human subject. Instead of just focusing on 'the lads' and what they said as individuals, I attempted to focus on discourse as practice, by exploring actual events such as parties, arguments, fights and card schools; relationships of love, friendship and community; 'the lads'' assumptions about others; and so on. This approach involved looking for the unities of discourse in the population of discursive events of what I describe as a leisure lifeworld. I attempted to both understand and articulate events which decentred the individuals who were engaged in them. I drew on the strategy time and again when I felt that 'the lads' were telling me something different from what I believed to be 'true' of their actions and beliefs. In this sense, the research was based on intuition and everyday knowledge, meaning it was as much pragmatically inspired as it was empirical.

This recognition of the efficacy of research strategies, which draw on both surface and depth, then, like Derrida's (1978) insistence on undecidability – the endless play of difference – alerts us to the possibility of undermining binary opposites to the extent that we should be able to assign to each of them more than one understanding. Concepts, after all, are like human beings, they are not simply good or bad but hold both and other possibilities. This is why Bauman (1992a: 114–48) can bracket together theorists as diverse as Hans Gadamer and Richard Rorty as 'postmodern' interpreters, because each of these theorists grasps what is required of an adequate mode of intellectual inquiry for liquid times. The fact that Gadamer organises his hermeneutic intellectual work in a deep sense, while Rorty, in company with Foucault, subordinates deep hermeneutics to surface hermeneutics, is neither here nor there. For Bauman these positions are commensurable in the sense that each inhabits a kind of post-scientific cultural world that has established superiority over its 'modern' rival. I should like to suggest that my own ethnographic project, which has made this paradigmatic leap, could be considered in a similar vein. For it has its roots among the same such 'poets' whose aim it is to create a hermeneutic revolution, both theoretical and empirical, combining interpretive visions. This brings me on to the last dimension of the critique.

Writing the ethnography

> Monsters cannot be announced. One cannot say: 'here is our monsters', without immediately turning monsters into pets.
>
> (Jacques Derrida)

In this section I discuss the writing of the ethnography. I argue that writing in ethnography post-poststructuralism operates in very different ways from conventional ethnographic approaches because it asks and answers different questions and operates with different ways from knowing the 'truth' about the social world (Rinehart, 1998). I argue also that as a researcher who has attempted to expand the sociological imagination in ethnography I have essentially been obliged to adapt my ethnographic writing as an 'alternative vocabulary' of pragmatic discourse, in Rorty's (1979) sense, because I found that existing ethnographic vocabularies were of no use in articulating what I wished to express in my writing.

As Rinehart shows us, conventional ethnographic accounts invariably attempt to 'capture' the research experience as accurately as possible, to increase both the 'reliability' and the 'validity' of the research. Typically, this approach explains the relationship between theory and method, problems associated with gaining access to the field, techniques of social research, analysing data and writing up the final account. Ethnographic studies of this kind contend that theory emerges from the research data and typically illustrate this by characteristic examples of data from field notes. William Foote Whyte's (1943) classic study *Street Corner Society* exemplifies this approach to ethnographic writing.

In clarifying what ethnographic writing post-poststructuralism essentially entails, Rinehart (1998: 204) could be describing my own approach:

> Authors attempt to replicate the sense of the experience. If something did not happen the way it was reported, recollection made it feel as if it did. . . . Truth, in this type of writing, is not a realist narrative but rather a sensual, magical, lyrical truth. The feel of the experience – verisimilitude – is what the writer is after. Exact recordings of words said are less important than what the sayer meant to say. How does the writer know what the sayer meant to say . . . immersion in the culture, in the world portrayed, and attention to context and detail.
>
> (Rinehart, 1998: 204)

Indeed, in an analogous way, the short episode at the beginning of this chapter attempts to 'reach' the audience and immerse it in the world of 'the lads', so that the audience can 'feel' that world and 'inhabit' that world. My writing essentially deploys the rhetorical strategies used by authors of popular fiction. The episode problematises and reveals a world that 'feels' very real to the reader, because I am able to elucidate a sense of the verisimilitude which constitutes the experience of the leisure life-world. The episode also 'reveals' a sense of the ambivalence the ethnographer feels about the Other (women) in the way that he is constituted in the text. The episode also 'reveals' how the author came to be accepted by 'the lads'. I could go on.

My alternative approach provides the reader with a glimpse of the meaning of the cultural imaginary (Castoriadis, 1987) of the leisure life-world by situating the discourse of 'the lads' within the sense of realism that produces it. As the reader will see in the following chapters this cultural studies approach deploys the rhetorical strategies commonly used by authors of popular fiction to allow the culture of the leisure life-world to 'reveal itself', to represent the 'self-evidential reality' of the discourse of the leisure life-world, which is constantly in the process of self-interpreting and self-deconstructing. In so doing it avoids both 'turning the lads into pets' and the subject–object split between myself (as the researcher) and the rest of 'the lads', which makes for an artificial separation in the research process. This is achieved through narrative 'episodes' which allow 'the lads' to 'announce themselves'; my academic self interrupts these from time to time, to add to, shift or refocus the discussion.

All in all, this approach to writing enables me to describe the 'cultural imaginary' (Castoriadis, 1987) of the world I have been exploring. That is, the whole realm of actions, feelings and desires of the leisure life-world in a discourse that 'the lads' themselves have constructed and which has constructed them. This approach works best, because at the end of the research process what I had was not a set of 'raw' data, in the conventional sense, but a form of 'tactics', in the Foucauldian sense, for revealing the 'realism' of the unities of discourse in the population of discursive events of the leisure life-world. I also had a means by which to give a voice to those whose story I was setting out to uncover. This approach to writing allows the culture of the 'field' to 'reveal itself' to the reader, to represent the 'self-evidential reality' of the world it reflects. This approach to writing lets the reader know a time and a place and the people involved much better than in conventional ethnographic accounts. Quite simply it enables the reader to see more. However, these texts do not speak for themselves: like all other narratives, they are ideologically positioned and it is nonsense to suggest otherwise. In the final analysis, my writing, more than anything else, confirms Foucault's point that how we classify and explain away social phenomena 'tells more about us, about our stance on how things are, than it does about any truth . . . It tells more about that which is true to the namer' (Rinehart, 1998: 201). For this approach to ethnographic inquiry is a way of 'making' culture which is contingent upon personal frames of reference, recognising the performative aspects of 'doing' research. In the end, this type of ethnography represents nothing more than my own fixed centre myth, established in my own inimitable way, which is unique to me. In this sense, the leisure life-world is my own personal narrative, my own form of discourse; that is, a 'true' fiction (Reinhart, 1998) which seeks to reveal verisimilitude, but which ultimately remains an imperfect story that is never completed.

My writing is better understood, not as an objective account, but as a subjective reading of the social world. The rhetorical devices used in this form of ethnographic writing are used not to replace reality, but to enhance it. Ethnographic writing post-poststructuralism recognises the limits of ethnography. This writing is best described as the world illuminating its sense of history and culture through an interpreter's reading. Meaning that a piece of ethnographic work of this kind is not about the world out there in the positivist sense, rather it is something in itself: a 'true' narrative fiction. It is the task of the author to bring the sense of realism to ethnographic writing. What I establish in the following chapters is a particular kind of textual performance. This approach is no less systematic and rigorous than conventional ethnography. But it is a form of interpretive intellectual work which understands that ethnography is better understood not as some direct correspondence to reality but empirically, pragmatically and intuitively through its application.

The analysis develops in two distinct ways, making for a synthesis rather than an analysis. The 'episodes' aim to describe the cultural imaginary (Castoriadis, 1987) of the leisure life-world. This approach to writing allows the culture of the leisure life-world to 'reveal itself' to the reader, to represent the 'self-evidential reality' of the discourse of the leisure life-world, which is constantly in the process of self-interpreting and self-deconstructing. This approach traces and reveals both the contingency and rational justifications at work within the discourse of the leisure life-world. It also reinforces Foucault's (1981: 10) argument that discourses may be both instruments and effects of power, but they are always at a point of 'reversal', at 'a starting point for an opposing strategy'.

The process and subsequent writing of the analysis follow a more conventional path, in that I turn to a range of theoretical writings to engage with and reflect on the episodes, to develop 'new' theory. This process should not be interpreted by the reader as a separate exercise; it is simply a stratagem that allows the author to realise the theoretical developments of the overall analysis.

Conclusion

The preceding discussion offered a critical discussion that drew on both the field research and poststructuralist theory in order to offer an alternative approach to ethnography. It also told the reader something about the difference between viewing this leisure life-world as set of signifying practices and viewing it as a density of concrete life experiences. A more concretely grounded understanding of the work of Foucault here was recovered and a conversation with him here was continued. This involved a sort of reinterpretation and reconstruction of my own, in which it was suggested that the 'story' of the lads would be scripted as much as a response to the limits of ethnography and its associated methodologies as to the literary turn in cultural studies, addressing a course of events which both define and make real the historico-cultural constitution of this leisure life-world.

The research approach underpinning the book, then, represents an attempt to explore – as well as explain and theorise – something about the leisure life-world of the lads. It is a work of the sociological imagination (Mills, 1959) developed with an effort to make discernible a model of ethnographic writing which is, in Bauman's terminology, 'made to the measure of liquid modernity'. This is achieved in the way it deals with the familiar; that is, where and how people live out their leisure lives in particular time and place.

This book also prefigures a shift from the sociological imagination as Mills conceived it to a post-scientific way of thinking sociologically in Bauman's (1990) sense, which supposes that in sociology there is an emerging interpretive sensibility (Bauman, 1987), which is underpinned by a way of thinking and understanding the social world that brackets together interpretive inquiry and hermeneutics (Bauman, 1992a). Bauman's project suggests a hermeneutic approach to sociology, which is necessary if we are to be successful in 'unconcealing' the myriad discourses that constitute the social world. Bauman's hermeneutic sociology shows us that to understand the social world we must attempt to understand the different discourses of which people are a part, in order to know where they are coming from; that is, what they know and what they say, their practices (what they do and how they do it), institutions (what they establish to carry out what they know and do what they have to do) (Natoli, 1997) and, last but not least, where they are going.

It was argued that this alternative way of thinking about the sociological imagination augments rather than replaces Mills's project. It does so by insisting that thinking sociologically is uncomplicatedly a demonstration of the interdependence of the sociological imagination of the author and the reality he is attempting to understand. As such it demonstrates that there is no epistemological split in the research process and that the sociologist is always already infiltrated with what and who is being researched. It also assumes that the outcome of any sociological endeavour is always very much part of the personal biography of its author. But if my research approach suggests total involvement, a complexity of identity and empathy, it stops short of being entirely biographical.

It has been suggested that the key strength of this type of interpretive inquiry lies in its ability to be 'up front' about its own weaknesses and in its sensitivity to the discursive, ideological and practical contingencies involved in 'making' sociological truth claims. Interpretation is not understood as an objective investigative orientation. It is seen instead as a critically argumentative and value-laden process. Implicit in this invocation is the recognition that empirical research will always remain partial and that the use of rhetorical strategies normally associated with popular fiction allows the researcher to fill a communication void. However, it is important to recognise that rhetorical devices are not used in this instance to replace empirical findings, but to clarify, reinforce and enhance them. This type of ethnographic writing attempts to stretch the boundaries of the sociological monograph by moving seamlessly from theory to ethnography and back again as the discussion requires. It makes the assumption that ethnography, as any good sociological writing, should be about showing us new ways to see as we seek more detail, greater insight, quirkier titbits of information to enhance our understanding of a social world we assume we already know quite well.

The impetus for this approach involves more than an attempt to describe an alternative model that rests on the notion of an epistemological critique of orthodox sociologizing, however. The author's argument is motivated more by practical matters. All the same, just as this approach does not claim that epistemological questions are extraneous to the sociological enterprise, neither does it ignore issues of ontology and ethics. However, instead of making absolute truth claims in the legislative sense (Bauman, 1987) my approach merely 'changes the subject' (Rorty, 1979) about doing ethnographic research. It insists, with Foucault (1980b), that 'reality' is grounded not merely in the rational thinking subject but in discourses of power/knowledge. That said, the analysis always places a premium on the contextuality and contingency of the local and historically specific social practices. Indeed, 'the lads' always emerge as both concrete and moving figures within the diachronics of this historical constitution.

Accordingly, my approach challenges us to continually question our various ontological positions in relation to the discourses that we produce through our sociological imaginations. What this book asks of readers on a more practical level, however, is that they temporarily suspend their own favoured positions and imagine for now that ontological questions do not apply. In relation to the leisure life-world of 'the lads', what the author is simply asking of the reader is this: for the time being take my word and join me in assuming certain things are 'true', and then, maybe, we can succeed in getting some good work done. And if we can inspire some critical dialogue, we will also have accomplished something along the way.

Notes

1   Discussing the way in which the concept of culture has developed in social anthropology in his classic essay 'Thick Description: toward an interpretive theory of culture', Clifford Geertz (1973) suggests that culture has become 'a permanent and enduring part of our intellectual armoury. But it no longer has the grandiose, all-promising scope, the infinite versatility of apparent application, it once had.' As such, Geertz continues impassionedly, we have come to recognise that the concept cannot 'explain everything, not even everything human, but it still explains something' and that the attention of latter-day social anthropology has shifted to 'isolating just what that something is'. Geertz goes on to tell the reader that 'it is this cutting of the culture concept down to size, therefore actually insuring its continued importance rather than undermining it'. That is the topic to which his book is addressed.

2 In recent years some anthropologists have begun to embrace the 'postmodern' turn. The later work of Clifford Geertz is particularly relevant in this regard, especially in his book *After the Fact* (1995).

3 Williams (1970) was concerned with the exploration of the 'knowable community' to unearth 'the substance and meaning of community'. However, he never underestimated the challenge of this task, for he understood that the idea that any community can be known and understood through people and their relationships is always going to be complicated.

4 Mullarky's (1999) excellent book explores all the major aspects of Bergson's thought.

5 The reader should not confuse the Foucauldian 'tactic' of 'gazing at the surface' with non-participant observation. Whereas the non-participant observation method seeks to understand what is going on from a neutral, detached perspective, the Foucauldian genealogist not only admits, but also celebrates, the subjective contingencies motivating what is 'revealed' through discourse.

Chapter 3

Initiation

Welcome to the Stout man

This chapter chronicles the leisure life-world which is 'the lads'' spiritual 'home'. It talks about 'the lads' and the kind of people we are. Around this discussion, it begins the task of tracing the genealogy of the leisure life-world and explaining how self and identity are constructed through the discourse of the leisure life-world. In order to achieve these two aims, in the first instance, the narrative focuses on the 'arrival' of Stout in the summer of 1979. This evokes a powerful scene which provides the hinge upon which the rest of the discussion in this chapter swings. For in that particular summer the leisure life-world was made singularly secure by a newcomer with a reputation for being 'hard'. It freeze-frames and rolls the credits at this point to reveal how Stout came to be accepted, but more importantly to offer the reader a sense of the verisimilitude of the leisure life-world to show how that world is both lived and understood by 'the lads'. The telling of the story takes the form of narrative 'episodes', which I interrupt from time to time, to add to, shift or refocus the discussion. This style of writing confirms that the relationship between the rest of 'the lads' and myself is not detached but, on the contrary, irrevocably discursive and passionately involved. It is also illustrative of the idea of complexity of 'the self as ethnographer' which was discussed in Chapter 2.

I should like to point out at the outset that this chapter is not a biographical analysis – though biography intrudes – but rather an impression of the historical continuity of the leisure life-world, considerably influenced by how it seems to me today. But what is written in this chapter is far from conclusive; in Foucault's understanding, things could not be anything different. For in the final analysis, this chapter, more than anything else, confirms Foucault's point that how we classify and explain away social phenomena 'tells more about us, about our stance on how things are, than it does about any truth . . . It tells more about that which is true to the namer' (Rinehart, 1998: 201).

The discussion reveals that to be at 'home' as part of the leisure life-world is to recognise the requirement not only to respond to prior discourse and social experiences and actions but also to respond in a fitting manner.

In rendering this portrait the chapter continues to remind the reader that the synchronics of 'the lads'' individual self-reflexivity and the diachronics of the leisure life-world as a historico-cultural constitution intersect, reinforce each other and stand in a coexisting relation, which is both complementary and antagonistic. However, the chapter does not in any sense attempt to write the history of 'the lads' in the conventional way that history is written. Neither does it attempt to try to reconstruct the minute details of the evolution of the leisure life-world. Still less does it attempt to trace the origins of the leisure life-world. As Derrida (1978) has shown us, undertakings of that kind are delusive, because origins are impossible to trace. To catch a glimpse of the meaning of the 'cultural imaginary' (Castoriadis, 1987) of the leisure life-world – my research approach recognises that it can offer no more than that – this chapter merely attempts to position this leisure life-world, this 'home', this 'community' within the sense of historicity and the realism that produces it. Consequently, the reader who is determined to gain entrance to this leisure world may arrive only at the ephemeral and transitory at best. Finally, this chapter also begins to divulge a sense of how the Other is constituted through the 'gaze' of the leisure life-world, which is explored in greater detail in the next chapter.

In short, and the above points notwithstanding, this chapter is really about getting to know 'the lads', but crucially it also allows me to set out the backcloth against which I begin to theorise the 'community' that is the leisure life-world of 'the lads' in the consequent chapters. In those chapters I also contemplate why 'the lads' carry on with this leisure existence by discussing what happened in the years after the mid-1980s, the decade when the leisure life-world changed, when everything in the leisure life-world came to seem the same yet different. In the subsequent chapters I also argue that the leisure life-world of 'the lads' is not a 'community' in the orthodox sociological sense (Durkheim, 1933). That said, I suggest that it is a postulated community (Bauman, 1995), a 'home', which has a contingent relationship to a place, which is the locality of Weston. As we shall see as the narrative in this chapter is developed, this relationship becomes one of particular significance once the collective puissance (Maffesoli, 1996) of the leisure life-world of 'the lads' sets itself in opposition to and seeks to undermine the material reality encountered outside itself. This latter point notwithstanding, before the chapter goes on to explore the 'cultural imaginary' (Castoriadis, 1987) of the leisure life-world, it is important to briefly describe the locality of Weston.

Our 'home', our 'community'

Geographical Weston, 'the lads'' spiritual home, is the village the two big hills – Stile Hill and Paupers Hill – of which rise up suddenly out of the stretched out landscape of south Leeds. Identified in the Doomsday survey of 1086 as part of the lands of a prestigious Norman family, Weston was in all likelihood one of the seven manors of Leeds. Much of the village of Weston was still recognisable until the 1950s, when Leeds City Corporation demolished most of the old buildings in the area. Thereafter Weston village was transformed suddenly and rapidly, with Richard Hoggart's (1957) Hunslet, into the inner urban core of south Leeds.

If in the years after the 1950s the landscape of the 'village' changed, the world of Weston – that is, the narrative for what Weston means and how it is understood, its residents and what goes on there – also changed: Weston became just another 'inner city' problem area. At the same time, geographical Weston was being swallowed up further by the continuation of the growing sprawl of Leeds. Today Weston is held in the tight grip of Leeds ring road, various trunk roads and myriad industrial estates in an urban triangle between, to its north, the M621 and, to its south, the M1 motorways.

Yet, for 'the lads', Weston is still and always will be an independent 'village'. A Weston frozen for ever into an imagined ambivalence, part belonging to 'the lads', part of the urban metropolis of Leeds. Weston is their territory. Weston is their 'home'. It is their kind of night out. Real pubs and real beer. And the tap room at the Farmer's Arms on the Halifax Road is their most agreeable meeting place. It always has been.

As we shall see, this imagined Weston holds an aura for 'the lads' which they can intermittently pull around themselves like a magic disguise. And when they are immersed in this 'home', this 'community', that disguise envelops them so completely they hardly know it is there. To such an extent that 'the lads' think of the leisure life-world as though it is symbolic of all human activity, as though they are enacting an intermittent drama of all that's right against all that's wrong, of good against bad, of the fantastic achievements that make 'the lads' the sure vanquishers in an imaginary and uneven game of contingency.

Enter the Stout man

Everyone, with the exception of Sean, was in the tap room and it seemed like most of us were already pissed. There was a Jam record on, *Eton Rifles*, nice and loud, Paul Weller was on the guitar, some other cunt was on the bass, and that hard-looking bastard, Rick something or other, was on the drums. As usual, we were going about our business. Scott was standing at the bar getting some drinks in. Colin was playing pool with some spastic he didn't even know (he has no style at all, that boring bastard). Stout, so called because of his vast bulk, was sitting with his back towards the bar. Stout stands less than six foot, and must weigh around seventeen stone. He is so thick-set that his clothes give the impression of being a little too tight on him. But he is no fat cunt, nor does he act like a fat cunt. Taking a long drink from his newly pulled pint, you could see him settling back and stretching one massive arm along the top of the defaced wooden bench. His meticulously shaved jaws stood out like giant watermelons as he sunk half the pint of dry cider in one.

Stout, as always, looked deadly. His image is lethal-looking, and it is meant to be. Stout was born in Weston not a stone's throw from his favourite drinking establishment. Stout has a life – a work life and a leisure life. Stout's work life is hard, he is a bricklayer. His leisure life centres on 'the lads'. He knows little, but he has one key skill: he is hard, very hard. He can inflict pain. That said, it isn't very often that he needs to call upon this skill, because his reputation precedes him. Nobody fucks with the Stout man.

The main order of business on this evening concerned Stout and the ritual act of his informal induction. Some of 'the lads' were still of a mind to block his entry, but Stout had been trying hard to become one of us. He'd had 'the lads'' DIY tattoo done already, which he was displaying on his arm, livid against his pale white skin. With his new tattoo the first part of his induction had been accomplished, but the leisure life-world demands self-sacrifice. He would have to hurt somebody – and somebody worth hurting too – to secure his membership. But Stout had come prepared. Tonight, you could tell, he was going to 'have' some cunt.

Stout, despite his hardness, is not exempt from the opprobrium heaped out amongst 'the lads'. And across the bar from Stout, and taking the piss out of him, was David D-ranged. Medium height, compact and lean, he is also a Westoner, born and raised in the Moor Road area. His hair is dark, but not as dark as Stout's, which is ebony. He is no way as big as Stout, but his shoulders are broad and muscular, his body firm. His complexion is surprisingly flush, given the blackness of his hair. But I suppose his colour is not so surprising, given the amount of beer and barbs the pillhead pumps into his body. D-ranged holds the attention absolutely: he is the proverbial 'head the ball' and attention-seeking child 'wanting to be loved' rolled into one, with a cherubic smile and psychotic gleam in his eyes. He was once discharged from the army, because he is fuckin' mental. In D-ranged's mind there are many twisted pictures. Most of them in some way are concerned with either sadistic sex or glorious slaughter. He is a sort of Byronic hero: both exciting and dangerous, but haunted by the remorse of a couple of unfinished performances. Following a fight with an Italian man in a pub in Leeds city centre, he once tattooed I'M GONNA KILL SPIKO BASTARD on his arm with a lighted cigarette. He said that he was going to kill the spik one day. The tattoo symbolises this pledge.

And then there was Sean. There is an art to being 'a lad' and Sean has this off to a tee. Sean is very much like Benno, irascible, sometimes mean, and always irreverent to 'outsiders'. A tall, powerfully built man, Sean, as always, was wearing a familiar neck of light brown hair: shaved to number one and tapered, not squared. He is an Irish Catholic who came originally from County Cork, with his parents, who moved to Leeds, via Glasgow, in 1975, when he was twelve. Sean's world is distinctively Westo-Irish. He was taught the Catholic religion at school and at church, Irish history and culture at home, and how to be 'a lad' on the streets of Weston. This means that not only does he know a great deal more about the Potato Famine, the Troubles and the IRA than anybody else, but also that he is as proud of his Weston origins as the next 'lad' is. Sean is Weston man built upon traditional Corkarian. He is also hard. And he likes to shag meaty fanny.

Sean and Stephen 'Benno' Benson are always arguing and both like a good scrap. Benno doesn't push the hard man routine as overtly as Sean; he also has the restraint and self-control denied to most Weston men. Sean, on the other hand, likes his own long, muscular legs, likes to use them to kick Miggy spastics. He kicks hard, always has. Grappling with the nature of his own enthusiasm for violence has never been easy for Sean. He had been fighting the night before this night and his left cheek was swollen. But at that moment, Sean was off exploring. Engaged in his usual preoccupation with chatting up some fanny, Sean was talking to some 'big' fanny in the 'best' room. Sean is a dirty bastard and his sexual odyssey between young girls, big birds and grannies is always designed to shock. Sean thinks of himself as some kind of expert, a connoisseur of fanny. He has his own subject and he is 'the lads'' leading authority. He knows everything there is to know about fanny. He could write his own thesis on fanny. There is good-looking fanny, ugly fanny, fit fanny, rough fanny, hairy fanny, bald fanny, beautiful fanny, classy fanny, married fanny – fanny *ad infinitum*.

The always neat-dressed, neat-faced Benno, has a sarcastic humour that is very much his own. Stephen is the very incarnation of integrity and honesty. This is something that deeply impresses everyone who comes into contact with him. The first thing you notice about him is his piercing blue eyes. They appear to stare at you curiously, almost aggressively. He is not a handsome man, though not in any particular way unattractive, just staighforwardly rough and brutish. He is above average height, slightly built, with short blond hair. He has large hands, three rings on three fingers on each, and bitten-down fingernails. He was wearing regulation Levi's jeans and T-shirt.

Sandwiched between the bar and the pool table were the Hogan brothers. Not quite lads, these cunts, but we love them just the same. John and Peter, both with round Irish faces dominated by hooked Roman noses. On this night they looked more alike than usual: with the medium-length brown hair, that square, freckled face, and the drooping and damp bottom lip. The Hogans emanate from a detached neighbouring tribe, and they examine, assess, even imitate us, and sometimes fight Miggy spastics with us, but with them we rarely exchange pleasantries. That would be conceding too much.

Then there was Louis. Louis is the fat cunt, to his mates. His hair is cut short and he is slightly jowly, with wire glasses pressed tightly against his fat face, giving him that ambivalent look of hardness and intelligence. Louis may be a fat cunt, but his body looks right, as if he is meant to be a fat cunt. Louis was holding out his fat tattooed hands and was taking two pint glasses from Scott. Scott as always seemed tall, rake-thin, wearing a denim suit and brown, spiked brown hair. He usually avoids looking people directly in the eyes. This is because he is a squint-eyed bastard. Scott always wears his hair short, shaved at the back. And he always wears black Levi's, black Adidas Samba trainers, and a white Fred Perry polo shirt. On the little finger of his left hand he was wearing a half-sovereign ring, a symbol of his love towards his girlfriend, Julie.

An interlocutory injunction

You can't quantify it, value it or identify it precisely. But the logic of 'the lads' goes as follows: Stout's hardness, Sean's hardness and charisma, Benno's 'I'll fuck anythingness', Scott's coolness, David's lunatic tendencies, Tony's eccentricity, Louis's fat popularity and Colin's boringness, individually, mean little. But when brought together, these individual personalities provide us with a collective sense of belonging, a masculine realism which unites us to such an extent that the individual differences between us are washed away into our collective mythology, which conceals both our personal wishes and individual desires. It is a convergence, a mutualisation of masculine Weston minds. The leisure life-world of 'the lads', according to this constitution, is the basic unit of our world, which accords each of us his sense of ontological security.

It is because of the ambivalence of the mystical and magical realism of the leisure life-world that there is no way of explaining what we are or our actions in a rational sense. We each are prodigiously loyal to one another. We look out for each other. We are sceptical about looking outside the 'home' for strength to keep the 'home' going. Everybody knows everybody else, and their business. We confide in things to one another that we would never reveal to anybody else. 'Outsiders' are treated with suspicion and are not to be trusted. It is always 'the lads' against the rest of the world.

Part two

We spent most of the day before in a pub in town, and that afternoon in the working men's club. We had spent the early part of the evening in the tap room at the Farmer's Arms, and now were making our way on the bus to the Setting Sun public house in Middleton, near Leeds. On this night, we were going up to Miggy to find some danger and some trouble. Because we hate Miggy and we hate Miggy bastards. Miggy bastards are the objectification of an intrusive outside world and that they are spastics, fuckwits and cunts, testifies to this reality.

On alighting from the bus, we walked down the last part of Miggy Park Avenue, a long road of council houses set back from grass verges littered with dog shite, and turned into Thorpe Road. In the dreary Miggy light it was darkening towards evening. Miggy is impoverished, always has been, in terms of its housing, its people and its pubs. Outside the main pub in Miggy, which is situated in a murky Miggy street with broken street lights, is a wind trap. All sorts of crap and rubbish from the Miggy estate blow into the car park and pile up against the front wall of the pub: curled ring pulls, dented beer cans, stubbed-out cig ends and spent matches, soiled plastic nappies, chip shop newspaper, empty chinky cartons and Durex foils. On the wall at the side of the pub somebody had written MIGGY WHITES ROOL OK in white gloss paint.

Through the early evening air came that rancid smell of Miggy. Miggy spastics smell worse than even Pakis. It came from the Expelair fans outside the pub, no doubt packed out with dirty Miggy spazwits, Miggy flids, Miggy dossers and Miggy cunts. There is the myth that most people who live on the Miggy estate are trying to leave it. But everybody else knows that dirty, spazzy Miggy bastards love living in the shit hole.

Little diamonds of broken glass decorated the door entrance where somebody had kicked in the bottom window of the inner door. The long passageway of the pub was lined with Miggy spastics in their full flower of youth. It didn't matter, though, because the marvel of the leisure life-world is that it is very much like an expensive car and we, its riders, always travel in certainty and comfort, even through danger-ous neighbourhoods. In the suffused and badly lit refulgence filtering through the single ceiling light, you felt a bit like a boxer walking through the baying crowd to his match with destiny. It was a bumpy, jolting journey to the bar. But in the manner of a petulant prize-fighter

Sean led the line well through the wall of bodies as we fought our way through the passageway to the large back room. We had to accept a lot of abstruse eyeballing before we reached the bar, but the feeling from the crowd of young pretenders in the passageway was pusillanimous, which made a change for Miggy.

We were an impressive-looking bunch as we entered the badly lit bar, which was reasonably clean and tidy, if threadbare. Not bad for Miggy. While Sean went to 'get 'em in', the rest of us were standing waiting for our drinks in the middle of the room, monitoring 't' crack', not really giving a fuck about the battle-scarred fixtures and fittings that had witnessed the scenes of millions of comings and goings, thousands of ups and downs between Miggy bastards. Tables, chairs and benches – chipped and burned – grouped here and there, some already occupied, most not. The decor, once dominated by gold and maroon wallpaper, was ripped and discoloured and drawn on. Stale and airless, the bar stank of Miggy spastics, horse shit and beer slops. Thick smoke from cheap cigarettes smouldered in the ashtrays. The tiled floor, which once held a chessboard pattern, was incomplete and matted with the years of Miggy strife, and gave off a vinegary smell of ancient beer slops.

A mongy old Miggy couple was sitting almost opposite us. There were also two young birds sitting in the room. Both had blonde bobs and were wearing short black skirts, and you can nearly see their dirty Miggy cunts. We never think about women except when they are in front of us, looking for some cock. And these two were looking for some cock, without a doubt. We could tell. But none of us lot would be seen dead fuckin' these Miggy scabs; even Sean. There was nothing doing in Miggy, so we decide to fuck off somewhere else. 'Home', to the Farmer's Arms.

Another interlocutory injunction

We have priorities. We accept, without articulating it, that our leisure is in some sense the antithesis of work, a reward for work or relief from work, and we buy the notion that work is something to do with paid employment and nothing to do at all with what we do together. The excoriations of the workplace are always perceived with hostility and thought to be demeaning. It is there that you cannot be yourself, where you are expected to forfeit your true identity, your sense of self-worth.

There is a sense of freedom from work and a sense of freedom to be had in the pubs and clubs of Weston and beyond and in the music that we love – ska, punk and pop – which animates our freedom. We have an idea of the leisure life-world as a sort of dream factory, where anything is possible. Whenever we get drunk – which happens every time we go out together – we have the most wonderful adventures. Drinking is what we do best. We know that if we don't drink we cannot have any fun. Drinking also brings us closer together and makes us more confident in what we do.

Like I said, we have a particular kind of outlook to life: do a job that pays 'good' money and live for the nights and weekends of leisure and pleasure. For us, a night of leisure means the pub and the night club. Besides drinking, four other pleasures emerge large in our lives: sex, gambling, sport and fighting. This means that fuckin' fanny, horse racing, card schools, pool, football and fighting play a major part in our leisure lives. Louis is the main gambling man: horses, dogs, cards, you name it. Sean and Benno are the supreme fuckin' men. We are all great drinking men. And Stout is the top fighting man. Going from pub to pub, we win some fights and lose others; each encounter bringing with it new adventures, small defeats and major triumphs. But, it must be said, we do not suffer defeats lightly.

Part three

The 'best' room in the Farmer's was quite crowded and the nearer to the bar you got, it seemed that the intensity of the atmosphere increased. We thought it should be a good night this. Familiar, Weston faces brightened up the bar and this felt a better place to be. Our unity incited us into being provocative and outrageous. We jeered and taunted some ugly-looking twats in the corner and Sean asked this fat young bird what colour knickers she had on and if she fancied a fuck. We felt all-powerful, uninhibited and free. Then it stopped. Suddenly we sensed the machinery of our private defence system clicking into first like an automatic gearbox, self-regulating.

Scott was walking back from the toilet and this ugly cunt stepped right into him to bar his way. His mates gathered round like flies around shit. They didn't look like Westoners. Without looking too closely we could tell that they were from Miggy, because they all looked the same. Everybody knows that incest is a local fuckin' pastime in Miggy. But who else would fuck the Miggy slags who mother these spastics? Most of the men looked our age. Though they each had that familiar spazzy Miggy appearance. These men had half-wit smiles on faces of cadaverous and taut-stretched skin. Malnourished, these cunts. Each of the cunts' hairs looked greasy. Head lice prevailed. And every other one had a tooth missing or a broken nose. These were Miggy cunts, all right. All strangers are Miggy cunts.

From the back of the group appeared a fliddy bastard older than the rest, in a tight-fitting shirt worn with use and discoloured under the armpits. At that point, the whole bar seemed to fall silent. Even the DJ turned The Stranglers off, not playing another record.

The cunt that was mouthing it at Scott was about our own age, but the flid was at least five years older. We knew who he was. And he was a hard cunt. The flid was also a big cunt, but he was still what you would expect. He was all cheap denims and affected speech, stammering something indistinguishable, while running the scabbed-up fingers of his disproportionately small right hand through hair stylishly awry through six months' grease. He had a mongy face like every other Miggy tit-head and he was looking in the direction of Stout. I monitored my own reactions as Stout glared back, fully alert and centred. My heart started beating faster and, like the rest of 'the lads', I could feel a sense of ecstasy arising within me.

The flid was wearing the expression of a typical Miggy spastic as he was staring at Stout with his squalid little eyes, mumbling something incoherent, in Miggy-speak. His face was a grey spastic's one, the greyness ground in, rooted in the interstices of his head. His Thom's shirt was raised up, revealing his bare back. The dealer boots he was wearing, once tan, were filthy. His massive jeans hung shape-lessly, revealing his buttock cleavage; gunmetal grey skin, enormous cheeks, a mass of shifting, rancid fat.

The flid was braced like a funky chicken as he prepared to do battle. He looked hard at Stout, trying to 'stare him out'. I felt, vicariously, in my own gut, the sense of intense anticipation that must have been in his. Stout in downing his second pint looked back at the spazwit. Stout was mean and tense, his face informed with an expectation of disregard. The flid looked assessingly at Stout's muscular frame. Although Stout was not as tall as the Miggy spastic was, he seemed to take on a more threatening shape. The flid talked hard but his spazwit face looked bothered. He absorbed Stout's status, and him, with a frightened and frightening gaze. Stout gave him, steadily, a Weston look. The suspense was deadly.

Stout's eyes focused with considerable intent on the dirty Miggy bastard, now; standing there in his fuckin' gyppo outfit, no doubt stolen off some other Miggy cunt's washing line. The flid was giving Stout some shit. Going on and on . . . But Stout wasn't listening. Then, inadvertently, the thick Miggy cunt tilted his chin forward slightly, inviting Stout to smash him in the face. It was at that moment – when the silence gathered and continued for what seemed to be an age – that Stout delivered the first blow.

Stout smashed the flid in the face and he found himself reeling several feet backwards. He fell, dropping on to his hands and knees. Catching his breath, the flid struggled up. Facing the Stout man, the flid was still courageously steady, but his face seemed suddenly bleak. Nevertheless, he rushed at Stout like a madman, in a blind rage now. But by the time he responded Stout was well ready for him and the graceless spastic fell again as Stout connected with another punch. The flid returned with a flurry of fists that held no fears for Stout, who connected once again. The flid seemed to have lost control of his legs now. In a manner spastic and unstylised, with no flexibility or grace, and much noise, he descended towards, sank to, the floor and his reputation fell in pieces around him.

At first the flid had moved easily, but he had soon visibly tired; and now he knew that he was in the shit. His bejeaned legs oscillated on the ground. His right eye was puffed and watering, deformed by Stout's fist, it seemed to spill into his cheek. There was a crimson smudge where Stout's knuckles had made contact with the fuckwit's temple. Stout wasn't stopping and sensed our approval as he pummelled the spazwit's head some more. With each punch Stout's membership unfolded and named itself to the rest of 'the lads'. In a short time the flid was no more. The room still smelled of Miggy bastards, but it also smelled victorious.

Various extensions to the original design of the pub had resulted in added security problems for the overworked and below-strength security staff of one. But Jeff the bouncer arrived as one of the flid's mates emerged from the crowd feigning to rescue his mate. But Jeff kicked him in the bollocks. The gonad tried to hide his distress but couldn't and clutched where his bollocks used to be. The spastic flapped about on the floor, like his mate: helpless, pissed and now fucked.

For almost everybody the bar soon returned to normal after Stout's vanquishing of the flid from Miggy. But, for 'the lads', the Farmer's Arms was a pleasure-dome. Stout had arrived. Watching this performance it was easy to understand how this lad stirred such emotions in the hearts of those who saw him. The leisure life-world has a badge of its own, and now Stout was a proud wearer. Stout would be revered for ever. It seemed as though there was nothing Stout couldn't do. Suddenly after he meant nothing to us he was everything. And we began to construct his life anew. This evening belonged to him. Long live Stout.

Thereafter, Stout's stature moved out of his person, almost angelically, like a heavyweight champion's, as if there wasn't any connection between him then and him previously. He felt like the star character in a box office success, floating into a new vision. This transcendental moment was to go down in the folklore of the leisure life-world.

An interlocutory injunction again

We picture Stout as man of hardness, of extraordinary physical prowess, and we cannot see him in any other way. We still remember the night he finally arrived. It is an image of Stout that lingers in memory, that bang and smack, and the punch in the face. The leisure life-world is a powerful community: attack it and it redoubles its efforts to fight back. And that night remains with us, as an inexplicable feeling of euphoria. To this day it is still talked about, its effects still felt. We never tire of the story. And time and again we have played out this scene, as if quoting directly from the unpublished discourse of our leisure life-world, as if narrating our leisure experiences in 'real' life. Every stupid cunt that has ever dreamt of fuckin' with the Stout man has tasted some of what the Miggy flid got on that night out.

Indeed, that was the beginning of Stout's enchantment with the leisure life-world of 'the lads'. For it was that particular night in the Farmer's that reconstituted Stout. Stout had ended the night out on a new footing. Before that night out, he had been no more or less than some big, hard bastard who was shaggin' David D-ranged's sister. All at once he was Stout the lad. He had also been apprehensive that he would always feel like that, feel like an intruder. And that his membership would ultimately be denied. But after his demolition of the flid it did not feel like that at all. For we at last understood the nature of where he fitted in, and the rest of it slotted very easily into place.

On a personal level, Stout's membership lent him gravitas and a new type of dignity. If there is such a thing as utopia, and if that is what Stout was looking for, it was with us that he had found it. For the rest of us, the euphoria of that evening buoyed us up over the months that followed. Stout's induction had been that type of night: the ratification of a new membership and as spectacular an occasion as we could wish for; all trust and bravado intact. And it laid a new rich texture. For we had an institutionalised power behind us, that had been enhanced with the transformation of Stout.

On being 'a lad'

In the above episode the reader saw that the leisure life-world of 'the lads' is somewhat prototypic, and as such it is highly dependable. It is set somewhere in the city of Leeds. Its protagonists are each different but also more than a little similar: they all, in some way or other, carry the look of the leisure life-world – in the way they dress, talk, walk and wear their hair, tattoos. The reader was also sensitised to the actuality that, for 'the lads' themselves, there is no need to see all this – those in the know, they always carry the leisure life-world in their heads, permanent – the feel of it, the smell of it. This suggests that 'the lads' have a special camaraderie, a 'perfect' relationship that can only be acquired between those who understand.

It should also be becoming apparent that an emotional force, a puissance (Maffesoli, 1996), which speaks of itself directly out of the discourse of the leisure life-world, underpins this relationship. And the reader will have begun to discern too that its key points of reference can be traced through the leisure life-world's own vernacular, which unifies its various stories. But before this relationship, which constitutes a particular kind of belonging – what Bauman (1995) calls a postulated community – is discussed in any further depth, in the rest of this chapter I both trace and explicate the meanings of selfhood and the strategies of identity making associated with the leisure life-world.

The following discussion applies some ideas originating from Heidegger's (1962) classical philosophical study *Being and Time*, which are developed more extensively through Ricoeur's (1991, 1992) hermeneutics to the leisure life-world to explain how the intersubjectivity associated with this life-world of 'the lads' is constituted through specific narratives of identity. The introduction of Bauman's hermeneutic sociology constitutes a critical supplementary perspective, which enables me to theorise the ideas surrounding these strategies of identity making to suggest that they make invocations to both 'solid' and 'liquid' objective criteria of categorisation.

In applying these ideas to the discussion already developed through the narrative episodes in the first part of the chapter this analysis charts the epistemological frameworks and ontological statuses associated with the being 'with' and being 'without' of the leisure life-world of 'the lads'. The reader will quickly grasp that this analysis is about the ways in which 'the lads' are *always* understood as particular characters in the leisure life-world's very own narrative. It will also be discerned that this discussion is about 'us' and 'them', the 'same' and 'other', and that it is through the discourse of the leisure life-world that (to adopt two of Paul Ricoeur's concepts) two contradictory but also complementary strategies of identity building are advantageously deployed by 'the lads': this of ipse-identity and that of idem-identity. This analysis also provides the backcloth against which 'the lads' encounters with the Other are understood and which are developed in more detail in the next chapter. As the reader will see, Ricoeur's hermeneutics suggests a dialectic of self and Other. Indeed, if narrative identity is the identity of the characters associated with this leisure life-world, it is also the identity which links ipse and idem. Basically, the following analysis suggests that these two identity making strategies – ipse and idem – operate conjointly to control the social space in and surrounding the leisure life-world of 'the lads'.

Identity building 'lad'-style

It is imperative to grasp at the beginning of this discussion that 'the lads'' identities cannot be understood simply as their own. They are contingent upon a time and a place and they are embedded in 'the lads'' mutual social experiences of the leisure life-world and are constituted through their relations with each other. As we have already begun to discern through the episodes described above, this process works through what Ricoeur (1992) calls the 'exchange of memories' that emphasises the ways in which 'the lads' are co-authors of their own shared discourse or master narrative. This 'exchange of memories' works through them sharing stories about themselves and others in a way in which involves cultural memory invoking particular characters. What is also significant about this 'exchange of memories' in terms of the leisure life-world is its power/knowledge (Foucault, 1980b): 'the lads' may be subjects in other people's stories and others may be the subjects of their own and in others' stories. But here in the leisure life-world none of these alternatives matters, for 'the lads' are unquestionably the exclusive master narrators of both their own stories and the stories of others.

As has been indicated already, this process of narration draws on two complementary strategies: the idem-identity strategy and the ipse-identity strategy. As Ricoeur shows, the idem-identity strategy seeks to secure for identity a sense of permanence by ensuring that the process of identity making is straightforwardly uncomplicated, by suggesting that the idea of identity has a rigid immutability which transcends time and space. 'The lads' are able to find the essentialist support for such a strategy in the discourse of the leisure life-world, which as we will see in the subsequent chapters is able to weather the ravages of time and change. 'The lads' believe and practise the supremacy of a passion over rationality, although they respect the truth of rationality, which informs them how to construct others (hereafter described as the Other). The idem-strategy 'lad' style is a performative procedure which draws on the Kantian category of *Einbildung-skraft* – literally the 'transcendental power of the imagination' – to construct the Other's 'true face' and 'schematise' its shape with concrete features (Žižek, 2002). Moreover, being 'solidly' modern, the idem-identity strategy of the leisure life-world of 'the lads' *always* makes invocations to 'solid' objective criteria of identification: women are always fanny, Miggy flids are always flids.

In relation to the leisure life-world this rationality enables 'the lads' to attach 'solid' modernist inspired visions of idem-identity to the 'surface' beings around them, like resplendent images more real than the actual bodies they obscure. As we saw in the first part of this chapter, the narration of the leisure life-world described others variously as 'flids', 'spastics' and 'fanny' living 'solid' modern lives, excluded from the 'liquid' world in which they 'really' live. For 'the lads', individuals or groups without the leisure life-world retain these identities precisely because they are external to its discourse, exhibiting a sense of fixity, continuous and immutable. The 'universal' truth of this rationality is what enables 'the lads' to divide themselves and others into two categories: 'us' and 'them', 'same' and 'other'.

'The lads' know that these mutually constructed discourses of idem-identity are but allegories; unfortunately they do not know – in truth they do not really care – how these allegories are interpreted by the Other. What the Other makes of these characterisations is neither here nor there. 'The lads' have their own version of the modern obsession with orderliness which in the leisure life-world is 'urgently undertaken and doggedly pursued' (Bauman, 2001c: 78). The Other litters what is otherwise an orderly place and must be dealt with accordingly. What prompts them to deal with the Other is the search for some order in a 'liquid' world of endemic disorder, and it is in 'their' leisure lives where 'the lads' perceive that utopia can be achieved.

This need to deal with the Other demonstrates that if the leisure life-world is about 'us', it is always manifestly about 'them' too, because 'otherness' is always at the heart of 'the lads' version of idem-identity making. The idem-identity, then, is always polysemic, in Ricoeur's terminology: a polysemy of otherness. These others are never persons, they are merely characters in the plot, which is a story of leisure written by 'the lads'. Moreover, these characterisations do not have to be 'real'; 'the lads' simply have to be convinced that they are. What is important for 'the lads' is the *meaning for them* of these characterisations of their version of truth, which is something that enables them to form what they perceive *is* the world when they are at leisure together. It makes sense to 'the lads' that they populate their leisure life-world with these characterisations of the Other.

These processes of narration also draw on the counter strategy of ipse-identity making. This counter strategy involves, for Ricoeur, the occasioning of self-identity making proper, which is always occasioned in the flux of everyday life. Ricoeur (1992), who, like Martin Heidegger, writes in the hermeneutic tradition, argues that every story about the world presupposes the world as it is through a kind of 'mythic stability', which enables its members to perpetuate their own world as distinct from others. Indeed, we have seen that when the 'lads' leisure together they bring forth a quite specific discourse that 'fixes' reality in a particular way around a narrative that perpetuates itself through this group of men themselves acting as the storytellers, characters in a plot and audience for themselves and one another. We have seen too that is achieved through the leisure life-world's very own cultural imaginary (Castoriadis, 1987).

The ipse-identity strategy works through the discourse of the leisure life-world in the following way: the figure of 'the lad' is always understood as a character in the leisure life-world's very own story line and is never imagined as anything other than through his experiences in the leisure life-world. In this leisure world each one of 'the lads' shares the condition of, to use Ricoeur's expression, a 'dynamic identity' that is specific to the story which is recounted each time 'the lads' come together: Stout's is the hardest bastard in the world, Sean's is hard and charismatic, Benno will always 'fuck anything', Scott is cool and D-ranged is always 'kicking off' with his lunatic tendencies. The leisure life-world has its own discursive and contingent temporality, outside commonsense notions of time and space, which constructs the identity of each of 'the lads', that is, what can be called 'his own particular narrative identity, in constructing the story told' (Ricoeur, 1992). It is then the meta-identity of the discourse of the leisure life-world that makes the individual ipse-identities of each of 'the lads'.

Ricoeur's ipse/idem thesis is essentially another rendition of the meta-physical critique underpinning Heidegger's classic study *Being and Time*, which emphasises the duality of ontologising implied by on the one hand the essentialism implicit to traditional Western thought and on the other Heidegger's own existential hermeneutics. 'The lads' might never have heard of Martin Heidegger but it as if from the essentialists they have learned how to reify others' identities, treating them as if they were surface beings, though beings of particular kinds: 'flids', 'spastics', 'slags', 'fanny'. As for themselves, it's as if from Heidegger they have learned how to give due justice to self-identity as a process of becoming; that is, to resurrect ipse-identity building as the more *authentic* possibility of Self-constancy. Heidegger (1962: 369) elucidates what this process of becoming involves:

> In terms of care the *constancy of the Self*, as the supposed persistence of the *subjectum*, gets clarified. But the phenomenon of this authentic potentiality-for-Being also opens our eyes for the *constancy of the Self* in the sense of its having achieved some sort of position. The *constancy of the Self*, in the double sense of steadiness and steadfastness, is the *authentic* counter-possibility to the non-Self-constancy which is characteristic of irresolute falling. Existentially, '*Self-constancy*' signifies nothing other than anticipatory resoluteness. The ontological structure of such resoluteness reveals the existentiality of the Self's Selfhood.

It is the emphasis on constancy and resoluteness and a perceived sense of authenticity that marks the characteristic features of being one of 'the lads'. This ipse-identity is both constituting of and constituted by the very particular discourse that is the leisure life-world, which integrates the past, present and future of 'the lads' into an existential continuity *Dasein,* which is marked by a veritable sameness. Indeed, as we have seen, the ipse-identity of 'the lad' as it is constituted through the leisure life-world relies on two important attributes that are assumed in this discourse: constancy and sameness. Their shared desire to conform to the discourse of the leisure life-world perpetuates the constancy and sameness confirmed by the ipse-identity of 'the lad'.

Contrary to the authenticity implied by ipse-identity, Bauman's (1992a, 2000a) work suggests that 'liquid' identity building lives on ambivalence; it is always about becoming rather than what you are – it is the struggle for identity, not identity itself, what we really want, what we really get off on. Be that as it may, 'the lads' idea of ipse-identity building in relation to themselves is *always* about what they *are* rather than what they want to become. Within the confines of the leisure life-world they are secure in the knowledge of who they are. This existential choice of the ipse-identity is what Heller (1999: 227) describes as a *leap*:

> It is not determined, although it does not take place without conditions. One can and cannot be aware of the leap. Authenticity means to remain true to the leap, to one's choice of oneself. *Authenticity is to remain true to oneself.* Authenticity has become the single most sublime virtue of modernity, for authentic people are the people who remain true to their existential choice, who are pulled and not pushed, who are person- alities. This also means that they get as close to perfection as a modern person can.

This latter point notwithstanding, 'the lads' recognise that the leisure life- world can only provide them with intimations of authentic selfhood, for if this discourse facilitates constancy and resoluteness it is also fated to be temporal. The following quotation, which paraphrases Rée's (1998: 34) explication of the contingency of Heideggerian authenticity, demonstrates very well the contingency that is integral to the authentic ipse-identity that is constituted by the discourse of the leisure life-world:

> Authenticity can never be a comfortable condition for 'the lads', how- ever. It means understanding themselves existentially, and making this understanding their own; but that entails accepting that they are no more than shifting networks of interpretations, without any internal 'essence' to hold their existence together, and this prospect may not please them. [In common with other men and women in liquid modernity] they would prefer to be something rather more substantial, so they flee from their authentic selves again and construe themselves as equipment or things of nature than mere beings-in-the-world.

Given the ambivalence of this central conflict, the ipse-identity of 'the lad' is best described as neither a secure or solid modern self nor an ephemeral (postmodern) surface being, but as a Self-constancy (Heidegger, 1962) achieved in response to the ambivalence characteristic of liquid modernity. Indeed, it is 'the lads'' desire to confirm the already existing reality of the leisure life-world that perpetuates the constancy of, in Heidegger's words again, *Dasein*. The ipse-identities of 'the lads', then, must be understood as both autonomous and self-reflexive, engaged in action, communally situated, in a life-world tempered by contingency. And it is the process of putting into discourse the narratives of 'the lads' which gives the leisure life-world its legitimacy and authority.

In Ricoeur's terminology the leisure life-world is ultimately 'the lads'' very own epistemology of 'attestation' that works in two ways, which are mutually dependent. First, the discourse of the leisure life-world operates

as 'the lads'' very own truth about the world, which is def
'Self-certainty' (Heidegger, 1962) that enables 'the lads'' to
to one another that it is in their leisure that they really can be them.
Stout the hard bastard, Sean the fanny man, D-ranged, Benno, Fat Louis
and the like. Second, it is through the selfsame certainty of this discourse
that 'the lads' can certify that their leisure world is 'free' from those others
whom it excludes: the 'flids', 'spastics', 'slags' and 'fanny' living 'solid'
modern lives, excluded from the 'liquid' discourse that has created them.

The leisure life-world is also based on Ricoeur's (1992) 'model of forgiveness', demonstrating one of the ways in which the sharing of memories goes
beyond mere recollection. 'Forgiveness' enables 'the lads' to block out that
which challenges or attempts to transcend the ontological framework that
underpins their leisure lives. That Stout 'knocks his women about', that
Fat Louis is 'a shit house' and that Benno's sister likes 'a bit of black
cock' means little if anything when 'the lads' are together. For Ricoeur, his
model of forgiveness points the way towards the opening up of a space for
ethics. However, the way it is made manifest in the leisure life-world is
through an ethics of contingency which dictates that 'the lads'' actions,
and their apparent values, are *always* contingent upon the discourse leisure
life-world.

This analysis of the leisure life-world of 'the lads' also confirms Ricoeur's
argument that if attestation is always a form of Self-certainty, it is too
always an epistemological position under threat through a 'hermeneutics
of suspicion'. Ricoeur (1992) considers that Self-certainty is itself always a
hermeneutics of the suspicion, precisely because self-identity as ipse, which
is attested through discourse, is always in need of interpretation and it
remains always bound to the dialectic between 'us' and 'them', 'same' and
'other'. For Ricoeur, as for Derrida and Foucault, if discourses have their
own 'specificity', they also always remain vulnerable to a point of 'reversal',
or some 'other' at 'a starting point for an opposing strategy' (Foucault,
1981). What also makes the leisure life-world fragile, in Bauman's scheme
of things, is that even though 'the lads' are hell bent on resisting 'liquid'
threats with their own 'solids', they are in truth merely would-be 'solid'
moderns, who really are not quite. This is because – to use a Weberian metaphor – what 'the lads' seek through the leisure life-world is a light cloak, not a
steel casing (Bauman, 2001b). Consequently the leisure life-world will always
remain haunted by the spectre of the Other.

Conclusion

In this chapter the reader has been getting to know 'the lads' and has seen
how they are the co-authors of their own shared discourse, which is the
leisure life-world. We saw that this discourse forms itself as a social and
cultural drama played out when 'the lads' leisure together. Unproblematic

it is not, and its protagonists intertwine in complex ways, but we saw too that they each sing from the same song sheet and in its volatile unity the leisure life-world forms itself into a narrative that reflects a concrete social context. We saw that when they are together 'the lads' conjure up what the poststructuralists would reject, that is, their very own 'finalising frame of reality', their own particularly 'solid' modern discourse. In Heller's (1999: 221) understanding, 'the lads', together as individuals, are autocephal, 'that is, enough for themselves. They are in no need of anyone or anything else'.

I introduced Ricoeur's distinction between the complementary strategies of idem-identity and ipse-identity making in order to demonstrate how 'the lads' control this social space during their leisure time together. We saw that what goes on outside features only as a backdrop to events within the leisure life-world, which is always played in wide screen, joining up the ipse-identities of 'the lads'. What is more, Ricoeur's Heideggerian-inspired hermeneutics enabled us to see that together the strategies of idem and ipse enable 'the lads' to construct and schematize through their own version of Kant's *Einbildungskraft* a leisure life-world that is constant and which allows them to maintain their sameness at the same time as controlling the Other through their very own normalising discourse. Indeed, the monologic imposed by the leisure life-world operates by establishing what Derrida (1998: 39–40), drawing on the Heideggerian metaphor of the One, describes as a sovereign foundation 'whose essence is always colonial [and] which tends, repressively and irrepressibly, to reduce language to . . . the hegemony of the homogeneous'. But we also began to see too that where there is the comfort of constancy and sameness at the centre of the leisure life-world, there is always the threat of instability and otherness at its periphery.

This chapter suggested that the Other becomes real to 'the lads' only when it populates their leisure world. However, it is 'the lads'' response to that threat and how they deal with the Other that I now turn. The following chapter examines the competing and contrasting understandings of the constitution of power/knowledge (Foucault, 1980b) in the leisure life-world. In so doing, it pays particular attention to the ways in which issues of 'us' and 'them', of 'similarity' and 'difference', are taken up, articulated, interpreted and contested in the leisure life-world. In relation to these the nature of this administration process is examined through Foucault's metaphor of the 'gaze'. The masculine and 'solidly' modernist normalizing 'gaze' of the leisure life-world is elaborated and its implications for the Other are spelled out. As we shall see, if 'the lads'' 'solidly' modern inspired version of the world 'out there' is essentially a rhetorical attack on alternative truth claims, it also has 'real' world implications for those who are not one of them.

Chapter 4

Administration

'Us' and 'them': the administration of the other 'lad' style

A night on the town

As we alighted from the bus by City Square, Leeds centre was jumping on this Saturday night. In the warm-for-May night air, town was everything that we could have hoped for – it was only sevenish, 'the lads' were in full swing and the streets were awash with barely clad fanny. The precinct off Park Row was teeming, as the throngs with thongs moved from bar to bar. While scores of people queued outside the myriad busy pubs, waiting to be let in by the ubiquitous doormen working In town on this night.

Four drinks and three bars later we entered one of the 'older' yet still popular weekend haunts in the 'rougher' part of town, close to the market area. It was a prodigious establishment, which invited drinkers, somewhat perversely, to share a milieu themed around an American 'Wild West saloon'. The pub interior was a cunning manipulation of chipboard, MDF and other Carol Smillie *Changing Rooms* DIY shite. As we entered it was almost surreal to see dreams of ours coming true on either side of the room: wall-to-wall fanny and some right lovely little split-arses as well. The 'Brit Pop' music was loud and the bar was full to overflowing, but given the fanny on offer the bar cheered us as it had done the week before.

It was around 9.00 p.m. now and the pub was loaded with a heightened atmosphere that is familiar to those who have experienced its like before. It had that type of atmosphere that develops from a combined sense of heady conviviality, heavy alcohol consumption, 'people on the pull' and, most crucially, through the coming together of working-class male strangers. Such an atmosphere facilitates the materialisation of particular brands of working-class masculinities. It was a 'town' atmosphere, a realisation of working-class masculine tribes on the move; Saturday night lives in transit.

At first blush, the stranger might have imagined that these hordes were fellow communards. And s/he could have been forgiven for making such a blunder; for you could see that many of the men shared a common accent and language, certain postures and gestures, and movement patterns. Most of the men were dressed much like other groups of working-class men out for a weekend night out in town on that particular evening, wearing typically: brand-named denim jeans, invariably Levi's; Caterpillar, Kicker or Ellesse boots, tag displayed prominently; and the ubiquitous checked buttoned shirt or stripy T-shirt, worn outside the jeans. Haircuts varied in style, but many were close cropped at the sides and the back of the neck – grade one or grade two. These were tribes of working-class men enjoying a night out in town, and their body language confirmed it to you.

You felt that the *status quo* was transient, rather than enduring; and so did the management, who were situated strategically throughout the cavernous room watching for any sign of trouble. To be sure, you were proved right as a local disagreement between two men at the back of the room turned into a fight. What ensued typified fights in busy town-centre bars, and is described succinctly by David Moore in his anthropological account of a skinhead subculture: 'the first sign is the crush of people trying to move out of danger of flying fists. This creates a ripple effect which spreads away from the violent epicentre' (Moore, 1994: 93). Within a few minutes, however, the relative calm was retrieved as the main protagonists were spirited away, by the black overseers, through one of the doors marked 'Private'.

'Fuckin' wankers, those fuckin' monkey men' (the bouncers). 'They were only 'avin a laugh,' remarked Stout. 'You can't do fuck-all in these pubs these days or yer out. Remember when we used to go in t' Yorkie bar? We'd have a fuckin' riot every week and no cunt would say a fuckin' dickie-bird. Are we off yet?'

Ignoring Stout, Benno had moved towards the small wooden dance floor and he quickly had his arms around the waist of a Geordie bird he had met in town a couple of weeks previously. Stout headed back to the bar and I offered to give him a hand. We queued impatiently for at least fifteen minutes. It was annoying, but a fact of life at this time of night, in this bar at any rate.

Two minutes back from the bar the Gallagheresque music faded and was replaced by a different but familiar tune which sounded more softly through the room. It was something catchy by Space: 'The female of the species'. Human shapes, most of them women, began to move towards the dance floor. People, inches apart, sharing nothing with each other but a desire to dance. The feeling of puissance soon accelerated as they moved in tandem, mesmeric.

D-ranged pointed and we collectively watched as the two motion-less figures of Benno and the Geordie bird became active, the former's shyness put on hold. They started to dance. As they moved, their footsteps were soon humming across the floor as Benno continued his embrace. We watched the two of them, starring like characters in the working-class dance production that is played out here at the Wild West saloon weekend in, weekend out. She was an extremely striking-looking woman, in her late twenties, with moderately Nordic features, and blonde hair plaited. Tall, she wore a halter-neck dress that showed off the Newcastle United tattoo on her left shoulder. Her companion looked dapper tonight. He wore his 'lads' uniform: Ben Sherman, Levi Sta-prest and large Pod shoes on feet supporting two legs which always seem to look too small for him. Delightedly he let go of her waist and instead danced around his prey, fulfilling the desire of a celebrant football fan who marks a victory and honours a hero: a graceless dirty bastard, dancing on two left feet like a demented chicken.

His muse was equally absorbed, but she was much more skilled in her art and was able to perform complicated steps. She spun, he tottered. She sideslipped, he stooped and fell. She also possessed the mark of a good dancer who has the ability to adapt herself to any partner, and in spite of him she was able to make them look as if they were dancing as one. The song ended. We clapped and Benno bowed. Stout had had enough by now and he repeated his earlier dictum: 'Are we off yet?' Benno was still ignoring him, though, because by this time he was indulging in a necking session with the Geordie bird – teenage in its intensity. 'Come on, y' cunt,' implored Stout, once again.

Shortly after we left the pub and headed back 'up our end' for the last half-hour of drinking time and the sure-fire possibility of a lock-in. On the way out, a man apparently nudged Sean as he passed through a particularly congested area of the pub. I watched closely as Sean called him a 'cunt' whilst staring intently into his face. The man did not volunteer a response.

Returning 'home'

Two streets away, a woman appeared to be standing waiting, like very many others have before her, outside the department store in the centre of town which has been the major meeting place of weekend revellers and dating couples since people can remember. She was of medium height, blue-eyed, and was wearing long, bleached hair. She was dressed in a smart short white cotton dress, with a minuscule black handbag straddled across her shoulder. Only the slightest hint of crows' feet, beginning to surface at the sides of her eyes, betrayed the fact that she is in her early thirties. She did not really stand out from the crowd, but if you knew her you would know, from the look on her face, that this woman felt as though she was beautiful on this particular night.

We knew the woman in the white cotton dress. She acknowledged us with a smile as we passed the department store on the way to the taxi rank. Each man proffered a greeting: a nod, wink and a 'Hello'. She could feel D-ranged's eyes scrutinising her body and she took care to avoid looking directly at him. But she did not seem unduly worried – 'Town is safe, because there are lots of people around.' Nevertheless, she reflected for a moment and paused to think that it was neither the first, nor would it be the last, time that she would be made to feel anxious under the gaze of such men. As we faded into the distance, D-ranged and Stout both expressed the opinion that they 'would really love to fuck that' (the woman in the white cotton dress) – given the opportunity, of course. D-ranged recalled that Daz Brennan had once fucked 'it' and had remarked what a good fuck 'it' had been too.

Soon we were queuing for a taxi at the end of a pedestrianised zone at the edge of the centre of town. Two young women were walking arm-in-arm towards the rank. The street was busy with people. How-ever, these women appeared to be engaged in a deep conversation and looked relatively oblivious to their surroundings.

With a suddenness that took her completely by surprise, one of the women was lifted from her feet. For a second she looked as though she did not understand what was happening, then she soon grasped that she was sitting on a man's shoulders and they were running towards the taxi rank. It seemed like a very long time before he put her down, but it was over in less than a half a minute. She was crying and her friend was hurling a torrent of abuse at the man. At the same time his seven or eight friends commended his action with the type of standing ovation that is given to football teams when they lift the FA Cup. Nevertheless the man's face told you that he was confused, and you suspected that he could not understand why the two women were being so unreasonable in their handling of the situation. My three companions also wondered 'what her fuckin' problem was'. After all, 'he only did it for a laugh'!

The Farmer's Arms

Back 'home' now, we headed for the bar in the tap room at the Farmer's Arms. It had been a long Saturday and much beer had been drunk; we'd been at it since dinner time. The pub was not full, but there were modest numbers of drinkers congregated mainly in huddles, minding their own business and keeping themselves enter-tained. Two couples were pissed and trying to play pool; a group of men propped up the bar while discussing what went on at work earlier in the day; five middle-aged men discussed football as *Match of the Day* came on the television screen at the side of the bar; and a lonely figure was sitting in the corner, next to the exit, having a long conversation with his near-empty beer glass.

We were now sitting with a party of five others – two women and three men. In the meantime, Stout and D-ranged were engaged in an animated discussion about 'fuck-all' (as D-ranged described it the following week). The rest of the new-fledged group, as much it could, attempted to ignore what was being said between the two.

Stout: You know fuck all; you're talkin' fuckin' shit, as usual.
D-ranged: Get fucked.
Stout: Don't point at me, y' cunt.

Enter Lucy, the pub manager and the 'bird' of fat Louis.

Lucy: That's enough, you two. Drink up. It's time you were gettin' off.
Stout: Come on, Lucy. I'm sorry. We'll keep it down, all right?
D-ranged: Fuck off, y' fat cow.
Lucy: Don't speak to me like that. If you don't leave I'll telephone the police. Now drink up and leave, please.
D-ranged: Where's that fat bastard? (Meaning Louis.) Look, if t' fat cunt wants me out, let him fuckin' try chuckin' me out. Is he hidin' upstairs?

D-ranged walked to the bar and shouted up towards the staircase at the back of the bar.

D-ranged: Get down here, y' fat cunt.
Lucy: Listen, David, this has got nothin' to do with Louis. I'm the land-lady. Please leave.
D-ranged: Tell that fat cunt I'm gunna pan him when I fuckin' see him.

The rest of the group reasoned – as best as it could – with D-ranged and he eventually left the pub. On his way out of the bar he repeated his threats towards Louis. He also started making aspersions about Lucy.

D-ranged: I don't know how he shags that. I'd rather fuck mi fuckin' fist. Pair a fat cunts.

Fists clenched, D-ranged continued to shout abuse aimed at Lucy and Louis as he walked into the night. The rest of the group carried on with the rest of its evening as if nothing had happened.

Introduction

It is 'the lads'' encounters with the Other which set the focus of this chapter. In Derridaean terms, the discussion deals with the meanings associated with the radical exteriority of the Other as constituted by the discourse of the leisure life-world, and as such the shadow subject of this chapter is the thorny issue of what is, in this world, constituted as truth and knowledge. The first part of the chapter discusses 'the lads'' dealings with women, while the subsequent analysis demonstrates how the leisure life-world deals with black men and black women. The work of Derrida is central to the whole analysis, while the writings of Foucault, Bakhtin, Cixous, Irigaray, Kristeva and Bauman provide further intellectual reference points.

The foremost aim of the first part of the chapter is to explore the leisure activities of 'the lads' and the normalising gaze of the leisure life-world by focusing on gendered binary oppositions. As this discussion makes clear, for 'the lads' there is no other species more 'other' than women. Drawing on the preceding episodes and further examples, which underpin typical events in 'the lads'' local and 'in town' leisure activities, this discussion sheds light on the dialectics of masculinities and femininities from the point of view of 'the lads'. It is suggested that what these episodes articulate is a sense of the prevailing masculinist discourse that is both constitutive and constituting of the leisure life-world.

Initially the discussion draws the reader's attention to the patriarchal assumptions underpinning the cultural production of the leisure life-world. In the context of these assumptions the chapter discusses gender relations, leisure lifestyles and masculinities (Hearn, 1996). In Foucault's (1972) meaning, the discussion explores the discourse of 'the lads' (what they know and say), their practices (what they do and how they do it) and their institutional achievements (what conventions they carry out to know and do what they perceive they have to do) (Natoli, 1997: 6). The chapter analyses especially the masculine lifestyle practices of 'the lads' in relation to the interplay between discourse and action. It moves from masculinities to men and examines 'the lads'' practices, social relations, assumptions and beliefs about 'the lads' and women as the Other. In this sense the discussion analyses agency and the discursive practices of 'the lads' 'in terms of the extent to which and the ways in which they are 'masculinised' rather than [speaking] of some independent substance of masculinity itself' (Hearn, 1996: 214). This approach recognises also that 'masculine' practices come to have distinct meanings and take on different forms in relation to the syntactical relations (Goffman, 1969) of 'the lads', in the midst of the social situations in which they materialise. The first part of this discussion analyses the masculine lifestyle practices of 'the lads', paying particular attention to Derrida's (1973) concept of différance,[1] to focus on the interplay between ipse and idem selves, in the leisure life-world.

It needs to be pointed out that although this analysis makes the lifestyle practices of 'the lads' the primary focus of attention, it does recognise, however, that women's practices, and men's and women's relations, are of crucial importance, too. Indeed, in relation to the gendered Other the analysis suggests that women's complicity is central to 'making' of the discourse of the leisure life-world. These latter points notwithstanding, the identity of women as Other is always treated as being under erasure: discredited and emptied of its meanings for the very reason that it is of 'them' and not of 'us'. As we shall see, for 'the lads' a clear sense of a dated and strictly 'solid' modernity of masculine practice is required if their leisure lives are to proceed as 'normal'.

In the second part of the chapter the analysis focuses on Derrida's 'play of difference' in relation to racialised oppositions. This discussion focuses on the 'consumption' of the black Other in the leisure life-world. It builds on the initial discussion of binary opposites by using Derrida's (1978) concept of the trace to show how the black Other influences and facilitates the leisure lifestyles of 'the lads' but is radically absent from that time–space, in the sense that it is perennially erased and denied a presence. For 'the lads', the male black Other especially must always be kept at a distance because it remains an indirect and local threat to their status and all the material aspects of their lives. 'The lads'' dealings with the female black Other stand in contrast to their strategies for casting the male black Other 'away from where the orderly life is conducted . . . either in exile or in guarded enclaves where [it] can be safely incarcerated without hope of escaping' (Bauman, 1995: 180). In marked contrast, we shall see that the female black Other is more 'welcomingly' absorbed into the discourse of the leisure life-world.

'The lads' playing with difference

Significant to the masculine ipse-identities of 'the lads' is their sense of difference from women. Key to this are the habitual ways in which 'the lads' construct their masculine identities and the implied discursive process of constructing what they do not aspire to – feminine identities – which is, to a major extent, achieved when 'the lads' differentiate themselves from women. The following cameos are indicative of this play of meaning and give weight to Derrida's (1978) concern with the 'play of difference' as a present time enactment (Gubrium and Holstein, 1994). First of all, in the rich flow of a typical Saturday evening at the Farmer's Arms we shall see how oscillating and ambivalent discourses are constantly assigned and reassigned, in the poststructuralist sense, in order to delineate the category 'woman'.

Colin and Jane at the pub

Colin and Jane are sat having a Friday-night drink in the lounge in the Farmer's Arms. Colin could see that Jane was clearly offended by the derogatory comments made about women by one of the two men standing at the end of the bar. Jane could not read her partner's face, though. Perhaps she did not care for the metamorphosis she saw. But I doubt that; she loves him completely and utterly. More probably the body language he was now presenting was not one she understood. For Colin was now in lad-speak. He drained his beer and put his glass down, hard, on the table. He then stood up and walked towards the two men. He tapped the man on the right once on the breastbone and then nutted him between the eyes. The man fell to the floor, but picked himself up surprisingly quickly. Throughout all this the gaze of his friend avoided Colin completely and he said and did nothing. The room was hot and the beer in the second man's glass looked flat and warm as he slurped it down, quickly and nervously; his free hand appeared to be shaking as it fumbled with the cloth of his trousers. It took barely half a minute for him to empty the contents of the glass and for the two of them to beg their leave. They made their exit swiftly, heads down and speaking to nobody.

In the following cameo Colin describes his account of the same incident:

Colin: I don't mind her being out when that lot are out, 'cos she knows what they're like; she i'n't daft. But it's when you get one at silly cunts out. We [Colin and Jane] were out the other night and we called in for one at t' Farmer's. A few at lads were in and Sean was there wi' a few mates from work. It wa' all all right until these two daft cunts starts. I'm sat wi' Jane and we're talkin' to Sean. This fuckin' dickhead looks at Sean and sticks his tongue out. His mate says, 'Have you ever seen a fuckin' tongue like that? All at birds beg him to give 'em some. He can never get his cock up, 'cos they all want his tongue.' This cunt then starts to pretend he's lickin' some bird's twat. I just lost it. I got up and fuckin' nutted the cunt and dragged him on t' floor. Next minute Sean's pullin' me off.

On the buses

Three months later, on a bus to the town centre.

It is 9.45 p.m. on Friday evening and the double-decker bus is no longer chock-a-block with people. It is making its return trip from the south of the city, heading along the main road towards the city centre. One cannot fail to notice the high-spirited group of men who take up the seats at the rear end of the bus. These are nine working-class men of between twenty-five and thirty-six years of age. They are dressed much like any other group of working-class men setting out for a weekend night out in town, and they've had a good few drinks.

Colin and Benno are particularly 'worse for wear', and they're trying, unsuccessfully, to chat up two young women at the rear of the bus.

Colin: Where are y'goin' tonight, girls?
No response.
Benno: Where are you goin'? Do you want to come wi' us?
Still no response.
Benno: Come wi' me, love, and y'could talk to Percy all night long.
Colin: Take no notice, love, he's all talk. But you can come wi' me, if
    y' want. I'll give y' some Weston cock.
The men are called by the others.
Benno: Leave it, come on. We're here. Fuckin' slags. I bet they're from
    fuckin' Miggy anyway. Y' don't know where they've been.

Sean and I are sitting drinking in the Farmers'. We have been discussing the above incident.

Sean: I wouldn't bring our lass out wi' that lot. No. They're a set a'
    perverts. Anyway, she'd find out all of mi secrets. I'm only kiddin'.
    (Laughs.) No, they would be fine with her; but I couldn't be me –
    the 'real' me, that is. I wouldn't be able to relax; I couldn't have t'
    crack. Anyway, there's some right rough bastards come in here,
    and I don't want her having to listen to them and see what they're
    up to. She's above all that.
T.B.: Stephen brings Denise, though, doesn't he?
Sean: Yeah, but who the fuck's she? He only met her about two month
    ago. He's just givin' her one; it means fuck-all. Half a' fuckin'
    Weston's fucked it.

Each of these narratives enhances our understanding of 'the lads'' attempts to both resist changing gender relations and at the same time construct their own interpretations of women, because, in Derrida's meaning, they show that the leisure time–space of 'the lads' is satiated with 'plays of difference'. This is because the leisure life-world demands a vision that places 'the lads', and those whom they encounter, at the 'centre' of its own ready-made discourse. In this centre-myth Weston men are 'men' and women are for fucking. The narratives elucidate how the past, present and future of women, seen in the mind's eye of 'the lads', is used at the local level to make the bio-graphies of women a 'present-time enactment' (Gubrium and Holstein, 1994: 697). In the Derridaean sense this process is 'artful, a complement to the play of difference'. However, contrary to Derrida's (1978) 'writing', this discourse is much more than a text or an artistic ruse; it is a social affair which is both locally informed and organised.

In the introductory section of the chapter we saw how David used a discourse which attempted to resist, through derision, Lucy's position as woman pub manager by attempting to strip her of her authority and sexuality through ridicule. Sean and Colin, in each of the above cameos, similarly construct narratives, through further 'plays of difference', which fix cultural attributes to women, to make them, in the terms of 'the lads', 'coherent and meaningful . . . circumstantially compelling life courses' (Gubrium and Holstein, 1994: 697). Here the dominant discourse of the leisure life-world is used to construct 'real' or 'authentic' idem representations of women. In essence, the prevailing discourse seeks to establish the leisure life-world 'reality' of women. That is, that most single women are 'fanny', and are treated as such; whereas women who have succeeded in becoming 'wives', or regular partners, command respect, and are treated accordingly. These women are endearingly called 'lass': 'our lass', 'your lass' and 'their lass'.

The research evidence illustrates also the contempt 'the lads' hold for women. Women are targeted as sexual objects and are defiled and abused if they do not meet the 'normalising' criteria or comply with the wishes of 'the lads'. Yet this conviction is not mirrored in 'the lads'' regard for fellow men; physical images of men do not matter in the same way. This latter point emphasises the working-class masculinised nature of the dominant discourse of the leisure life-world of 'the lads'.

The two narratives featuring Colin elucidate a further characteristic of the dominant discourse of 'the lads'. That is that 'the lads'' definitions of criteria for what is moral and ethical are much the same as their 'treatment' of women. 'The lads'' moral position is infinitely malleable. In the first cameo, featuring Colin, he defends his violent actions on the basis that he is 'protecting' Jane from the odious practices of the two men. Yet, on the bus to town, Colin is justifying his behaviour on account of the two women being 'a couple of fuckin' slags from Miggy'. These ambivalent actions are illustrative of the moral relativism inherent to 'the lads'' behaviour. They are also indicative of the point that, if this rigid and simplistic discourse follows a specific code, it has no deeper meaning located beneath the surface.

The narratives also demonstrate how the discursive practices of 'the lads' decentre women in order to multiply the 'authentic' meanings of the idem-identity woman. Such representations of this polysemic female self transgress the simple good/bad 'girl' dichotomy prevalent in many interpretations of gender relations (see, for example, Moore, 1994), however. What these episodes do is explicate the uncomplicated complexity of the female self's polysemic character in the discourse of the leisure life-world. 'Real' women do not matter in this discourse; they do not exist. There is no hypostatised self assumed behind women's performance as 'fanny', 'bird', 'slag' or whatever. This is because their performance is always staged in the mind's eye of 'the lads'; that is, women are scripted in the performance of a heteroglossia (Bakhtin, 1981).

Bakhtin's concept illustrates the central importance of the contingency of the discourse of the leisure life-world. It also brings our attention to the conflict between the 'voices' of 'the lads' and the female Other to illustrate the direct competition between the 'official' language of the discourse of the leisure life-world and the 'unofficial' language of women. The discourse always articulates a particular view of the world, and this heteroglossic performance is scripted *for* the Other rather than *of* the Other: the women involved are volunteered by 'the lads' to perform in dialogic concordance with the 'truth' about women promulgated in the leisure life-world. This discourse attempts to inculcate the 'truth' that women are passive and malleable; the subject woman is an identity that can be controlled, protected or ridiculed by 'the lads'. How this discourse operates is suggestive of Irigaray's (1985a) view of the power of the masculine cultural privilege to construct women's identities and how in this process women are always excluded. And in the leisure life-world these versions of women are always constructed and judged by 'normalising' sexual criteria. This heteroglossia as it is spoken on behalf of the female Other can also be understood through Kristeva's (1986) concept of 'delirium', that is, a knowledge about women 'disturbed' by desires of 'the lads'. In Kristeva's meaning the leisure life-world represents a meta-discourse of a 'presumed reality' about women that is constituted less as 'truth' than as a wish.

While these multiple but extremely limited interpretations of the polysemic subject woman make sense to 'the lads' and to women, in the sense that we have seen that to some extent they are constitutive and constituting of women's actions, they comprise only one story: that of the prevailing discourse of the leisure life-world. 'The lads' may think that they know women but they know only the faces and the bodies they see. However, the research evidence would seem to confirm the argument that the dynamics of masculinities and the power of the phallus are likely to hold sway in gender relations (Cixous, 1975; Irigaray, 1985a, b; Kristeva, 1986). In the Deridaean meaning, women constitute the inassimilable Other, which enables the discourse of the leisure life-world to operate by virtue of their very exclusion (Derrida, 1974b).

Yet the point that the dominant discourse of the leisure life-world is to some degree constitutive and constituting of some of the women's actions would seem to indicate a further 'decentring' of the self as Other and, to an even greater extent, stress its polysemic nature. Yet women cannot simply be read off as the objects of 'the lads'' own narcissistic invention. They have a pivotal role to play this game of domination, too. Women do have some choice in the matter and in the 'complex structure of gender relations . . . the interrelation between different forms of masculinity and femininity plays a central role' (Demetriou, 2001).

In marked contrast to their interpretations and constructions of women, the research evidence suggests that, for 'the lads', this public world of leisure is one in which their own 'authentic' ipse-identities can be realised and separated from their family commitments, work, financial commitments, religious affinities, other leisure activities and the like. However, as Featherstone (1995: 119) points out, 'the prospect of a unified single identity may be impossible or illusory as [people] move between various identities'. The uncertain and risk-ridden liquid modern era, then, demands not only economic flexibility but also a *palimpsest* identity, 'the kind of identity which fits a world in which the art of forgetting is an asset' (Bauman, 1997: 25). In the light of these observations we can see that, as a consequence of their own marginality, 'the lads' look forward to their 'nights out' together because they perceive that these nights will induce a sense of freedom: freedom from the constraints of their everyday servitude (including work and respite from emancipated women) and freedom to be themselves: 'authentic' and 'solid' modern men. In this sense 'the lads' are resisting societal change by trying, fallaciously, to find and display their core or 'authentic' ipse-identities.

These latter points emphasise and reflect the dialectical relationship between the theories of the sociology of the postmodern and poststructuralism, which together underpin this discussion, that is, the disagreement about whether agents do or do not exist subject to their own identity, by consciousness, in a self-reflexive and embodied sense, or whether they are firmly products of discourse. The preceding analysis would appear to show that the achievement of selfhood is implacably ambivalent: individual reflexivity may be all-pervasive in liquid modernity (Bauman, 2000a), but how identities are constructed in the leisure life-world is also indubitably subject to discourse. Discourses might have incisive and penetrating structuring principles, but as the work of Foucault (1981: 10) shows, they also provide a point of 'reversal' . . . 'a starting point for an opposing strategy'. As this research shows, difference is open to the emancipatory and it can facilitate cultural diversity. Notwithstanding the language that prevails, the following account is, in more ways than one, indicative of this alternative aspect of difference:

Benno: A lot of these birds today are, well, weird. Y' go boozin' in town today and no cunts, especially t' birds, has got a Yorkshire accent. Me an' Gez Wilcock picks these two up a couple a month ago and they were full of all sorts a' shit. They had pint glasses and fuckin' posh southern accents. I think they wanted a bit a' Yorkie rough. Bye, they were hard work.

All we did wa' argue wi' 'em about women and equal rights and that shit. That one I got wan't bothered about that shit when I 'gave her one' at her flat. (Laughs.) Funny, though, she wan't interested in seein' me again. I've seen her since but she wan't interested.

Playing with difference: black style

In this second discussion the leviathan does not arrive in a feminine form; it emerges as a trace (Derrida, 1974a). The trace is comparable and related to Derrida's concept of *différance*. Faithful to poststructuralist form, however, the exact meaning of the trace remains imprecise in Derrida's work. For Ritzer (1997: 120), though, Derrida's (1974) trace emerges as 'the role played by the radical other in the sign', which can be recognised by its 'absence of presence' (Spivak, 1974: xvii). For Derrida (1974) the trace is always a positive effect, never a negative one (Krell, 1989). Yet at the same time the trace is that which is continually effaced from the present; it is that which carries with itself a mark or indication of a 'perennial alterity' (Spivak, 1974: xxxix). In what follows the discussion uses Derrida's idea of a trace to develop an analysis of 'the lads'' leisure time–space activities in relation to the black Other. Evidence suggests that this racialised Other fulfils the role of the trace impeccably in the leisure life-world of 'the lads'.

It is first of all worth re-emphasising that Derrida is, of course, concerned with language as writing and that his reference to the trace refers to words and meaning that are continually 'under erasure in writing' (Ritzer, 1997: 120). However, the following discussion suggests that the concept of the trace can be used to analyse the leisure lifestyles of 'the lads' in relation to their relationships with black men and black women. First of all, I deal with the male black Other, who is conspicuous by his absence, not only from the social network but from the pubs and clubs of Weston and central Leeds.

At the working men's club: traces of the black Other

It is a hot July evening and I am with some of 'the lads' at Halifax Road Working Men's Club. Unusually, there are about eight of us. Somebody has hired a room for 'a do' and we've joined the party. It's 11.30 p.m. and the room is full. This place, like that studied by Hobbs (1988: 230), is 'white man's territory'. There are 'no Pakis or nothing, it's like the way things used to be before the niggers moved in'. The Halifax is in the centre of the Paki world of south Leeds.

To anybody else this could have been any other working men's club in Leeds. A concert room. A games room. Bingo. A 'turn' every Friday, Saturday and Sunday. But to us the Halifax is a habit, and it is not like any other club. It is comfortable and comforting; whatever bad goes on in the world goes on outside the Halifax in the nearby streets outside the metal fences surrounding the club. The Halifax speaks of once upon a time, same place, where you knew where you stood, certain. When the children in the streets were white and well mannered; father was at work and mother was in the kitchen; when you could leave your back door open with the assurance that nobody would steal the consumer durables that you did not possess. The Halifax is our club; it is just like 'home' used to be before the Pakis arrived.

Someone shouts, 'Let's get up' (on the dance floor): it's 'Heatwave' (an old Motown song by Martha Reeves and the Vandellas). And we get up, approximately seven of us. We dance, or, more precisely, we try to dance, for the duration of the song. As we leave the dance floor David says, 'I love that music. Good fuckin' dancin' music – if y' can dance, that is! Great fuckin' record.' The scene, played time and again, is once again static, frozen in hyperreality, a well worn photograph of gyrating bodies and smiling and happy faces 'dancing' to soul and ska all night long. Well after midnight, four of us leave the club in the pursuit of 'something hot, like a good curry or a chinky'. Relishing the prospect, Benno says, 'It's good to be back.' (He has recently returned from a holiday.) 'We couldn't get a decent curry in Benidorm.'

Black men in the leisure life-world

Like Hobbs's (1988: 133) 'chaps', 'the lads'' appreciation of black culture has nothing to do with the local indigenous black population. It emanates from appreciation of black food and black entertainers. Local black people are treated as the racialised Other and remain pariahs. Hobbs's respondent Mick elucidates:

> [T]he coons made it worse. Paki's never 'ave council places, do they? They buy places: a bit shrewd. But the coons, I could never stand them. When I was at school there weren't any at our school. Now there's no whites. My sister-in-law still lives there, and it's like a fucking jungle, the muggings and that.
>
> (Mick, in Hobbs, 1988: 134)

Sean, in talking about the time when he and some of 'the lads' worked in the Channel Islands, makes a similar point:

Sean: The locals were thick bastards, and the pork 'n' cheese [Portuguese], all they did is work and send their money home. We had fuck-all to do wi' 'em. But what really made it great wa' the fact that there were no fuckin' Pakis, it wa' fuckin' great. It wa' like bein' in Ireland or England thirty year ago or so.

Benno, on the other hand, while confirming a similar point, shows how local Asian men have been forced out of the pubs of Weston:

Benno: Y' never a see any Pakis in t' pubs round 'ere. Y' used to in t' Cavendish Arms, years ago, but they wun't dare go in there now. It's rough as fuck. It got petrol-bombed a couple a' year ago. There's this family a' losers, a think their called t' Maloneys; they got clotched [barred] by t' landlord, so they fuckin' petrol-bombed it. Fuckin' mental cases. Them cunts are just like fuckin' Pakis, bits a' fuckin' shit; they'd con or rob y' t' first chance they fuckin' got.

The role played by the black Other in the leisure time–space of 'the lads' can be understood through Derrida's concept of the trace. Black culture plays a key role in determining the leisure lifestyles of 'the lads' – even though black people, but particularly men, appear to be absent from that leisure time-space. More precisely, black culture is both at once conserved and effaced in the leisure life-world. The black Other influences and facilitates the leisure lifestyles of 'the lads', but is radically absent from that time–space, in the sense that it is perennially erased, denied a presence. The preceding cameos not only elucidate the perennial postponement of the black Other in the leisure life-world; they also emphasise the differences distinguishing that Other.

These cameos both emphasise and articulate the ambivalence attached to the black Other in the leisure life-world. 'The lads' do not have any black friends and very few black people frequent the pubs and clubs where they drink – even the pubs and clubs which they patronise in Leeds city centre. Yet we saw that the trace of black culture(s) (black music, black athleticism, black cuisine) is found in and plays a key role in facilitating the 'great nights out' and the shared memories of 'the lads', yet the black Other, particularly in its male form, is perennially erased through the discourse of the leisure life-world.

Black women in the leisure life-world

Black women are treated differently from black men, as the following quotation from Stout shows:

Stout: It's like Scott, when we were in town a couple of years ago, he pulled this black pussy and shagged it, tongue job, the lot. Next minute he's sayin' that they're [black people] okay and all this bollocks. I'm sure

he'd 'ave said same about her brothers, wun't he? [Laughs sarcastically.]
He just wanted a bit o' black pussy, din't he?

As Stout pointed out at a later date, 'Scott always did love his lovely juicy
black pussy.'

As we have seen already, references to female genitalia figure significantly
to represent women in the context of the fixed and closed symbolic realm of
the discourse of the leisure life-world. Woman in her limited number of guises
must be continually reaffirmed and her sexed body continually recreated.
That black woman is constructed as black pussy rather than black fanny
marks her difference from white woman. Black 'pussy' is also much more
ambiguous than the male black Other and it is precisely because of its
perceived 'slipperiness' that the means by which a social relationship with
it is made possible. Black pussy is interpreted as an immovable 'feast' and
is devoured as a form of exotic 'fruit'. Moreover, with black pussy bodily
secretions take on a particular significance. 'Juicy' is mobilised in the
discourse of the leisure life-world as a recurring and insistent signifier of
black pussy. If the male black Other lingers *physically close* while remaining
spiritually remote (Bauman, 1991: 60), vomited forth, the female black Other
stands in a rather different relationship to the leisure life-world. Black pussy's
complicity is fundamental to this game of social domination, but if it is its
'lovely' 'juiciness' that allows 'the lads' to both at once devour and colonise
the black female Other, it is the metaphor of the phallus (Irigaray, 1985b)
that is perceived as essential to replenishing the 'juice' or the 'slipperiness'
needed to sanction this strategy of social domination.

Drawing on Bauman's (1995) use of Lévi-Strauss's critical distinction
between anthropoemic and anthropophagic strategies of social domination
enables us to gain a more complete understanding of how the leisure life-
world deals with black men and women conjointly. In his discussion of tribal
moralities towards strangers, Bauman suggests that strategies of oppression
do not merely seek to exclude outsiders, they operate also to polarise
them. Borrowing from Lévi-Strauss, Bauman (p. 179) argues that, in every
game of social domination, social groups employ, conjointly, anthropophagic and anthropoemic strategies of oppression towards outsiders: the
two strategies are only effective precisely because they are used in conjunction. Social groups employing anthropophagic strategies gobble up, devour
and assimilate outsiders, whom they perceive to carry 'powerful, mysterious
forces'. In marked contrast, those employing *anthropoemic* strategies towards
outsiders metaphorically throw them up, casting them into exile, 'away
from where the orderly life is conducted . . . either in exile or in guarded
enclaves where they can be safely incarcerated without hope of escaping'
(*ibid.*: 180).

Specific to the black Other the research evidence presented here suggests
that these two strategies can be seen to be operating both individually and

as one in the context of 'othering' in the context of the leisure life-world. What makes its social domination of the black Other complete is that the leisure life-world employs both the *phagic* and the *emic* strategies as one. For its way of dealing with black Other is at the same time both *inclusivist and exclusivist* (Bauman, 1995). Bauman elucidates how this twofold strategy operates:

> The first 'assimilates' the strangers to the neighbours, the second merges them with the aliens. Together, [it] polarize[s] the strangers [black women and black men] and attempt[s] to clear up the most vexing and disturbing middle ground between the poles of neighbourhood and alienness – between 'home' and 'abroad', 'us' and 'them', To the strangers whose life conditions and choices [it] define[s], [it] posit[s] a genuine 'either–or': conform or be damned, be like us or do not overstay your visit, play the game by our rules or be prepared to be kicked out from the game altogether. Only as such an 'either–or' do the two strategies offer a serious chance of controlling the social space.
>
> (Bauman, 1995: 180)

This strategy of administrative control which reflects the discourse of the racialised hegemony of the leisure life-world relays coherent enough messages to the black 'Other': we will consume your food and your women; we will dance to your music – borrow it, even; you can play for our football teams if you like (as long as you are winning); we will borrow your fashions, your chic, and your cool and style. (See also the celebratory acts of the mainly white England cricket team (when it wins!) as a trenchant example.) Be that as it may, do not let this lead you into believing that you can ever really become one of us. We do not want you getting too close; we do not want to live near to you or to leisure with you. You can surely understand why, though, can't you? Yes, you are mysterious and exotic, but you remain 'ignoble savages' (Hall, 1992), and that means that you will always remain untrustworthy and potentially dangerous. The black Other is foreordained to remain a trace in the leisure life-world of 'the lads'.

Conclusion

The various narratives represented in this chapter have emphasised most clearly the importance of leisure to 'the lads'' sense of identity. In the leisure life-world 'the lads'' desire, seek for, the 'solidly' modern. Masculine ipse-identity, which has been marginalised, or has altogether ceased to exist, in other aspects of his public life, is realised and exposed to view, and his fellows accept it for what it is. That 'solid' working-class masculine identity, as we have seen, can be violent, and in this chapter the discussion has thrown light upon some of the more egregious masculine practices of 'the lads'.

What is the point is that, regardless of anything else, the fact that he has denuded what he *perceives* to be his 'authentic' masculine ipse-identity means that 'the lad's' remembrance of times past is continually constructed afresh. In the postmodern sense 'the lads' have their own 'resident ways of bringing to presence what is absent' (Natoli, 1997: 196). Within the leisure life-world, they contrive a surrogate reality, a presence that stands in for what they cannot be in other areas of their lives. This leisure life-world, which in the next chapter I describe as a postulated community, as a separate sphere and DIY custom-made channel, not only enables each of 'the lads' to identify what he perceives to be his 'authentic' ipse-identity, but validates his truly 'solidly' modern, working-class sense of masculinity.

We have seen also, in the discussion of this 'solid' modernity of masculine practices, that, as women's shifting position evolves and increasingly comes to vilify men's own positions, so these men resist the material practices of gender changes in seemingly paradoxical ways. A paradox is that 'the lads' resist the material practices of gender change by reacting with curt and abusive attitudes, language and behaviour which not only reflect, but also make manifest, their own doubts and anxieties. None the less, the leisure life-world provides them with a site to forcefully assert their masculinities in 'solidly' modern ways. The anxieties 'the lads' feel about the hauntings of their present liquid condition are rooted in their anxieties about them-selves. They live in a sociality where structures of masculine domination prevail, where no one distinct meaning of masculinity gains ascendancy, no group of men is dominant, no woman is being dominated in any singular sense, and no ground exists for any one principle of gender liberation. None the less, the leisure life-world provides 'the lads' with a site to assert forcefully their masculinities and amplify 'solidly' modern features of 'manliness' in seemingly more modern than modern ways. This resistance to changing gender relations is a forceful affirmation of working-class masculinity at a time when that form of masculinity is being radically deconstructed, and in Connell *et al.*'s (1982) meaning is most fittingly described as hyper-masculinity. The effect of this form of hypermasculine representation allows 'the lads' to amplify 'solidly' modern features of 'manliness' in ways in which their meanings seem apparently fixed, but are in reality merely 'temporary retrospective fixings' (Weedon, 1987). Indeed, we have seen that what it means to be a 'lad' is contingent upon local frames of reference.

This chapter has also explored, in relation to othering, the meaning of the complexity of identity and selfhood. The research shows that the self and identity are a product of discourse in the Foucauldian sense. In the ways that 'the lads' make meaning, the female idem-identity is constructed through a heteroglossia of difference which portrays women as fanny, pussy, birds, fat ugly cows, slags, Geordie birds, wives, 'just' girlfriends, and the like. That women can be subjects of their own and in others' stories is neither here nor there in the leisure life-world. This analysis showed also the importance of power/knowledge to these meanings and highlighted the 'contingency rather than the fixity' (Woodward, 1997) of gendered relations. As we have seen, 'the lads'' actions, and their apparent values, are never more than contingent upon the immediate situation which gives rise to them. From the analysis it becomes clear that there is no guarantee that what is seen as acceptable moral behaviour in one situation will be acceptable moral behaviour in any other.

The discussion showed also that women do not necessarily have to be present to be vilified by 'the lads'; as has been indicated already, 'the lads' have their own 'resident ways of bringing to presence what is absent' (Natoli, 1997: 196). However, this polysemic identity of woman cannot be reduced to simulacra, in Baudrillard's meaning. The sort of self and identity constructed in this discourse may be ambivalent, fleeting, episodic, fragmented and tentative; however, they are an outcome of social interaction, in the sense that they are present or 'centred' in experience. As we have seen, 'the lads'' 'solidly' modern practices attempt to fix cultural attributes to women, to make them, in the terms of the lads, 'coherent and meaningful . . . circumstantially compelling life courses' (Gubrium and Holstein, 1994: 697). If this polysemic subject of woman is 'postmodern', it is 'grounded' in interpretive day-to-day practice. Gubrium and Holstein (1994: 698) endorse these conclusions:

> The self is centred; it is mediated by diverse local cultures, competing discourses, and the gambits of practical reasoning. Variation in interpretive practice provides for self's multivalent and polysemic reality. This does not mean that self is a floating signifier akin to the postmodern radicalization of Derrida's play of difference . . . If it floats, it does so within the bounds of its social and descriptive organization.

Indeed, another key point of this chapter was that the meta-discourse of the leisure life-word of 'the lads' is to some degree constitutive and constituting of women's actions, which confirms a further 'decentring' of self and identity, which to an even greater extent stresses its polysemic nature.

This chapter also focused on the consumption of the black Other in the leisure life-world. It used Derrida's concept of the trace to show how the black Other influences and facilitates the leisure lifestyles of the lads, but is radically absent from that time–space, in the sense that it is perennially erased and denied a presence. If the leisure life-world demands a vision that places 'the lads' at the 'centre' of a particular discourse, we saw too in both this and the previous chapter that in this centre-myth Weston 'lads' are 'lads', Miggy men are cunts, women (both black and white) are for fucking but all black people remain, the Other. For 'the lads', the black Other is also always kept at a distance because it remains a direct and local threat to their status and all the material aspects of their lives. When the Other is the indigestible it still always remains unassimilable to the leisure life-world, allowing the discourse to continue to function by virtue of its very exclusion. However, the trace of the black Other always remains a potential threat because it is mysterious and exotic and untrustworthy and dangerous.

'The lads' live perceiving that the split between reality and hyperreality is critical to their individual sense of ontological security. As we shall see in the next chapter, for 'the lads' the leisure life-world is *the* pivotal point in a fragmented life, which allows them to fashion a sense of order out of the disorder of the everyday. It provides their escape from the myriad anxieties, uncertainties and ambivalence inherent in liquid modernity. 'The lads' perceive that they grew up as 'real' men, as part of a dominant 'solidly' modern masculinist (Connell, 1995) and white hegemony, and as we have seen, that distinction as such is not something that they will relinquish willingly. The affronts that they have had to suffer in the light of women's emancipation and the shift to a more egalitarian and multicultural society are truly that: a bad dream from which they are powerless to awaken. In this sense, 'the lads' are resigned to their fate; they know that their collective weekend leisure experience is just a break. However, in the quotidian of the contaminated and uncertain liquid world of the present they continue to rehearse their parts, biding their time, until 'real' life in the perfected social order of the leisure life-world – when the Other can be transformed – resumes as normal on a Friday or Saturday night.

Note

1 For Derrida (1973) difference is still seen in the conventional meaning; that is it is perceived to operate – as it has always done – through the process of making 'distinctions', in Bourdieu's (1984) sense. Indubitably, in Derrida's scheme of things, any process of differentiating implies inequality, prejudice, discrimination and the like. Indeed, implicit in his conceptualisation is the recognition that difference is conceived of the dialectics of power relations. However, for Baudrillard (1988, in Ritzer, 1997), difference comes to be of ever more import in 'postmodernity', for what we come to desire is no longer objects 'but rather we seek *difference*, and by being different we acquire social status and social meaning. [In postmodernity] it is *not* pleasure, not the pleasure of obtaining and using an object we seek but rather difference . . . we have a continuing, lifelong need to differentiate ourselves from those who occupy other positions in society' (Ritzer, 1997: 82).

Alluding to the Saussurean concept of *langue*, which gives primacy to the process of differentiating in exploring the 'value' of what is said and what is not said in speech situations, Woodward (1997: 35) suggests that 'binary oppositions – the most extreme form of marking difference – are essential to the production of meaning'. Woodward then takes Saussurean logic a step further, using the work of the feminist poststructuralist Cixous (1975) to argue that *all* binary oppositions, not only masculine and feminine identities, should be seen as unequal in the sense that they are always gendered. In Cixous's meaning, processes of power, which are culturally mediated underpin binary oppositions and 'suggest that women are

associated with nature rather than culture and with the "heart" and the emotions . . .
[and that men are associated] with "the head" and rationality' (Woodward, 1997:
37). For Cixous, as for Derrida, there is always inequity in binary oppositions.
Decisively, however, Cixous puts the onus on gender differentiation. Be that as it
may, there is a further dimension that applies to Derrida's meaning of difference,
which makes it a difference with a difference, namely a *différance* (Harland, 1987).

Objectively this means that Derrida's notion of difference also indicates a
deferral, an 'interposition of delay, the interval of *spacing* and *temporalizing* that
puts off until "later" what is presently denied' (Derrida in Harland, 1987: 138).
In this second meaning, *différance* – derived from the French verb *différer* –
which is cognate with the English verb 'to defer' – 'brings into play the notion of
an action *in time*' (Harland, 1987:138). Distinguished as it is by this second meaning
of *différance*, the signification masculinity is more than the ontological antithesis of
femininity; it exists by dint of its *deferring* of the meaning femininity. Yet the
signification femininity that is deferred is merely held in abeyance as a present
time enactment (Gubrium and Holstein, 1994). In Derrida's sense, femininity
waits in the offing; and, in time, its meaning that is deferred by masculinity will
be realised: the meaning of the signification femininity will flow into and pervade
the signification masculinity, and vice versa. Consequently, for Derrida (1973),
différance becomes a feature of the *same*, which should be made distinguishable
from the *identical*. However, binary oppositions themselves are not synonymous
with each other and, in Cixous's (1975) scheme of things, it is inevitable that
masculinity will preside over femininity.

Nonetheless, Derrida helps us to locate the promise of resistance to masculinist
discourses. Such potential is, of course, undoubtedly ephemeral, for masculinist
discourses, and the representations that constitute them, as we have seen through
the leisure lives of 'the lads', are capable of rapid and adept modification and transformation when challenged. This implies that any masculinist discourse and, by
implication, the masculine–feminine dichotomy, cannot ever be transgressed to
effectuate an alternative post-patriarchal gender order. Indeed, in the Derridaian
world, opposites always remain unstable without ever constituting a third way
(Harland, 1987).

Chapter 5

Communion

Individually, together: the self-constitution of community 'lad' style

> Utopias afford consolation: although they have no real locality there is nevertheless a fantastic, untroubled region in which they are able to unfold.
>
> (Michel Foucault)

'The lads' in 1998

In a piss-saturated doorway next to the entrance to the town-centre pub a sickly young bird sporting a blanket over her knees was begging for money. She was flaunting her little tits and scabbed bare arms. Her nipples protruded like two tab ends under her thin polycotton T-shirt and her elbows glowed, incandescent, in the autumn dark of a Leeds Saturday evening. Her face was blank. Popped up next to her was a bit of card, the remnants of a McDonald's Happy Meal carton. Printed on it was that postmodern piteous spiel: HOMELESS PERSON, PLEASE HELP. Benno must have thought it wasn't an evening for being a 'homeless person'. Either that or he was showing his appreciation of the nipple show, because he threw a pound coin on to her blanket as he passed on his way into the pub.

It was the first thing we heard when we entered the pub. The sound of The Specials belting out 'Nite Klub'. It seemed to fit easily with the conversation that had followed us into town, which had been steeped in nostalgia and memories of the lives and times of 'the lads'. Talk was about football and fanny, accompanied by more nostalgia, for the comradeship and the social cohesion of the past. The evening, like the bus journey into town, was to spin itself out like a familiar web.

The pub was one of those that we had frequented often. Nearly twenty years ago we first entered this place – or rather one of its previous incarnations, the Golden Cock – and became for the first time 'town' 'lads'. These days prostitutes, simpletons, wasters, lesbians, shoplifters, smackheads, dealers and other breeds of slime like to

meet there, and so still do we. In the context of the 'new' brand of
Leeds pub this place sticks out like a rotten molar in an otherwise
healthy set of teeth. Inside it is dark and brooding, the chief effect of
which is to make it even more appealing to us.

Sean was the first to arrive after us. Scott, who was still wearing his
black jeans, came next, accompanied by Alan, a 'mate'. You could see
that Scott's style still remains jerky, full of pregnant pauses and re-
arrangements of his bendy limbs, but he is no longer the booze-
soaked figure of old. Slim, dapper and with a brush of platinum grey
hair, at thirty-five he remains in dauntingly good shape, looking as
much like a new millennium man as one of 'the lads'. There's a lot to
be said for marriage. Ten years back, Scott looked like a rich man's
version of Nick Cotton whereas now he looks like a cross-eyed
George Clooney. It was Scott's first night out with us for a long time.
Scott had always liked it in town. He likes it better than in Weston. As
for this Alan cunt, in normal circumstances he would not have been
allowed to come out with us, but time had forced him on to the scene.

Stout and Colin were the last to arrive, and what a fuckin' combination they were. Colin went back to the 1970s, Ben Sherman,
Sta-prest trousers, suede head and loafer shoes. It was a sort of post-
skinhead Joe Hawkins look. He always thought he was a stylish
bastard. Stout was different, at another point on the sartorial scale:
dyed black hair, black shirt, two-tone waistcoat, blacks trousers and
black Chelsea boots. Fuckin' Roy Orbison without the dark bins.
Stout is terrified of age and this performance attempted to show that
he is unconvinced that age is stalking him. You can tell he thinks that
he is exempt and that the ageing process applies only to others.This
reconstituted Stout is also schizophrenic, both lamenting and exulting.
His life bounds from gloom to animation. Away from 'the lads', and
invariably in a state of depression, he becomes anonymous – his
features pale and sickly – holed up in some poxy little council flat
near Miggy, of all places! Back with 'the lads' he is elated, vibrant –
his face cracks, his eyes glisten and his demeanour becomes electric.
He was like this now as he looked towards Sean.

When Sean and Stout met they engaged in a mighty hug, rudimentary and childlike backslapping and the sort of unchanging mutual
cheer that recalls all Cup Final winning goals. I knew how Stout felt
about seeing his mate. I saw it just then; I saw it as Stout stood watching Sean. I saw it in his eyes, in his stance, in the movement of his
hands fretting up and down his trouser legs. Seeing all of this, I just
knew how Stout felt. The two of them grabbed a bottle of lager each
and drank deep, not because they were necessarily thirsty but
because it seemed the expected thing to do. Then Stout flung his
long and thick black hair back over his head, with a play actory

gesture of his hands, before sitting down 'touchy feely' next to his best mate.

With all fashions being *de rigueur* in liquid modernity, Sean's uniform has remained stoically unadapted: Levi jacket and matching jeans, his Kicker boots with tag displayed prominently. His head is shaved except for a clump of matted hair on the top, plastered to his head like a tight skull-cap. In the 1970s and 1980s we had let our hair grow a bit longer, and that's what we tended to stick with, but as the hair has thinned and fashions have changed we tend to wear it short and shaved – with the exception of Stout, of course – and today it is difficult to distinguish between the shaven-haired and the naturally balding men in the group.

The conversation was soon filled with displays of mutual exclusivity that betrayed Alan's sense of not belonging to the group. But it didn't matter, because everybody ignored the cunt anyway. You've got to watch cunts like that, because they'll always take advantage if you give them so much as an inch. This cunt was an infringement of the rules and Scott should really have known better. He, on the other hand, we took back in. Scott has earned his badge and he was back with a bang, dominating the conversation as usual. An intimate knowledge on Scott's part of our lives and times, coupled with the most rudimentary familiarity with our most recent exploits, was sufficient to reveal to him that the leisure life-world he had left was the same as that to which he had returned. We felt like he was once again back with 'the lads'. It was like coming back to a rock band. Scott was the member who had been playing with other people and now he'd come back 'home'. We were on stage together once again and it felt great.

An interlocutory injunction

When we are together there is a sort of silence at work, but not the literal silence when there is no actual conversation – the animating spirit of the leisure life-world ensures that there is never any quiet when we are together. Scott understands this. There is also always another sort of silence at work in which a wordless conversation takes place, the product of an intimacy and of intuitive interpretation that has been years in the making – the undertow of all that is unspoken between us, which is much. Scott will always be part of that.

We also know that the current *Zeitgeist* is the enemy of the leisure life-world. We are aware of the liquid fate that is in store for our world. We know it is coming closer all the time. We know, but we do not discuss it together. On this issue we also choose to remain silent. Not because we are afraid of what this implies, but because we do not wish to endanger our mutual commitment, our attempts to save what can be saved.

Back to the night out

As we drank, each of us spoke enthusiastically and passionately, with frequent recourse to our communal lexicon, not merely of 'the lads', but for a little while – and only a little while – about the tedium of life beyond our world, of women, families and work. Other than that we followed the pattern of the leisure life-world to its ill arranged letter. The music was loud and you could dance if you wanted. We were sitting down because we didn't dance, couldn't dance, pretending we didn't want to dance, though it was our reluctance to look like cunts that really made our decision for us.

We drank our beer faster than was good for us. But we were free once again and we knew what we were going to do with this freedom now that we had it. We talked voluminously of 'the lads'. Of 'the lads', and then of 'the lads'. We read a few more pages from our mutual discourse. Conversation moved from subject to subject, moving one way and then the other. We finished each others' sentences, and communicated, more remarkably, without speaking at all. With a real affinity, and in the spirit of the communion that exists between each of us, we used gestures known only to ourselves. We drank and we drank. As the evening moved on we felt ourselves become fully one. We were exuberant, on the rampage, heady with booze and 'the crack'. The leisure life-world was humming, its mechanisms in fine fettle. Outside it there was nothing else.

There were some differences, of course. But these were endured with the minimum of complaint, for we each recognised that we were inculcated in a discourse that far outstripped anything external to it. For we conversed and supped our beer, as intimate, extraordinary, and puissant forces together, pushing, as we had throughout our leisure lives, against the rising tide of change. Holding it back, for the moment at any rate. It was the same when we were young and it was the same now, years later. During all of this, our bodies were almost motionless; our cognisance of anything external to us dulled by the collective euphoria, the weed and the drink. We were the same age, thirty something, but now, sitting together in the fantasy of the leisure life-world, it seemed to us as though we were ten, or fifteen, years younger still. We read together, at once from our collective memory and from the text of the present moment. As if by magic, the leisure life-world had regained its supremacy. But it was all right, because it was a bar, and it was 10 0'clock on a Saturday night.

The voices of The Specials once again filled the room. Everybody in the bar seemed to be caught up in 'Too much too young', lost in the song. Then some spastic smashed it. The bar exploded. Two spoon-heads were knockin' fuck out of each other at the other end of the room. Sean dragged Scott up from his chair and took a firm hold of Stout with his other hand and the three of them shifted with the crowd to watch the scrap. But it was soon over. The doorman grabbed the main protagonist's sleeve and hauled him bodily towards the door, relative calm retrieved. We went back to our beer and a short time later moved on. We left an assemblage of Bud bottles on the table, and these would remain there as trophies of our exploits. 'The lads' were back, once again.

The fun and excitation did not stop then, and it did not stop there. There was a lot of drinking that night, and the next week, and the week after that. From that night onwards we met on each consecutive Saturday for another five weeks. Then things sort of drifted. In liquid modernity, nowhere stays wondrous for very long once you are there, and the leisure life-world is not any different.

An interlocutory injunction again

As Dean MacCannell points out (1992: 109), in the years during which the world really became, in his understanding, postmodern – during the late 1970s and 1980s – the 'drifters', 'bums', 'tramps' and 'winos' stopped being 'drifters', 'bums', 'tramps' and 'winos', and became, rather, like the young bird with the nipples, 'homeless persons'. At the same time our world changed, too. One by one, other elements crept into our lives. Alongside the leisure life-world crept all-consuming shapes that were women, love, cohabitations, marriages, divorce, children, financial responsibilities, the continual threat of unemployment and increasing public and private regulation. Regulation in the bedroom, at work, in the pub, every fuckin' where, you name it. We also glimpsed what we imagined were better, more fulfilling lives elsewhere. But these imagined utopias have proved to be, more often than not, ephemeral.

Time after time we have seen one comforting myth after another taken apart. So, like everyone else, we have tried to come to terms with the hard truth. We feel the transition from 'solid' modernity to 'liquid' modernity as a deep betrayal, as a blow almost physical. We have had to accept that the world today is full of cunts and that they will fuck you good and proper if you give them half a chance – just like that Alan cunt. We have learned to be aware. Besides, why should we have anything to do with insubstantial cunts like that?

We have also learned to close our shutters to guard against our mutual home-made models of ourselves losing credibility and the intricate cogs of our masculine realism from being damaged. We have suffered setbacks of all kinds; but still we emerge intact. This is because we keep our own narratives alive in our collective memory, our private gallery, which is the ambivalent legacy of our youth. It may have been turned into a sort of heritage museum for ageing lads but the leisure life-world continues to earn its keep. This museum is certainly not popular with most people, primarily because it advertises itself as being mindful of strangers, and it tempers information about itself with unappealing displays. But its members are select and we are here of our own volition.

The trappings of the leisure life-world may at times weigh heavy on our shoulders. This is because our life is not simple. It requires patient understanding, imagination and the power to endure constant adversity. Yet a feeling of 'home', of belonging, of happiness, always prevails. Without the leisure life-world we feel naked and exposed. Within the leisure life-world we resolutely protect what we love – our values, our ideas, our culture, each other. The marvel of 'the lads' is that we have the tenacity of spirit to go on fighting in spite of this troubling admixture of seduction, added responsibility and increased control. And the desire for a better life may be a powerful one, but the desire to be together has remained stronger. For a part of us will always be drawn back, to our rampaging and our madness. Now in our thirties, heaven is 'home', and 'home' is the leisure life-world. What is great about the leisure life-world is that it never completely loses its potency, because there is never any form of culmination or ending attached to it.

Yet, even with 'the lads', things have changed, have become ambivalent. Everything has come to mean the same yet different. Yet it is still the same – a sort of leisure life-world Mark II. Determined to maintain our sense of belonging, a refashioned and reconstructed 'lads' has emerged. In terms of our leisure lives, this means that we now hold a cool disregard for the present and the uncertainty of the future, and what we embrace is the past. It is a new chapter in our existence. However, this new chapter requires nothing new, only our continued commitment. Today we may only occasionally be able to identify happiness by felicitation; to make the leisure life-world manifest and enjoy it for what it is. We might not have accepted this contingency, but we have adapted to it, and have coped with it. This is because, despite what we insist, we are flexible, we are much like other men and women in liquid modernity – palimpsests. As Smith (1999: 154) notes, Bauman argues that, accordingly, living in liquid modernity is permeated with 'the contingency of events and the insecurity of being'. And the kind of identity demanded of liquid modern men and women is a *palimpsest* identity, 'the kind of identity which fits a world in which the art of forgetting is an asset' (Bauman, 1997: 25). There is a sort of transience to the leisure life-world that allows for this contingency. Some of 'the lads' come and go, and sometimes they stay away for considerable periods of time, but when they return to the fold their apostacy is never held against them. Scott returned to us as if he had never been away. That night out was the first time for a long time that he had felt the visceral sensations of the presence of the leisure life-world, which was, for him, nothing short of electric.

At twenty we wanted each other and each other absorbed us. At thirty-something, while retaining a similar facade – a temporary 'home' – we now have the best of both worlds, because we have found the key that enables us to restore paradise in our lives. Over the years we may have acquired different needs, but we still hold a strong desire, a nostalgia, to maintain a hold on our sense of collective meaning, that sense of belonging and together-ness that only we understand. Only we know the intensity of this desire, which feels as if our ontological security depends on it.

In the past, when conditions were more or less ideal, travelling the path of the leisure life-world was not a difficult task. In recent years, however, adhering to that path has become more a duty. In order to be able to resist the corrupting influences of the outside world that we have to endure, we know we must be blessed with inner resources of a truly superhuman order. Yet the kind of life offered by this enduring condition of 'home-lessness' is accepted more readily by some than by others. Scott, as we saw, is not so in love with the leisure life-world twenty years on. Today the buzz of the leisure life-world no longer has the same deep resonance that could once halt him in his tracks. Today it is still there, but it feels much less powerful. Nevertheless it still has this nagging subliminal power, which has survived from back then to now, as it continues to reverberate on the edges of all our leisure lives.

Stout, on the contrary, is still marvellously in love with it all; he is still resolutely under the leisure life-world spell. This is plain for everyone else to see. You can tell it from what he says about the rest of 'the lads'; you can see it in his face, in the drop of his jaw, see it as he stands amongst his compatriots in the Farmer's Arms. It is etched in his body language and in the way he is in awe at being with the rest of 'the lads', in the movement of his lips, in the way he drinks his beer, in the way he continually touches, lovingly caresses, his mates. And in seeing this you know quite precisely what he is feeling – we each know this because we ourselves used to feel like that about the leisure life-world once upon a time.

Stout perceives that everything has changed; nothing is as it was before, yet everything is still the same. 'The lads' have changed but they have not been away. How come? What has happened to 'the lads'? Stout ponders upon this issue ceaselessly. He resists everything that has transpired to change us. This desire to eliminate all shadows of doubt is his *raison d'être*. Even the tiniest shadows in the most hidden corners of the leisure life-world must be blotted out.

For Stout, being 'a lad' is very simple. To be 'a lad' your commitment must come with no ifs or buts, it must be absolutely unconditional. It must come from the heart. And you must really understand, really know, totally. All this is not easy – it takes a great deal of loyalty – but the rewards are tremendous. Indeed, once you have got it you no longer need to concern yourself with anything else, the rest just happens. Today, however, with the exception of Stout, none of us wants to stay here always, all the time. The burden of being-with and being-for is too great.

This is not to suggest that any of us really embraces the contingency of our belonging. This non-acceptance makes us, in truth, refugees, in the sense that we retain passionate feelings about a world we have been obliged to leave, to the extent that we continually seek to return and take shelter there. For we know that we were not always refugees and have not learned to love the unfamiliarity associated with the material reality of the fragmented and risk-sodden liquid world. Contrary to Seabrook (1982), the core membership of this leisure life-world perceives – no, knows – that we grew up in a 'solid' world of certainty, only to be betrayed by our encounters with adulthood. When we became adults we discovered that life is perennially insecure.

We hope that we have not given the wrong understanding. An impression of a life as anachronistic leisure could not be more illusory, as the above glance at the spectacle of the leisure life-world promptly shows. We are alive and kicking. And paradoxically it was the disappearance of the leisure life-world that secured its infinitude. This change hasn't aged us or made our times together moribund or morbid melancholy. It merely seems to have taken us back in time. This is the first thing that you notice about us today, our renaissance.

When we are together we feel released from what the philosopher Schopenhauer described as the 'racking' of everyday life, set free, in touch with an intimate source that is ours, only ours, and where this our own work of art lives. We see our leisure as a means of leaving the realm of illusion – what most people describe as reality – and entering the real, where cures and solutions to problems might be perceived. These days, we sometimes have to wait long for these moments, but when they come they feel even more intense, even more sublime. When it is time to leave, it is stupidly difficult to let go, but that is what is required. We know this. But in letting go, we can come back again tomorrow to that same deep seat of passion – our own leisure life-world – with all its riches and freedom. The discourse of the leisure life-world has its own logic; and its narratives are so persuasive, they need no argument. So we will waste no more time justifying our behaviour to you.

Contemplation

In Chapter 3 we saw that 'the lads'' individual identities are constituted through a narrative which secures them through a Self-constancy (Heidegger, 1962). The analysis developed so far in this chapter has suggested that the leisure life-world also achieves its sense of communion by dint of a constancy, which extends across time, revisiting and reliving past moments, without congealing into any one given moment. Moreover, it has been suggested that 'the lads' invoke through this process of reiteration a present the very futurity of which contains both a certain and a not too distant past. Competently video-taped, the leisure life-world could be used as a Weston version of a dated form of a 'solid' modern working-class masculinity.

Yet we have also seen that 'the lads' themselves aren't asking to be admired as works of the imagination – they are simply relics of the past, and are trapped in a cycle of performance and display. Indeed, the activities and manners of the protagonists of this leisure life-world appear to be locked in a past very specific to their youth, and a night out in this leisure world feels like late 1970s and early 1980s retro without the irony. We have seen too that 'reality' is magnificently reinvigorated in the leisure life-world, 'lad'-style, and that this reanimation is more than nostalgia. It recollects the past forwards, not backwards, disassembling and reassembling the present by explosively penetrating its mucilaginous and melting the flimsy shreds that hold the wider fragile world of liquid modernity together.

The thing is that 'the lads' simply choose to leisure alongside 'solid' modern working-class versions of themselves of the kind that in their everyday lives they have let pass them by, to resist the socio-cultural, political and economic vicissitudes of a rapidly transforming liquid modern world. They essentially have a 'solid' modern leisure life coupled with a 'liquid' existence. A 'solid' life which has gone but is redeemable and a 'liquid' existence, now, which has to be endured. There the leisure life-world operates, tucked snug, if a little out of place, into the weekend night life of Leeds. It could simply have grown of its own accord, you feel – made from the very heart of Leeds. As if it were very much a production of a time and a place, suspended in the night-scape like a time capsule, with its machinery intact, in spite of everything around it humming their own different tunes.

The ultimate appeal of this leisure life-world for 'the lads' is that for each of them it fulfils both a need, which is their mutual longing for 'home' and 'security', and a concomitant desire for the quotidian of the non-rational – in the form of leisure, play and pleasure. For 'the lads' the leisure life-world is *the* pivotal point in a fragmented life, which allows them to fashion a sense of order out of the disorder of the everyday world of liquid modernity. The price of the freedom offered to 'the lads' by liquid modernity is the loss of a fixed cultural identity, which must subsequently 'be searched for and somehow restored'. And it is through the leisure life-world that they set about this restoration process.

The leisure life-world makes manifest a sense of communion associated with the lives and times of 'the lads', but it is not 'community' in the orthodox sociological meaning. The leisure life-world is better understood as a postulated community (Bauman, 1995), veritably a 'cloud' of community (Lyotard, 1988), which is a work of imagination stimulated by the anxiety of the present and the uncertainty of the future, and 'the lads' live, perceiving that their task is now to find that point – in their leisure time and space – where they can feel at 'home' to assert their 'true' ipse-identities.

'The lads' living with anxiety and without certainty

As has been well documented, Anthony Giddens (1990) suggests that our experience of modernity is akin to riding a 'juggernaut'. People are more anxious today as they now live in a more uncertain world. Bauman's sociology reinforces Giddens's argument when he shows that liquid living is manifestly changeable and we have been forced to contemplate living with a permanent sense of ambivalence. Characteristically, we experience life as a constant oscillation between a sense of belonging (feeling at home) and loneliness (homelessness), familiarisation and disorientation, and permanence and fragmentation. The actuality of 'the lads' experiences of liquid living would appear to confirm Bauman's prognostication.

'The lads'' anxieties about liquid uncertainty are manifested in different ways. As Sean puts it:

> Things have changed. Like Scott, you never see him any more. Well, not much. Fair play to him, though; he's got a wife and three kids and a cunt of a job. He has to work loads of hours for shit money. Same wi' me. I work more hours; you can't afford to knock back work, 'cos you don't know when it will come again. It's same at home, our lass wants this for t' house and that for t' house and two fuckin' holidays abroad a year. Then we have to go to Ireland to see mi mam and dad at least every other year. It's all pay out. Fair play to our lass as well, though; she does her bit. She works full time.

These anxieties are also evident in the words of Colin, who describes his experience of splitting up with his partner of two years. Colin's experience, if not strictly typical of the rest of 'the lads', elucidates well the shift in personal relations that each of them has to deal with in the course of their everyday lives.

> It didn't come out o' t' blue, really; I had a good fuckin' idea. I'd suspected summat for months. She reckoned she 'an't known t' cunt long an' that she'd never shagged 'im. Oh yeah. Anyway, she came in from work one night and said that she had met someone else and that she wanted *me to leave*. I fuckin' cried, I cried like fuck. Our kid said, 'Why din't y' knock fuck out of her and him?' 'Oh yeah,' I said, 'you talk bollocks.' I begged her to *let me stay with her*, but she said that she didn't love me any more. Simple as that, really. (Ironic laugh.)

Giddens (1992: 8) argues that today we are witnessing a sexual revolution in which personal life has become a more 'open project', producing 'new' demands and anxieties for both men and women. A particular consequence of this transformation in the gender order is that, if relationships have not necessarily become more equitable, they have surely become more uncertain. Moreover, this uncertainty is manifested in different ways for men and women. The above quotation elucidates very well the uncertainty in Colin's personal life, particularly in the way it conveys his unmistakable scepticism about his partner's 'story' surrounding her decision to end the relationship. The quote explicates also the self-reflexive realisation of Colin's subordinate position to his ex-partner, as it is he who is asked to leave, and it is *he* who has to beg *her* to let *him* stay. In the everyday world of Colin's personal life expectations about gender roles have clearly changed. It is no longer the case that women expect to get married and thereafter sit tight through troubled times. In this sense, the quote is also suggestive of Bauman's (1998: 75) point that in liquid modernity men and women alike 'surround [themselves] with a sanitary belt of uncommitment' as they increasingly become frightened of pledging themselves long-term to relationships.

The effects of these sorts of personal uncertainties become exacerbated for 'the lads', not only because they prefer not to understand women's sensibilities, but because they 'choose' to live in different areas of south Leeds: Rothwell (Scott), Morley (David) and Churwell (Louis), apart from each other, returning 'home' to Weston only on their nights out together. The mutual support emanating from the social network remains on the whole removed from their everyday lives 'outside' the leisure life-world. This is because the leisure life-world requires a particular type of togetherness: one that demands that its members do not bring with them any uncertainties or dilemmas. There is an unwritten rule that all leisure life-world encounters must be unproblematic. This is because the leisure life-world represents above all else 'leave of absence from the wearisome and the worrisome' (Bauman, 1995: 47) condition of individuality that each of 'the lads' has to carry; it is not a cure for this encumbrance.

Their isolation is also intensified under the conditions of uncertainty about work. Each of 'the lads' is in semi-skilled or unskilled work that involves shifts, contracts or requires a great deal of movement. Their work is, by design, more often than not, both 'risky' (in terms of earnings and personal safety) and temporary. Bricklayers, roofers, painters, scaffolders, drivers in small operations in both the 'formal' and the 'informal' economy. For 'the lads', uncertainty at work is a persistent reality, a 'natural' part of their work identity.

'The lads' also perceive that there is a disintegration of 'community' in Weston and that they are witnessing the emergence of an altogether different locality, one that is impersonal, alien, fragmented and crime-ridden. Stephen explains:

TB: So, you moved back down to Weston?

Benno: Well, all mi family's down this end. But it's not t' same as it used to be, is it?

T.B.: In what sense?

Benno: Well, fuckin' everything. Half at' cunts round here only talk when they want to. I was comin' home from t' supermarket last week and a' saw Jimmy Cash and their lass; they both looked other fuckin' way when they saw me. About three week ago they wa' 'avin' t' big conversation wi' mi in't Farmers'! Fuckin' wanker. Then there's smell a' fuckin' curry everywhere. The Paki bastards are comin' over (the park) in their fuckin' droves now. Did y'know that they've bought Paddy Shearon's old 'ouse now? And there's loads a' lazy smackhead robbin' bastards everywhere. Y' never see 'em; they only come out when every other cunt's in bed. Do y' know, mi old lady went on 'oliday; she wa' only away a week an t' cunts had broken in t' house. T' whole thing's well fucked now.

'Outside' the leisure life-world, anxiety and uncertainty are experienced in myriad ways for 'the lads'. Paradoxically, however, it is those, like Benno, who still live at 'home', in Weston, who perceive that it is they who experience this dual ordeal of anxiety and uncertainty most acutely.

The postulated community of the leisure life-world of 'the lads', or, the leisure life-world Mark II

The leisure life-world as 'the lads' experience it today can be interpreted as an individual, collective and reflexive response to living with liquid anxiety and uncertainty. As a consequence of this, I want to argue that it makes sense to describe the leisure life-world as a postulated community (Bauman, 1995). Bauman's idea of the postulated community is basically another rendition of Williams's (1970) intuitive 'knowable community', which was discussed in Chapter 2. But labels are not important to 'the lads'. What matters to them is that the leisure life-world has the 'look', has the 'feel', of a 'community', of a 'home', and this is why it makes sense to describe the leisure life-world using Bauman's conceptualisation.

Interestingly enough, once upon a time 'the lads' would never have felt they had a compulsion to speak of their 'community', of their 'home'. There was no need to because the two distinguishing characteristics of the leisure life-world were its sense of 'naturalness' and the certainty that it 'always has been' (Williams, 1976). In the manner of Williams's community the leisure life-world of 'the lads' as it once was to them is no more. Still, we should not be too surprised by this, because as Bauman (2001b: 11–12) points out:

Community can only be numb – or dead. Once it starts to praise its unique valour, wax lyrical about its pristine beauty and stick on nearby fences wordy manifestoes calling its members to appreciate its wonders and telling all the others to admire them or shut up – one can be sure that the community is no more . . . 'Spoken of' community (more exactly: a community speaking of itself) is a contradiction in terms.

The leisure life-world as it is imagined by 'the lads' today is not a community in the orthodox sociological meaning; it is 'not even *imaginary* (any mental image would be too specific, too constraining) – but postulated . . . [For 'the lads'] what is postulated is *having* a home, not a particular building, street, landscape or company of people' (Bauman, 1995: 97). Like Foucault's (1998) heterotopia or Lyotard's (1988) 'cloud' of community this postulated community – or more appropriately understood leisure life-world Mark II – is at the same time both 'mythical' and 'real' and it operates betwixt and between the mundane and the spectacular of the quotidian as a temporal discontinuity. It is a borderline 'integratory and interstitial space' where identities are performed and contested. As a 'borderline work of culture' it 'renews the past, refiguring it as a contingent "in-between" space that innovates and interrupts the performance of the present' (Bhabha, 1994: 7). This postulated community never underestimates the power of symbolism for that which it stands for, and it allows us to see the extent to which 'the lads' recreate the world in their heads and the extent to which they recombine and imagine these cognitive frames collectively. Indeed, it is a self-reflexive of truth, which comes after, not before, the individual choice (Bauman, 2000a: 169), and this is why it makes sense to interpret the leisure life-world in the 1990s as a Mark II version.

As I have said already the leisure life-world of 'the lads' achieves its sense of community by dint of constancy (Heidegger, 1962). It is such a notion of unity, a converging without congealing, that distinguishes the leisure life-world Mark II. It is not in any way fixed at any given moment in time, it is rather a contingency and a process reality. Analogous to Maffesoli's (1996) neo-tribes, it is reflexivity and individual autonomy that centralise this postulated community and occasion its unity and continuity, however fragile the unity and continuity are, given the ambivalence which is inherent in liquid modernity. As we have seen, for 'the lads' the leisure life-world is unproblematically their only 'true' home because it is only there that they perceive that they can each achieve some kind of meaningful belonging.

Unlike Maffesoli's tribus, however, there is also an enduring persistence of continuity that marks the pivotal and distinguishing feature of the leisure life-world of 'the lads'. In the sense described above, the postulated community of 'the lads' is best understood as a diaspora, which has been obliged to disperse at the hand of liquid conditions. Today 'the lads' may (sometimes) leisure together, but they essentially live in different worlds. Like the rest of us, they have been obliged to carve up the world in different ways, live in different worlds (Rorty, 1991a).

It would be all too easy to dismiss the type of togetherness associated with this life-world as not worth very much, but it is, for each of 'the lads', of direct significance for his existential security, because this life-world is the profound expression of a group of individualised men, each of whom is over-whelmed by the living realisation of his own solitariness. Indeed, there is an importance to the leisure life-world that can be understood only in the context of 'the lads'' lived experiences of liquid modernity, and the leisure life-world confirms Bauman's (1997) argument that, with liquid modernity, it is not community but the liberty of the individual that becomes the over-riding value. The leisure life-world Mark II is a time–space to which each of 'the lads' turns for the imagined and imaginary version of the ritual enact-ment of community, entering and exiting post-haste as soon as any trace of obligation – beyond the confines of that immediate setting – is demanded. In this liquid world 'the lads' live, perceiving that their task is now to find that point – in their leisure time and space – where they can feel at 'home'. For it is here, in the time of liquid modernity – the age of anxiety, risk and uncertainty – that the lads, like so many others amongst us, articulating a nostalgic long-ing for the sureness of the past, 'exercise a bit of picking and choosing between the remaining residues of old "certainist" modernisms' (Jenkins, 1995: 7). 'The lads'' quest for certainty is well illustrated in the words of Colin: 'It's only when I'm out wi' t' lads that I can be what I am and do what I want; I don't have to change for no bastard.'

In the leisure life-world, the feeling of uncertainty diminishes significantly – for a while at any rate – once each of them makes 'the lads' the centre of his attention. Stout elucidates:

> There's about seven or eight of us, or a' should say there wa' – no, there is – who look after each other. It's not that simple, though, today. We used to see each other most nights and every weekend. But most of t' lads have kids an' mortgages an' that, now. But underneath we're all t' same. I an't seen Scott for about six month; he lives in Rothwell these days. D-ranged lives in Morley, but he manages to get out. But it don't matter. An' a bet we all an't been out together for about eighteen month. But we still keep in touch. There's this, like, unsaid thing, I don't know what it is. We all think t' same, feel t' same. Arr old lady thinks I'm fuckin' mental, but she dun't understand. Do y' know, I can go down to t' Farmer's for weeks on end and see no cunt, just usual dick 'eads. Then, like last week, it wa' weird. Stout, Scott, Benno, and Colin Machin were out an' it wa' fuckin' great. We ends up at this birth-day 'do'; it wa' t' best night I've had for years.

This experience of 'homelessness' is in no way exclusive to 'the lads'; as Bauman (1998: 77) remarks, 'Nowadays we are all on the move.' For Bauman (1995) liquid modernity does not signal the re-emergence of the Tönnies-type *Gemeinschaft* community. Rather it replaces rootedness with strolling, playing, tourism and vagabondage. From Bauman's (1992a: 134) perspective it is also important to recognise that liquid modernity *had* to become an age of community, 'of the lust for community, search for community, invention of community, imagining community' or, more accurately, postulated communities, because, in becoming 'conscious of its true nature' (Bauman, 1992a: 187), reflexive modernity (Giddens, 1991) inevitably had to reconstruct itself in what has turned into an era of uncertainty, fragmentation, doubt and anxiety, risk, contingency, ambivalence and irony. Into the bargain, universal reason is thrown into doubt, and uncertainty becomes the responsibility of the individual: all doubts and fears become private property. In which case, for Bauman (1992a, 1995, 2001b), it was bound to happen that the anxieties and uncertainties of liquid modernity would bring a need to share.

However, this yearning for a feeling of belonging, of 'home', manifests itself in forms of togetherness which vary considerably from the traditional models of community promulgated by orthodox sociology. Today 'community' is imagined to offer an assemblage of 'self-assembly kits' as a means to make our 'DIY escape' (Bauman, 1992a: xviii) from the manifest uncertainties of the market place of everyday life. In a later book Bauman provides evidence of these 'new' forms of togetherness. What each has in common is a sense of depthlessness and impermanence: 'like in the case of many other commodities purchased for sale, the durability of the goods is less than fully guaranteed and the customer's rights are less than fully honoured' (Bauman, 1995: 49). Bauman's argument has an underlying discourse which suggests that community relationships in liquid modernity are almost certainly always ephemeral surface phenomena, destined to disappear as people move between social groupings. Akin to 'the lads', most other men and women today are without a permanent 'home'.

These important points notwithstanding, what the leisure life-world Mark II serves to confirm is not merely the precedence of the liberty of the individual over the collective, but also the significance of a postulated sense of community, as it comes into being during 'the lads'' nights out together. This marks a response to the incongruity between the 'same' and 'other', the difference between 'us' and 'them'. Indeed, what is clearly apparent from the discussion developed thus far is that it is when this difference is realised that a sense of community in the leisure life-world is confirmed, even though, at the very same time, that feeling of postulated togetherness must also be put under erasure in the Derridaean meaning, fated to be put off until further notice, both maintained and preserved as it is as a moment suspended in 'lads'' time. To paraphrase Bauman (1992b: 21), the leisure life-world has no other firm ground than its members' commitment to stand on, so it lives as long as the attention of 'the lads' is alive and emotional commitment is strong. Otherwise it would most probably vanish.

In their leisure 'the lads' experience only intimations of a return to a deeper, more certain world that has in reality disappeared: solid modernity 'has come to be known to us mainly through its disappearance. What we think the past had – is what we know we do not have' (Bauman, 1997: 87). On top of that, the appeal of this 'home' is experienced ultimately as ambivalent and is very much contingent on time and context. This is because, in common with other men and women in liquid modernity, each of 'the lads' is guided by the wider discourse of individualism, and he is a reflexive individual, who is guided by the will of himself, rather than by the will of others.

Yet the ambivalence of this longing for 'home' is intensified all the more as liquid modern conditions make 'the lads' as reflexive individuals ever more aware of their insecure present and uncertain future. Moreover, it shows that the turn to this 'home' or 'community' evinces the seriousness of 'the lads'' leisure as they seek to experience the ultimate in being and meaning through their shared identities. As Jacques Derrida (1970) might say: with this certainty 'the lads' can be sure that their anxieties will be mastered.

From a rational perspective 'the lads' achieve the unthinkable, neatly reinventing a familiar past and achieving utopia in one fell swoop. However, things are not as 'perfect' as they seem, a lamentable truth they each always discover. Indeed, the sense of community associated with the leisure life-world always remains of an 'until further notice' sort, melting into air the moment 'the lads' think that they have secure hold of it. The friendship established between these men may imply community, but their autonomy and sense of individual self-reflexivity always throw both the existence and the homogeneity of community into doubt. Indeed, at the same time that community is affirmed in the leisure life-world it must also be put under erasure in the Deriddaean meaning.

Conclusion

This discussion was not so much concerned with an endeavour to retheorise community based on reflexivity and difference (Delanty, 2000) as with Bauman's (1997) concern that, with liquid modernity, it is not community but the liberty of the individual that becomes the overriding value. If 'the lads' share a postulated community that is imagined, it is imagined not because its members will never know most of their fellow members, in Anderson's (1991) sense, but because the demands and opportunities required by liquid conditions disperse and fragment collectivities, such as community, to form new *habitats* (Bauman, 1992a), within which the liberty of the individual, not the collective, is now the overriding value.

'The lads' have in truth abandoned concern for community and have introduced commitment to friends. What matters more than anything else is 'the lads', and essential to each one of them is his social acceptance and his own individual well-being. The leisure life-world may be demanding of observance, but it is fickle in its allegiance. The leisure life-world thrives on the contingency of community without responsibility; it couldn't operate without this. It is knowing that its door is always open, that they are not shackled to it and that they are at any time free to leave that maintains 'the lads'' commitment to the leisure life-world. This fickleness is also witnessed in the ways they surreptitiously blot out the parts of their shared history that they do not wish to confront so that their leisure lives are as much a product of their collective imagination as of their past.

Nevertheless, I agree with Anderson that in the minds of each member of 'the lads' lives the image of their communion, which *can be* conceived as a deep-felt mutuality. I agree with him also that it is an imagined community in the sense that it is limited by its strictly demarcated, though elastic, boundaries, beyond which lie ways of being and living that take the form of various threats, anxieties and uncertainties. Finally, 'the lads'' version of the postulated community, like Anderson's imagined community, is sovereign because it came to maturity at a particular stage in history when freedom was hardly unequivocal. However, its stage in history is not the same as Anderson's – when freedom was only a rare and much cherished ideal. It is a time when freedom depends on one's ability to consume: the age of liquid modernity. And what 'the lads' consume in the leisure life-world is the image of their communion.

We saw that 'the lads' lives are straddled between an enchanting past, an inhospitable present and an uncertain future; the former being the place they imagine as 'home'. This is a 'solid' vision of 'home' that is achieved in a liquid world through their mutual explorations of their past, and this 'solid' vision is ubiquitous in the leisure life-world of the lads. The leisure life-world of 'the lads' is that of an unchangingly homogeneous masculine working-class culture rooted in a 'solid' modern *idée fixe*: the very antithesis of the tormentingly intrusive heterogeneous and 'liquid' world of the present. For above all else it is certainty that their collective past contains. This collective use of memory as a secure and certain historicity within the leisure life-world can be taken to illustrate the interiorisation of the discourse which shapes this shared 'home'. This most rigid pattern is not imposed from the outside. It is the pattern made from within, collectively, a mythology for their leisure activities, a mythology that brings them a cramped delight which they protect by putting all possible space between others and themselves. As we saw in the last chapter, if the postulated community implies a temporary safe haven from 'the lads'' anxieties, it also implies social closure and exclusion for those who are not 'one of them'.

As has been pointed out, the leisure life-world can be understood, in Bauman's (1992a) sense, as an ever tractable mechanism for expressing self and identity *and* a spurious sense of belonging in a liquid world: a postulated community which is imagined to provide certainty where everywhere else there is uncertainty. The temporary togetherness of the leisure life-world presents 'the lads' with an opportunity to take respite from the feeling associated with being refugees and to 'unload the burden of individuality' associated with liquid modern living (Bauman, 1995: 47), to return 'home', to be supported and made to feel secure. In this sense the postulated community represents, for 'the lads', a culturally and themed weekend getaway, a short break to old certitudes. Given what each of 'the lads' wants – diversion, escape, excitement, combined with a sense of love, comradeship and community without any long-term involvement – they are extremely well served by the vicissitudes of the leisure life-world. The truth of the success of the leisure life-world lies in its ability to balance the unending spinning of a particular tale – the story of themselves is the one 'the lads' never tire of – with the most satisfying of leisure experiences. In this sense 'the lads' are the solifidians of their leisure *par excellence*. As we shall see in Chapter 7, even when they are apart, elsewhere, 'the lads' can still be together in their leisure time.

Yet the events that constitute the leisure life-world offer happiness only by felicitation. These events may provide the wonder that makes the incumbents of this closed world feel all at once so right, so good, so safe, but these ephemeral narcotics involve individual self-gratification, not the marvel of a collective will. This leisure life-world, with its cure for 'homesickness', constitutes one of those self-defined communities, *conceptually* formed 'by a multitude of individual acts of *self-identification*' (Bauman, 1992a: 136). Though this postulated community provides nothing more than a DIY shelter, a 'home', it is a cure for *individual*, not collective, 'homesickness'. More than that, it is 'no real house of brick and mortar' (Bauman, 1995: 48); it is above all else a community of self-convenience, inhered by those too self-absorbed to settle anywhere for too long. The truth is that the leisure life-world Mark II is a facade. Like other solid modern commodities the building of this 'community' has been gutted and has been replaced with a soft, liquid centre. As we have seen, it merely offers 'the lads' – with the possible exception of Stout – a 'perfect' way to recharge the batteries. 'The lads' yearn for a safe, 'solid' modernity, but through their leisure create what is essentially merely a simulacrum of a masculine working-class culture already spent. In many ways the postulated is a community without community, a community beyond culture itself. It is a bolthole maintained between a solid past and the immediate, liquid space beyond, which leaves unresolved the tension between appearance and reality. As we shall see in the following two chapters this postulated community is there and not there, neither dead nor alive. It is always ten, fifteen, twenty years ago, yet it is always now.

Chapter 6

Mythologisation

On being together: the mundane and the spectacular of the leisure life-world

From time to time their collective sense of belonging seems to mean more to 'the lads'; when its discourse vitalises the leisure life-world with a breath-taking intensity. This spectacular leisure experience is intimately bound up with 'the lads'' conception of the postulated community. Such occurrences – as this chapter will demonstrate – are the animating spirit of the leisure life-world. These episodes, when customary descriptions of time and space collapse, evoke in 'the lads' a collective feeling of belonging that is amplified beyond conscious understanding.

Leisure experienced during these spectacular episodes is different from, though not unrelated to, what is routinely experienced by 'the lads' in the leisure life-world. For this sense of community is also an experience of the mundane quotidian; a belonging conceived of an imaginary working-class tradition, enduring friendships, language, myths and memories, which make its historical continuity possible. This historical continuity is also rooted in the *puissance* (Maffesoli, 1996), or 'will to live', that shapes the communal spirit of 'the lads', giving their leisure life-world its vitality and group identity.

There is a sociology that describes such communal leisure experiences as a 'separation' from 'normal' life, a liminal stage of marginality (Shields, 1991; Rojek, 1995), a 'time out' response (Moore, 1994) to 'paramount reality' (Cohen and Taylor, 1992). But, from this point of view, leisure is important only in the sense that it provides liminoid situations (Turner and Turner, 1978) which contribute to the functional equilibrium of the social system (Parsons, 1951). For as Rojek (1995: 88) points out, when thought about in this sense, leisure thresholds of spontaneity and manumission cannot at any time be of any real facility, because although they may subvert 'reality', by giving rise to social conflict, challenging the *status quo*, or even facilitating a spurious sense of belonging, they remain 'inauthentic', or 'safe', because they do not survive the return to 'normality'. For Rojek, as for Victor Turner (1973), inside the leisure liminoid both time and space become changed, but 'real' time and space remain out there, undisturbed.

In this chapter I argue that this type of sociology's demand for rational explanations and for more 'science', at the expense of the non-rational, represents both its limitations and its philistine attitude towards popular culture. In an effort to repair this tendency, this chapter is illustrative of how sociology should relate to the quotidian, rather than to the rational organisation of 'society', with its hierarchies, centres and false dichotomies, which tell us more about the intellectual predisposition to order things than about everyday life. From my perspective, the social world of 'the lads' appears not only as rational, but as sentimental, affectual (Maffesoli, 1996), enchanting, exciting, mystical, erotic, aesthetic and magical, as well.

This chapter develops Turner's conceptual framework from an alternative position, to generate new theory through an analysis of the leisure life-world of 'the lads', paying particular attention to the cultural geographies of 'the lads'' leisure exploits. It is argued that Turner and Rojek are wrong to stress the divide between the liminal stage of margin and 'reality out there' and that there is, in the leisure life-world of 'the lads', an underlying continuum, and a progression from the mundane to the spectacular. Within this analysis, the roles of discourse, myth and memory are revealed to play a vital role in shaping the collective identities of 'the lads', transforming actual events into recollections and, thereafter, 'new' leisure experiences. These processes, which involve 'the lads' having recourse to powerful oral histories, become the myths, the 'true fictions' (Denzin, 1989) of the postulated community, the stories through which the leisure life-world of 'the lads' is sustained.

This chapter focuses attention on that area of their leisure lives that is 'the all-embracing myth', that which contains the underlying truth about 'the lads'. The chapter argues that this area can be located only by reference to an ideal of leisure, which provides the key to the 'reality' of 'the lads', to reveal the postulated community's sense of continuity, belonging and truth. In the absence of a community proper, 'the lads' must look elsewhere for a sense of unity. It is in their leisure that they can enjoy a sense of 'higher' belonging, without having to commit themselves to a community in the orthodox sociological sense. The leisure life-world makes this possible because it thrives on the contingency of community without responsibility; it couldn't operate without this.

In the myth of 'the lads' there is a seamless progression through time and space. As we saw between Chapters 3 and 5, they can move from 1978 to 1998 without batting an eyelid. Within this process, memory plays a vital role in shaping their collective identities, transforming recollections to actual events. The process of recounting memories, which involves their recourse to oral histories, become the collective myths 'the lads' leisure by. Their past is their mutual mythology, which they plunder for tales and explanations about themselves, which remain for ever lucid and clear. The point of these narratives is not whether the events they describe really happened, but what they mean for 'the lads'. And 'the lads' not only create their own mythologies, they also make use of extant 'solid' modern mythologies, such as those connected with hegemonic masculinity, as we saw in Chapter 4.

In this chapter the evolution of the myth of 'the lads' is traced through an extant body of theory. The chapter proceeds in a manner that will appear slightly different to the reader, for the course of the discussion deals more with concepts related to the theory of the mundane and the spectacular than with the more familiar theme of the analysis developed thus far. This approach is adopted because of the difficulty involved in advancing a synthetic approach that attempts to merge both rational and non-rational interpretations of the leisure life-world.

The anthropology of Victor Turner provides the starting point for discussion. Turner's concepts of *communitas* and *liminality* present an interpretation of the leisure life-world which leads to the conclusion – not surprisingly, given that these concepts are constructed within the orthodox framework of structural functionalism – that the experiences of 'the lads' are best seen as a 'separation' from 'normal' life, or a liminal stage of marginality. The crux of this discussion of the work of Turner is that if a fundamental understanding of the leisure life-world is to be grasped, his theory must be adapted to come to terms with 'the lads'' 'liquid' predicament, recognising the underlying de-differentiation of contemporary sociality.

The major issue to be raised in connection with Guy Debord's concept of the commodity spectacle does not directly concern what the spectacular is as such, but rather one important thing that it is not: real. For Debord (1995 *1967*), the spectacular encounters that shape the leisure life-world of 'the lads' make manifest an 'unreal unity'. However, the subsequent analysis goes on to show that, in 'the lads'' meaning, the commodity spectacle is paradoxically fundamental to their unity and plays a crucial role in their form of praxis.

My discussion of Baudrillard's concept of the hyperreal offers an advanced vision of the leisure life-world that challenges even the complexity of Debord's thinking. Baudrillard's work illuminates the enigma of a world which has now lost all contact with reality. Yet, using the concept of the hyperreal, it is possible to develop a 'new' understanding of the leisure life-world, and in my own audacious scheme of things, to argue that, for 'the lads', the sign becomes a signification – as opposed to the signification becoming a sign – in terms which reverse Baudrillard's logic of commodification. Contrary to Baudrillard (1983: 65), for 'the lads' the 'social' still exists.

Standing between my discussion of the spectacle and the hyperreal is a review of the sociology of Michel Maffesoli, which maintains that every social group acts 'as if' it is a community, potentially and actually. In view of this outlook, and because of its concern with the vitality of the social world, Maffesoli's sociology offers us a way to conceptualise both the mythical and the mystical aspects of the leisure life-world and to show how they relate to mundane and spectacular 'laddism'. Within the context of this discussion, the work of Zygmunt Bauman is utilised to temper Maffesoli's impulsive predilection for the ideal of unfettered community, in a way that firmly anchors sociology in the reality of the contingency and ambivalence of 'liquid' modern social relations.

Finally, I present my own theory of the leisure life-world of 'the lads', which builds on the insights of these extant theories and my own rhetorical account of the mundane and the spectacular – which follows in the next section – to offer a more conventional interpretation of that leisure experience. What is significant about this 'new' theory is its ability to knit together and elucidate a whole range of leisure experiences, of which hedonism, drinking, dancing, and fighting are only the most obvious, to a specific goal, which is the togetherness associated with the leisure life-world of 'lads'.

What precedes this core discussion distinguishes between the mundane and the spectacular to illuminate the 'affective feel and the cognitive "truth"' (Rinehart, 1998: 204) about the leisure life-world. I make these two categories discrete for two further reasons: first, for discussion purposes and, secondly, to elucidate the range of experience associated with 'the lads'. However, in the actual expression of the discourse of the leisure life-world, 'the lads' make manifest a continuum between the mundane and the spectacular, with the spectacular being their 'ideal' leisure experience.

The mundane and the spectacular

Get Drunk

You must always be drunk. Everything is there: it is the only question. Not to feel the horrible burden of Time breaking your shoulders and bowing you towards the ground, you must get drunk without stopping.

But on what? On wine, on poetry, or on virtue, after your fashion. But get drunk.

And if sometimes, on the steps of a palace, in the green grass of a ditch, in the dreary solitude of your own room, you wake up, with your drunkenness already lessened or gone, ask wind, wave, star, bird, clock, everything that flees, murmurs, rolls, sings, speaks, ask what time it is; and wind, wave, star, bird, clock will answer you: 'It is time to get drunk! Not to be the tormented slaves of Time, get drunk without stopping! On wine, on poetry, or on virtue, after your fashion.'

Charles Baudelaire

The mundane

The tap room at Farmer's Arms, on Halifax Road, is Sean, Stout and David D-ranged's most agreeable meeting place. They love the tap room for itself, but they also love it because it provides the backdrop for their favourite transformative challenge: the mundane meta-morphosis into 'the lads'. A strictly observed ritual that, while not exactly fixed, carries much more than a faint echo of the grand old days of the lives and times of 'the lads'. This room is where the mun-dane quotidian of their leisure life-world often starts and ends. The tap room is 'the lads'' territory. Their spiritual home. Their kind of being together.

In recent times the tap room has, like the rest of the pub, slipped into almost total decay. The prevailing impression the room provides is that of broken glass and boarded windows, stains, risk and disquiet, a disturbing history of past encounters, not of destructive violence or hate, just the unforeseen consequences of a lot of insignificant scuffles and squabbles.

The significance of the fixtures and fittings is lost on 'the lads', whose collective insouciance permeated the shabby room on this Saturday night. There was Sean, Stout, D-ranged, Benno, Colin and myself. Cigarettes were lit up. Five out of six were smoking, contribut-ing in no uncertain terms to fill the room with a grey haze that hung heavily, thick with the all-pervading smell of nicotine and spilled beer. Six out of six were slurring their words in 'pissed-up' conversation. Six drunken friends who were fast becoming the surviving regulars from the days when this tap room really did belong to 'the lads'. Six out of six who refused to accept that this moribund place was anything but 'home'.

As the evening pressed on, the background exploits of 'the lads'' imagined and imaginary past soon became the foreground of the present moment. Not a little effort and a lot of drink were all that was needed to provide them with a forum for this expression of their togetherness. As the beer flowed, they soon began their reconstruc-tion. As always, Stout looked so sure, so strong. Like some god to whom 'the lads' could always trust both their safety and their destiny, his decisions would always be right, his 'hardness' and street wisdom tacitly understood. While D-ranged transformed from a quite ordinary thirty-something bloke into that perfectly psychotic young man who was discharged 'on medical grounds' by the army in 1982. Sean, with his good looks and his muscular physique, became 'Sean the knob', and Benno turned into his sidekick: 'I'll fuck anything in a skirt, because y' don't need to look at mantelpiece when you're pokin' t' fire, Benson.' Colin metamorphosed into the 'boring bastard' he undoubtedly always is on these occasions. While Tony became once more the victim of his own eccentricity, required to play the role of chief sage and master narrator in a fantasy where his contrariety is only marginally valued. Six transubstantiations completed before ten o'clock.

The six quickly moved to an even more demonstrative state of inebriation. And, as they continued to drink heavily, they exchanged highly edited versions of their lives and times: the lives and times of 'the lads'; narratives constructed with an accuracy perfected with plenty of rehearsal. They soon got back to the nights of allegorical certainty: of the all-day sessions and 'afters' drinking, of the shagging in pairs, of the nights of the four Es (erection, entrance, ejaculation and, if you're lucky, some 'ead [head]), of the gang fights with the inevitable victories, the 'internal' arguments, the card schools and the ventures into 'town'.

They were no longer individuals, they were 'the lads' now, and they behaved as if their collective sanity depended on this narrowness of vision – the ability to select the elements vital to their survival: the great truths 'the lads' leisure by. They built up this fantasy until it possessed the tap room and filled it with their peerless vitalism. Oblivious to anybody else, their all-pervading group aura seemed to lace all the disparate talk and laughter in the room into a groundswell of pleasurable discourse. The drinks continued to come and the mood remained festive. Their consumption for the evening was high now and the leisure life-world was omnipresent. Then, just as they completed the fantasy, they destroyed it.

At 11.30 they had sunk the last beers of the evening and, like a post-Taylor football stadium, the tap room emptied abruptly, smashing the fantasy of the leisure life-world at the same time. When they disbanded 'the lads' did not arrange to meet again, same time, same place. For that would have been some kind of admission, some kind of weakness, as if they needed one another. Which of course they did, but this they could not acknowledge publicly.

The night had passed without incident, but not without event. For 'the lads' had lived out a fantasy that was both real and pleasant to them. A fantasy that was materialised by myth and ritual. A fantasy that had been accomplished. They had kept the leisure life-world alive, tenaciously refusing to let its image become obsolete. The continuity of the leisure life-world had been confirmed once more. And if they had cared to view their work, there would have been general agreement that they had added brilliantly to the already well established discourse of the leisure life-world, that self-absorbed and self-contained 'community' of 'the lads'.

The ambivalence of all of 'the lads'' nights out is that they are the same, and different, and then every now and again there arrives a night out that is ranked special, a spectacular event that underscores the nature of all their nights out. Such as the night in the summer of

1997 when 'the lads' went to a night club in Leeds city centre. A night out which began like any other.

The spectacular

Elevenish on a summer evening in Leeds city centre is not so beautiful to most people. But it is fantastic if you are 'a lad'. There's more beer to be drunk, there's lots of 'fanny' to look at, and the night is still young. The added bonus is that you can be together, talk together, not about anything special, just 'the lads'. 'The lads' had been out since 'half six', but there was still an exciting night ahead. It was 11.15 when they poured out of two taxis and stumbled towards a club they frequent only occasionally. It is a prodigious establishment, buried in the guts of a monolithic 1960s shopping centre.

The doormen who greeted them at the dark front entrance were wearing their council permits on cap-sleeved T-shirts. 'The lads' each tried to pass through the front door individually, as they wanted to avoid getting 'knocked back'. But, to even the most casual observer, they seemed to share something that was all too apparent. Was it their fashion sense, gestures, smell, jokes, language, desires, discourse or sense of togetherness? Regardless of this common impediment, they all passed through this first test without any difficulty.

The night club was swarming with people, and so was the moving dance floor beyond the bar. Bouncers were situated strategically throughout the club watching for any sign of trouble. 'The lads' went straight to the bar and ordered a round of drinks. The bottled beer arrived, expensive, not weak, but insipid, served with profit in mind, not the stuff 'the lads' were used to, but their sense of taste was blunted by their desire to fit in and their state of inebriation. They found some seats and talked as best they could against the cacophony of the 'techno-shite' that was being played by the DJ, while supping themselves closer to oblivion. Benno was on the pull. He had spotted some 'tasty-looking fanny' near the moving dance floor and was determined to 'get his end away'. Nobody else could give a fuck. Although the music was disappointing, there was plenty more beer to be drunk. It was a group decision to stay put for the time being.

Some two hours later the beer had subverted their reticence. And they responded in kind, by hitting the dance floor with a crapulent aplomb. 'The lads' danced for most of the rest of the evening. Once again they were in full flow. Pregnant with the confidence heavy alcohol consumption brings to working-class men, they were now dancing at a remarkable pace, and oozing a prodigious degree of conceit. They sang and danced to the 'techno-shite' as if it was Tina

Turner's 'Simply the Best', a song that *had* been written for them. The other dancers gyrated around 'the lads', but they didn't even notice them. Even Benno, who had fulfilled his ambition to pull, was oblivious to those around him as he danced up close to his new-found love. She was an extremely striking young woman, with her blonde hair rolled into a bun. She could have been Baby Spice. But to Benno she was just another 'piece of fanny'. A beautiful body – yes. But only a bird. Not a 'lad'.

The dance floor was crowded. People ebbed and flowed around them like tidewater, in psychedelic confusion. Their bodies moved less awkwardly to the beat of the music, minds racing; they felt younger by the minute. Benno hitched up his Levi's and jumped on Stout's front, kissing him full on the lips in the process. Thereafter, the two embraced in a sort of binate eurhythmics. The rest of them danced in an uninhibited mutuality. They could sense each other as they moved, serenely now, not having to concentrate all their efforts on staying upright, not tripping, not falling over. Seven long hours after they had started on their adventure, and now they were once again in utopia. They felt good, felt ecstatic, felt paradisiac, felt as if they were wholly together, sitting on top of the world. Once more they felt that *puissance* (Maffesoli, 1996), that 'eruption' of a communal 'will to live'; and it was masculine, exciting, mystical, erotic, aesthetic and magical, all over again. It was like one of those recurrent dreams where 'the lads' are permanently fixed in time, back to where they started from, back 'home'. It was a 'top' night out. Indeed, it was to become one of the spectacular narratives, the myths, the collective memories, a really 'real' night out with 'the lads'.

More than that, this particular night out was to become a 'new' ritual narrative linking their past to their present. For in time-honoured fashion it conveyed the quintessential meaning of the leisure life-world to each of them in a cultural code that only they understand. An intensity of a sense of the affectual (Maffesoli, 1996: 72–8), communicated by an extraordinary mutuality for which there is no rational descriptor.

Two, three, four years on, this 'new' narrative works to continue to link the diminished present of 'the lads' with the glories of their past. It acts simultaneously as an advertisement for their well-being and as a sense of their continuity, calling 'the lads'' attention to the overwhelming enticement of the enchanted world of the spectacular.

VictorTurner: communitas, liminality and anti-structure

For Turner (1973) the concept of liminality literally means a 'threshold', a place 'in an out of time', which provides the individual with a

spatial separation from the familiar and habitual, constitutes a cultural
domain that is extremely rich in cosmological meaning, conveyed
largely by nonverbal signals. Liminality represents negation of many
of the features of preliminal social structures, and an affirmation of
another order of things, stressing generic rather than particularistic
relationships.

(Turner, 1973: 213–14)

All liminoid experiences include both personal and transpersonal elements.
Yet the liminoid, while reaching beyond the experience of the individual,
depends on a unique existential (and by implication individual) encounter.
Fulghum (1995) argues that the most powerful dimension of liminality is
its solitariness; the way it emphasises the individual's separateness from
others. Yet this issue is never resolved by Turner, who chooses to emphasise
the shared experiences of liminality through the concept of communitas.

The concept of communitas is distinguished from that of *community*,
which, in Turner's (1973: 216) terms, is properly seen 'as a geographical
area of common living'. In common with Parsons (1951: 91), Turner
makes the naive functionalist assumption that a locale is a necessary foundation for the functioning of community: 'a community is that collectivity the
members of which share a common territorial area as their base of operations
for daily activities'. In much the same manner as Maffesoli (1995), Turner
insists that the concept of communitas surpasses and subverts the utilitarian
and rationalistic structures of society. Communitas 'expresses a very concrete
and communal unmediated communication between people, which it is
suggested, arises spontaneously within groups sharing a similar commitment
or position' (Thompson, 1981: 6). The experience of communitas 'strains
towards' an openness (Turner and Turner, 1978) and provides a return to
the social group denied by the manifest inequalities inherent to bourgeois
society. These mystical experiences of togetherness are captured within situations of liminal 'margin' and communitas 'remains open and specialized, a
spring of pure possibility as well as the immediate realization of release
from day-to-day structural necessities and obligatoriness' (Turner, 1973:
217). Turner (1973: 193–4) identifies three types of communitas: *existential
or spontaneous* communitas, *normative* communitas and *ideological* communitas. I shall briefly discuss each of these below.

Existential communitas represents an explicit, total and authentic coming
together of a social group, which undermines the capitalistic commodification of relationships encountered in a sociality founded on economic aliena-
tion and class, gender and racial inequalities. Participation in existential
communitas involves, for the individual, total dependence on the dialectic
of the self in relation to others and, when existential communitas occurs, it
is liable to provide those experiencing it with a return to the unfettered

social group of 'homogeneous unstructured, and free community'. For these reasons the existential communitas experience is always likely to be transient.

Normative communitas develops where existential communitas persists and the social group develops a need to organise and make its position more secure. Turner stresses, however, that this more lasting form of existential communitas should not be confused with utilitarian social togetherness, such as Durkheimian *mechanical solidarity*, for example, which is likely to have structural antecedents and be built on bourgeois-rational *Gesellschaft* (Tönnies, 1955 *1887*)-type foundations. For Turner, communitas-type social groups tend to have non-utilitarian, enchanted and primordial origins and, in this sense, invariably surpass 'the utilitarian and functionalist aspect prevailing in the surrounding economic order' (Maffesoli, 1996: 79). Finally, Turner (1973: 194) defines *Ideological* communitas as 'a label one can apply to a variety of utopian models or blueprints of societies believed by their authors to exemplify or supply the optimal conditions of existential communitas'.

For Turner (1973) the concept of social anti-structure evinces most fittingly the sense of interpolation experienced in thresholds of liminality. Yet this concept connotes a definite pattern and structure associated with day-to-day existence at the liminal stage, giving the go-ahead to what is, in 'the lads'' meaning, a 'will to happiness', 'where the whim of the moment dictates the pace and direction of activities' (Thompson, 1981: 36), and signalling at the same time an abrogation of the dominant social order of things. In respect to my own analysis, the irony is, of course, that it is a sense of a 'solid' modernist social *structure*, not *anti-structure*, that 'the lads' look for in the leisure life-world.

On the face of it the spectacular leisure activities of 'the lads' would seem to correspond to existential communitas, the mundane to normative communitas and the discourse of 'the lads' (the stories they tell about themselves) to ideological communitas. However, the leisure life-world of 'the lads' is underpinned by a process of de-differentiation, making for a messiness that is underemphasised in Turner's account, and this is why I have chosen to describe it with the underlying continuum of the mundane and the spectacular. Perhaps the separation of concepts – communitas, liminality and anti-structure – I have emphasised is an artificial distinction that neither really bears out, nor truly reflects, what Turner is attempting to describe. Be that as it may, Turner's story corresponds with a larger discourse of structural functionalism associated with the sociology of Talcott Parsons, which makes it a story that misreads the quotidian of the imagined, imaginary and magical in people's lives. The leisure life-world *is* a key part of the *real* lives of 'the lads'. Indeed, just because it is a world of leisure, pleasure and frivolity, which is governed by the non-rational, does not mean it is beyond the threshold of *reality*. The leisure life-world may be fantastical, but it is the *social reality* of 'the lads'' mutual leisure experiences.

The commodity spectacle

> The spectacle erases the dividing line between self and world, in that self, under siege by the presence/absence of the world, is eventually over- whelmed; it likewise erases the dividing line between true and false, repressing all directly lived truth beneath the real presence of falsehood maintained by the organization of appearances. The individual, though condemned to the passive acceptance of an alien everyday reality, is thus driven into a form of madness in which, by resorting to magical devices, he entertains the illusion that he is reacting to his fate.
>
> (Guy Debord, 1995 *1967:* thesis 219)

In a similar way to Turner, Guy Debord's (1995 *1967*) situationalist critique of the commodity spectacle suggests that the spectacular encounters that shape the leisure life-world of 'the lads' make manifest an 'unreal unity' that 'masks the class divisions on which the real unity of the capitalist mode of production is based' (thesis 72). In Debord's sense, the notion of the spectacle is a sham, suggesting that the leisure life-world of 'the lads' is merely the material construction of the illusion of community. This is because the inexorable march of the spectacle means that the leisure pursuits of 'the lads' are disposed to become mere images of resistance, because of their complicity in the capitalistic relations of production and consumption. In fact, for Debord (1995 *1967:* thesis 42), all acts of resistance involving leisure are likely to be forestalled in the spectacle. This is because at the same moment 'the spectacle corresponds to the historical moment at which the commodity completes its colonization of social life'.

However, when Debord describes the all-pervading commodification of society through the spectacle, he does so in very different terms from Baudrillard. Debord describes the society of the spectacle in terms that make explicit his Marxian idealism, making comparisons with Baudrillard a confrontation between 'modern' and 'postmodern' theories. In marked contrast to Baudrillard's nihilistic hyperreality, in Debord's scheme of things there remains hope of escape from the commodity spectacle. For 'the spectacle is not a collection of images; rather, it is a social relationship between people that is mediated by images' (Debord, 1995 *1967:* thesis 4).

There is an explicit link between Debord and classical Marxian approaches and the Frankfurt school (Marcuse, 1964), in the sense that he infers that people's relationships to the spectacle present new possibilities for their exploitation. However, in Debord's avant-gardist scheme of things there is an attempt to distinguish between the commodified, that is, distorted and fetishised situations of the spectacle and 'authentic' or essential situations, which are undistorted by capitalistic relationships. Debord suggests that by moving away from the spectacular to the 'authentic' practice of *détourne- ment*, people can gain a sense of 'real' meaning in their lives. *Détournement* involves 'the integration of past or present artistic production into a superior environmental construction' (Internationale Situationniste, 1958). Jenks (1995: 154–5) explains what the practice of *détournement* entails:

> The two principles of the practice are: (a) that each re-used element from a previous context must be divested of its autonomy and original signification; and (b) that the assembly of elements must forge an original image which generates a wholly new meaning structure for the parts, through the totality that they now comprise.

In effect, what Debord is describing is a compound strategy of deconstruction and *bricolage*, for putting 'new' and 'original' meanings back into social situations which are most effective when they advance non-rational responses to the commodity spectacle (Debord and Wolman, 1956).

The trouble is that Debord makes the fundamental Marxian error of trying to distinguish between the distorted and the undistorted (essential) nature of things. The practice of *détournement* providing an overly simple linear movement from the distorted logic of the commodity spectacle to a situation of undistorted essence and redemption. Debord's reified conception of the 'world out there' confirmed as the pre-set schema for 'authentic' human relationships. In this sense, Debord misses the point that there is (no)thing that is uncommodifiable in the version of capitalism associated with 'liquid' modernity and that:

> popular culture self-commodifies. It doesn't resist the power of the market. It can't. Popular culture doesn't pretend to be outside the culture; it's already inscribed in the flux of culture, including, of course, the market metanarrative. Unfortunately for that metanarrative, however, is the fact that popular culture, with a passport to go anywhere it can to make a profit, often finds itself reflecting unsettled, problematic values and meanings. *Nothing is meant to counter market values but the possibility yet remains that countering values can be made conceivable.*
>
> (Natoli, 1997: 179–80, my emphasis)

In Natoli's sense, and contrary to Debord, the discourse of 'the lads' sets itself in opposition to and seeks to undermine the commodification of relationships encountered in a sociality dominated by the market metanarrative. What 'the lads' are trying to escape in this sense is the power of the market meta-narrative that imposes on them an existence which is not really 'theirs'.

David D-ranged elucidates what this entails:

I think that when I'm out wi' t' lads it's t' only time I really feel I belong to summat. It's all about what y' feel in 'ere (makes a fist and thumps his chest). Our kid, an' his mates, they don't 'ave fuck-all like that; all they care about is t' next car, t' next 'ouse or whose woman they can fuck next. They're all cunts. They can't see what it's really about, 'cos they're so much up their own fuckin' arses. Half o' those cunts ignore yer, if they see yer out on t' streets. Stout, Sean, Louis an' them, they're all cunts, in their own ways, but they'd do owt fo' yer. An' I'd do owt fo' them.

As 'the lads' might say: 'Today most of our entertainment comes from the past, even though complemented now by the 'retro' industry that dominates the market place of popular culture. We know that what we have has such and that it pulls, for us, a real emotional punch – the music and the fashions of our mutual past. We also know that the logic of the market, with its passport to go anywhere it can to make a profit, tries to squeeze us for all we are worth. But we've sussed those cunts out too and we exploit them for what we can get out of them.'

Yet the discourse of the leisure life-world has no conscious political ambitions and remains both incoherent and underdetermined. In the following quotation, de Certeau could be describing the leisure life-world and the practices of 'the lads' on a night out in Leeds:

> The ordinary practitioners of the city live 'down below', below the thresholds at which visibility begins. They walk – an elementary form of this experience of the city; they are walkers, *Wandersmänner*, whose bodies follow the thicks and thins of the urban 'text' they write without being able to read it. These practitioners make use of spaces that cannot be seen; their knowledge of them is as blind as that of lovers in each other's arms. The paths that correspond in this intertwining, are unrecognized poems in which each body is an element signed by many others to elude legibility. It is as though the practices organizing a bustling city were characterized by blindness. The networks of these moving, intersecting writings compose a manifold story that has neither author nor spectator, shaped out of fragments of trajectories and alterations of spaces: in relation to representations, it remains daily and infinitely other.
>
> (de Certeau, quoted in Jenks, 1995: 156)

The quotidian of the mundane and the orgiastic experience of the spectacular

The nature of the spectacle is to accentuate, either directly or by euphemism, the sensational, tactile dimension of social existence. Being-together allows us to touch: 'The majority of the people's pleasures are found in the pleasures of the crowd or the group' (A. Ehrenberg). We cannot comprehend this strange compulsion to group together without keeping at the forefront of our minds this anthropological constant.

(Maffesoli, 1996: 77)

There is another way in which the mundane and the spectacular might be interpreted and that is through the sociology of Maffesoli. Maffesoli (1996) uses the Bergsonian method of intuition to locate 'community' somewhere between the mythical and non-rational described in the philosophy of Nietzsche and the *conscience collective* theorised in the sociology of Durkheim. However, whereas Durkheim's sociology tended towards rational analysis, Maffesoli shuns purely rational argument, and, in this sense, his sociology tends towards synthesis rather than analysis. In Maffesoli's sociology of postmodernity, neo-tribalism adds the sense of the 'orgiastic' and the 'magical' to Durkheim's rational interpretation of the *conscience collective*.

For Durkheim (1951) the quotidian of all collective existence is made up of collective representations, which are inimical to individual representations. In Durkheim's sense, then, the postulated community of 'the lads' represents a *conscience collective* of experience and is not, therefore, 'real' in the commonsensical meaning, but a representation of their group mind, which consistently attaches itself to them collectively. Discourse plays the similar role for those theorists writing from a poststructuralist position as the *conscience collective* does for Durkheim.

Reasoning sociologically, in the Durkheimian sense that, because the *conscience collective* represents the 'totality of beliefs and sentiments' (Durkheim, 1933: 79) common to a community, there are two specific assertions that can be made about the collective representation of 'the lads'. First, that this community reflects the ambivalence of the hopes and fears of 'the lads'. Second, that the discourse of this community is relatively autonomous and functions according to its own rules.

For Maffesoli (1996) community is not at all community in the traditional sociological sense; it is reflexive, which precludes absolutism and enhances the individual's capacity to become a member of other communities. Moreover, for Maffesoli, community-type social groups, or tribes, tend to have non-utilitarian, enchanted and primordial origins and, in this sense, invariably surpass 'the utilitarian and functionalist aspect prevailing in the surrounding economic order' (Maffesoli, 1996: 79). The knowledge and power which create the sense of community between 'the lads' is what Maffesoli calls *puissance* (will to live). For 'the lads', the *puissance* that animates the leisure life-world collapses the restrictions imposed by social fragmentation. Bauman elucidates what the *puissance* of neo-tribalism entails:

> Perhaps we live in a postmodern age, perhaps not. But we do live in the
> age of tribes and tribalism. It is tribalism, miraculously reborn, that
> injects juice and vigour into the eulogy of community, the acclaim of
> belonging, the passionate search for tradition. In this sense at least,
> the long roundabout of modernity has brought us to where our ances-
> tors once started. Or so it may seem.
>
> (Bauman, 1997: 79)

I have argued consistently in this book that 'liquid' living involves a greater
awareness of the self as an autonomous individuality, leading inevitably to
less social cohesiveness. However, during the mundane and the spectacular,
the distinctions between 'the lads' are dissolved. And the idea of the individual, which, Bauman (1997) argues, is of the utmost importance for the
good life in liquid modernity, is notable only by its absence during the
mundane and the spectacular, but particularly in the latter. For the discourse
of the spectacular gives a far greater intensity to the sense of belonging than is
normally experienced in the mundane/quotidian of the leisure life-world of
'the lads'.

In this sense, the fictitious reality in which they normally live is, for 'the
lads', reversed when the 'real' meaning of life is revealed in the spectacular.
And, contrary to everyday reality, the spectacular makes manifest a leisure
world almost entirely particularised by significations. Moreover, the form
of knowledge that underpins the discourse of the leisure life-world of 'the
lads' establishes a relationship between the knower and the known that
dissolves the simple subject–object dichotomy, and so too blurs the distinction between what 'really' took place and what is imagined by 'the lads'.

In the course of the leisure spectacular, the mundane experience of being
'a lad' detaches itself from the familiar circumstances of the everyday to
initiate an emotional aura where 'passion is expressed, common beliefs are
developed and the search "for those who feel and think as we do" takes
place' (Maffesoli, 1996: 12–13). Spectacular 'laddism' is not only experienced
more vividly in terms of sensation: it also seems to mean more, for it functions 'as if' it really exists (ibid.: 19). And its meaning, which is by now out
of all proportion to its everyday function, can no longer be described in
terms of rational thought, which seems inadequate to express the sense of
the magical associated with both the mundane and the spectacular.

The spectacular, in particular, appears to be capable of producing in
awareness a sense of belonging far in excess of the needs of the autonomous,
reflexive individual described in the sociology of Bauman and Giddens.
Bauman (1997: 2–3) finds particular significance in Freud's concept of the
pleasure principle, which emerges ever more forcefully as a consequence of
the 'liquid' modern 'will to happiness' and its never satisfied striving. However, for Bauman the authentic experience of pleasure is always that of the
individual, not the collective.

Another major difference in Bauman's work is his interpretation that the 'liquid' 'will to happiness' is guided in all cases by a hedonistic rationality which is always satisfied – for a short time at any rate – by the consumer logic of the market meta-narrative. Such a reading fails to grasp the role of vitalism in the leisure life-world of 'the lads', which is shaped by affectual, magical and communal feelings, rather than by instrumental rationality. Bauman's theory is insufficient because it is based on his own ontology, which is not the ontology of 'the lads', who are immersed in a constant struggle to reunite themselves with that 'solid' modern world to which they believe they belong and from which they have been separated. This is the seriousness in the leisure life-world that is understated in Bauman's scheme of things.

Maffesoli (1996: 13) repairs this tendency in no uncertain terms in the following quotation, to describe what could easily be the manifestation of the leisure life-world of 'the lads'.

> Whether in the context of the network of tiny convivial cells or at a favourite local pub, the collective emotion becomes concrete, playing on the multiple facets of what Montaigne called the *hommerie*: that blend of greatness and turpitude, generous ideas and venal thoughts, of idealism and convinced worldliness – in a word: man.

Just the same, there is a contingency to the apparent all-pervasive mutuality of the leisure life-world which relates to Bauman's word of caution about the 're-emergence' of community, or tribalism, in liquid modernity, and which must be noted in relation to this discussion. The leisure life-world of 'the lads', while being a close-knit mutuality, is at the same time a temporality – governed by the contingency rather than the fixity of liquid events and social relations. For 'the lads'' actions are never more than contingent upon the immediate situation which gives rise to them. There is also an ambivalence to the spectacular world of 'the lads' which must be noted in this context. The leisure life-world it reflects, while being recognisably safe and familiar, is at the same time both dangerous and unfamiliar. In this sense, the spectacular is not dissimilar to the festival world of the carnivalesque.

The carnivalesque is a blanket term that refers to those traditional, historical and enduring forms of social ritual, such as festivals, fairs and feasts, that provide sites of 'ordered disorder' (Bakhtin, 1984; Stallybrass and White, 1986), where social rules are broken and subverted and where one can explore one's 'otherness', secret desires and most intimate pleasures. Featherstone (1991: 79) argues that the carnivalesque:

> involves the disconnected succession of fleeting images, sensations, de-control of the emotions and de-differentiation which have become

associated with postmodernism and the aestheticization of everyday life . . . the carnival involves the celebration of the grotesque body – fattening food, intoxicating drink, sexual promiscuity – in a world in which official culture is turned upside down.

This study suggests that the more enduring locations of leisure, such as the city centre, continue to be the most visible and discernible sites where people are most likely to encounter and experience the carnivalesque. We have seen also that the carnivalesque (spectacular) of the leisure life-world is often experienced at a rapid pace, in ways that are often unpredictable, contradictory and dangerous. Indeed, risk is inherent in the carnivalesque and is its essential attraction. However, this research suggests also that most people's experience of the carnivalesque is two-edged: it is at the same time a site of both the emancipatory and the unequal. As we saw in Chapter 4, 'the lads'' enjoyment of the carnivalesque (spectacular) is often had at the expense of women. Indeed, for those who do not fit the 'solid modern mould', particularly women, the more modern than modern leisure experience surrounding the life-world of 'the lads' is encountered as anything but pleasurable.

The hyperreality of the leisure life-world

A tormenting thought: as of a certain point, history was no longer real. Without noticing it, all mankind left reality; everything happening since then was supposedly not true; but we supposedly didn't notice. Our task now would be to find that point, and as long as we didn't have it, we would be forced to abide in our present destruction.

(Elias Canneti, quoted in Baudrillard, 1998: 4)

The epistemological and ontological frameworks underpinning the arguments developed in this book differ fundamentally from the postmodernism of Baudrillard, which postulates the argument that it is the infinite questioning of rationality that leads to the demise of the 'grand narrative' of modernity (Baudrillard, 1983). It is the postmodern view that, in trying to find the ultimate truth, in seeking ground for its knowledge, rationality unavoidably lays the foundations for its own destruction. In Baudrillard's postmodern world it is rationality that produces nihility. Nietzschean nihilism is the ultimate consequence of rationality. Once rationality has been banished from the 'business of life', there can no longer be any single objective reality, nor any observation that is not merely postulation; what we have is nothing more than 'the play of signifiers . . . in which the code[1] no longer refers back to any subjective or objective "reality", but to its own logic' (Baudrillard, 1975: 127). Postmodernism's postmodernity is a depthless, 'hyperised' asociality; individual agency is irrelevant, 'the individual is nonexistent'

(Baudrillard, 1981: 75). Indeed, Baudrillard's postmodern schema gives priority to the 'sign over subjective ideas' and the 'antisocial sign over the social sign' (Harland, 1987). Although the work of Baudrillard is limited by the lack of an adequate metaphysical framework for interpreting his own postulations, his insights help us to overcome Debord's tendency towards essentialism.

During the 1990s Baudrillard used the quotation that precedes this section on a considerable number of occasions, to develop his argument that the year 2000 would not necessarily not happen, and even if it did, we would not know anything about it. This non-event would or would not occur, owing to the fact that, for Baudrillard, the human race had already turned its back on history. Indeed, in Baudrillard's third order of the 'Wholly Trinity of Revolutions' (Simulation), history – and reality – has disappeared; 'there are only simulacra' in postmodern hyperreality (Baudrillard, 1993: 120). Not unsurprisingly, given the reasoning of such an argument (which is typical of him), Baudrillard can easily be discarded – as he often is, of course, as the postmodernist *nonpareil* of nihilism.

Paradoxically, however, Baudrillard argues also that it is possible to make a stand against the hyperreal in this society of shit, where 'so many messages and signals have been produced and transmitted that they will never find the time to acquire any meaning' (Baudrillard, 1989b: 30). Revolution, in the Marxian sense, is no longer possible, of course, because the social no longer exists. For Baudrillard (1993) resistance can be accomplished only through the use of pataphysics.[2] Baudrillard's pataphysical schema is not unproblematic, though, as it presumes that resistance to the disappearance of the real is imaginary. Indeed, it could be nothing else in hyperreality.

In the essay 'The world according to Jean Baudrillard', Bauman most clearly makes the point about liquid modernity being anything but hyperreal:

> To many people, much in their life is anything but simulation. To many, reality remains what it used to be: tough, solid, resistant and harsh. They need to sink their teeth into some quite real bread before they abandon themselves to munching images.
>
> (Bauman, 1992: 155)

As we have seen, the means by which 'the lads' construct and reconstruct for themselves a postulated sense of community through the routine of the mundane and the spectacular is anything but imaginary. Those narratives may be imagined, but they are certainly not imaginary.

Be that as it may, Baudrillard's discussion of the disappearance of the real cannot be cast aside so easily – and we have more than a cursory interest in it for the purposes of this analysis. The view developed here is that Baudrillard's thesis is not as daft as it seems and that it can have a direct relevance to our own task; that is, if we can put it to use to analyse the 'lads'' affectual (Maffesoli, 1996) and magical attempts to reconstruct a 'solid' modern sense of being and belonging.

It is possible to utilise Baudrillard's schema, without having recourse to its more precarious proposals. As I have suggested throughout this analysis, if we are properly to understand 'the lads' as a sociological generation (Abrams, 1982), we must be able to see the 'world as it is' from their point of view. Baudrillard's thesis is of direct relevance because it enables us to grasp the quintessential point that, from the terms of reference of 'the lads', and in the commonsensical meaning of the word 'real', 'liquid' changes are *perceived* as not 'real', as unreal. For if 'liquid' modernity is in reality their present condition, in their leisure time–space, 'the lads', can, and do, choose to live by the remains of a certain, 'solid' modernist way of life. In that leisure time–space of the mundane and the spectacular, the reality of their present condition can be subverted – for a short time, at any rate. In this sense 'the lads'' resistance to the 'liquid' conditions emerges as a particular kind of hyperreality. I will illustrate what I mean by paraphrasing the afore-mentioned quote from Canneti, quoted in Baudrillard (1998: 4):

> A tormenting nightmare: as of a certain point, the social world was no longer real for 'the lads'. Without noticing it, with liquid modernity, all mankind had left reality; everything happening since then was supposedly not true. For 'the lads' this meant that, regardless of the unmitigated inculcation their habitus had inscribed and bequeathed them, they, white, working-class men, were no longer supreme. 'The lads' supposedly didn't notice, but they themselves know different. Their task now would be to find that point – in their leisure time and space – where they could resist liquid changes and, individually, assert still that monosemic identity of the 'true' 'modern' man. For as long as 'the lads' didn't have that sense of ontological security, they would be forced to abide in their own present destruction.

Indeed, as we have seen already, 'the lads'' perceive themselves to be of the 'perfect world' conceived in 'solid' modernity, and 'one remaining forever identical with itself, a world in which the wisdom learnt today will remain wise tomorrow and the day after tomorrow, and in which the life skills acquired will retain their usefulness forever' (Bauman, 1997: 12). In 'the lads'' sense, liquid modernity is perceived as not 'real'; and, contrary to con-ventional wisdom, their leisure time and leisure space provide them with the means by which they can challenge and undermine the 'irrationalities' of their present condition. Contrary to the so-called 'real' world, in their leisure time and space, life can *appear* still to be of the certain, 'solid' modernity.

Consequently, for 'the lads', the certainty of 'solid' modernity is required if their leisure lives are to proceed as 'normal'. Leisure provides the means by which they can challenge and undermine the 'irrationalities' of liquid conditions, a modern world where it is no longer sufficient or desirable, socially, politically or economically, to be a 'real' man. Contrary to conventional wisdom, when each of them makes 'the lads' the centre of his attention, his leisure life appears still to be of the more certain 'solid' modern world. However, we must not make the mistake of misunderstanding the leisure life-world of 'the lads'. The mundane and the spectacular are *not* of a 'solid' modern world, they are of the individualistic liquid modernity. As Bauman continues to show, past experience of the modern world, 'as we tend to reconstruct it now, retrospectively, [is] known to us [only] through its disappearance' (Bauman, 1997: 87).

I am proposing that 'the lads'' leisure experiences manifest themselves as hyperreal. However, I do not have in view a hyperreality in the sense that Baudrillard means – a depthless, 'hyperised' asociality. My approach does not deny the existence of 'reality' in Baudrillard's sense but suggests that we live in multiple representations of it, 'each reality believing and arguing that theirs is no mediated reality but the reality in itself' (Natoli, 1997: 198). Time moves on but the leisure activities of the 'the lads' remain fixed within a 'solid' modern discourse. The past is key to 'the lads' because it brings to the present what is absent. To be sure, the 'lads'' leisure lives are anything but simulation and are very real. Expressed in another way, the hyperreality of 'the lads'' leisure lives is best described as 'solid' modern resistance to 'liquid' change. This understanding of the hyperreal presumes that 'solid' modern ideologies, perfectabilities, biases, prejudices and the like take on 'new' hyperreal tendencies and meanings in liquid modernity. In 'the lads'' meaning, the sign becomes a signification – as opposed to the signification becoming a sign – in terms which reverse Baudrillard's logic of commodification. Contrary to Baudrillard (1983: 65), for 'the lads' the 'social' still exists.

The eusociality of the leisure life-world of 'the lads'

> And yet it is the very fact that reality and the past do exist that we are endlessly drawn to them, re-engaging both as 'insidious ideological political fashions change'. The past is put in motion in terms of the motions of the present, And the present is neither at rest nor monologic nor settled before one horizon. There is no fixed order of observing in the present nor could there have been a fixed order to be observed in the past. What is said about the past is said by observers, and we have countless observers and ways of observing.
>
> (Natoli, 1997: 165)

'The lads' inhabit a hyperreal leisure life-world in which there appears to be a clear logic – it could hardly be any different from a 'solid' modern perspective – in which time is both regressively sequential and episodic, and in which anything under the narrative of 'solid modernity' is possible. The leisure life-world is a time and space dominated by an illusory solid modernity of leisure experience, and the spectacular represents its culmination. But this hyperreal leisure life-world is an imagined modernity shaped by non-rational feeling. The dynamics of the leisure life-world may relate to a 'solid' modernity, but the masculine, the exciting, the mystical, the mythical, the erotic, the aesthetic and the magical determine them.

In the self-same way, the leisure life-world dissolves the problem of fitting together the needs of the individual and the collective. In this intersubjective world (Ricoeur, 1992) each of the individual needs of 'the lads' manifests itself as the collective need of the group – in a transient but persisting sense – once each of them makes the leisure life-world the centre of his attention. This ideal of community collapses the rational modernist order of things and enchants the leisure life-world. The ultimate appeal of this leisure life-world being for 'the lads' that it will fulfil their longing for 'home' and security and their desire for the quotidian of the non-rational (leisure, play and pleasure). Yet, at the same time, this 'we' of 'the lads' knows that 'I' am only involved in a game, because 'we' and 'I' know that this 'will to happiness' cannot be sustained and that the transient leisure of the life-world remains pleasurable only because 'we' get together only intermittently. And 'I' know that although the leisure life-world is central to my leisure and pleasure, it is not central enough to the way of life that 'I' cherish and am committed to in 'reality'. But:

> by 'pretending', we are participating magically in a collective game . . . reminds us that something like the 'community' has existed, does exist or will exist. It is a question of aestheticism, derision, participation and reticence all at once. It is above all the mythical affirmation that the masses are a source of power. This aesthetic game or sentiment is collectively produced just as much for oneself as for the power which orchestrates it. At the same time, it allows one to remind this power that it is only a game, and that there are limits which must not be breached.
>
> (Maffesoli, 1996: 49)

There is also a seriousness in this game that is a vital part of this 'solid' modern leisure. Orthodox synthetic sociology, with its hierarchies, centres and false dichotomies, and its orderly notion of linear time and dissociated space, is an inadequate body of thought for analysing the mundane and the spectacular of the leisure life-world. For as the present is swallowed up by the past, linear time and separately divided space cease to be discernible in the rational sense.

Both the present and the future are understood vaguely as an absence and possibility, which by force of circumstance will inevitably become heavily affiliated with the historicity of the narrative of the leisure life-world; as if by necessity, growing constantly and spectacularly out of the past. Time experienced in this way necessarily impoverishes the present, meaning that the present time disappears; in this sense the experience of the leisure life-world is timeless. But timelessness is a particular way of experiencing time. The present moment is indubitably imbricated in the past, in particular through 'the lads'' existential sensations and experiences and practical leisure. The past is no longer experienced as absent from the present, but as an integral part of it. This takes place at that moment when 'the lads' set about the present with a great deal of absence that they want to fill with presence and the narrative of their past becomes required reading.

The discourse of 'the lads' achieves this transmogrification of time in two distinct ways. The first is by taking historical episodes involving 'the lads' and recreating them as vividly as possible, so that they feel as 'real' as present experience, without the oppressive associations of the actual present. As we saw in the two episodes described above, both mundane and spectacular nights out play a key role in this respect. So does gossip. Gossip serves as the 'glue' holding the leisure life-world together and is 'used to strengthen the group in its belief in what it represents and in its activities. It [unfailingly] possesses the truth – theoretical, existential, ideological' (Maffesoli, 1996: 145–6) about the 'lads'. The second transmogrification of time involves a fusion of experiences of the past with those of the present to such an extent that the distinction between the two times becomes, in Baudrillard's sense, hyperreal. In effect, the prospect of realising the past is bought at the cost of losing contact with the 'real' world, as we saw in the episode describing the spectacular.

These connections with the past sometimes materialise between consecutive nights out, but as often as not they relate the present to a narrative from the more distant past, if that narrative happens to offer something more meaningful than recently developed ones. The present, therefore, includes an imaginary sense of the meaning of the past, also experienced concretely through material action and performance. Such a sense of the past plays a key part in both the episodes described above.

However, these two episodes cannot be understood in isolation, or as identical; they must be recognised in relation to each other and to other narratives. They refer to part of a larger body of related leisure experiences, in that they are fused, as we see throughout this book, by striking parallels operating at both the direct level of describable leisure experience and at a highly abstract existential level, emphasising the ambivalent relationship between the negative (loneliness and anxiety) and the positive (belonging and secure) aspects of 'the lads'' predicament. 'The lads' themselves recognise the imaginativeness of this intellectual correspondence, but the creativity this involves comes to a stop once some unifying notion of leisure experience has been achieved. For both the existential and the discursive knowledge that sustains 'the lads' is to be found in the ready-made discourse of the leisure life-world. This knowledge is ample to make further imaginativeness unnecessary.

The episodes show also that 'the lads'' leisure experiences tend to follow familiar patterns of development, in that they often begin with unorganised meetings in the local pub and time and again culminate in spectacular drunken binges, providing each of 'the lads' with an ecstatic and spectacular recognition of what he perceives to be his 'real' ipse-self in this postulated community. However, the normality of 'the lads' is often no more than a 'good' session in the Farmer's Arms, reflecting the mundane of the quotidian of the leisure life-world.

However, the knowledge which creates and sustains this postulated community always provides the possibility that *any* night out *could* become spectacular, meaning that even the most mundane encounters offer the potential of thrill and excitement. Mundane nights out are best seen, then, as partial realisations of the spectacular. In this sense the leisure life-world makes manifest a continuum between the mundane and the spectacular, with the spectacular being the 'ideal' leisure experience. These observations appear to qualify Derrida's (1973) point that there is always inequity in binary oppositions. This does not mean of course that the leisure activities of 'the lads' are necessarily underwritten by a predetermined order, but it demonstrates the underlying power and knowledge of the discourse driving the leisure life-world.

The two episodes indicate also the extent to which alcohol is intimately tied up with the leisure life-world. 'The lads' tend to 'celebrate' their unity by consuming prodigious amounts of alcohol. Heavy alcohol consumption helps to propagate 'the lads'' idea of the 'truth' about the leisure life-world. It also has the desirable effect of accentuating the visual, the aural and the aesthetic, and increasing their awareness of their sense of unity with one another. Popular music is another vehicle through which 'the lads' penetrate the leisure life-world, the other means of entry, as we saw, being the discourse of the leisure life-world, including gossip, soft drugs and alcohol. Popular music symbolises memory and it also reflects the past, because particular songs evoke particular meanings for 'the lads'. In this sense, popular music plays a key role in conferring a sense of the past to the present. Popular music, like 'the lads'' DIY tattoos and dress code, also provides a sense of 'permanence' that enables 'the lads' to make believe that they can resist the palimpsest mentality that is all-pervasive in the liquid condition.

In the absence of a 'real' sociological community in their lives, 'the lads' must look elsewhere for a sense of belonging. The leisure life-world presents 'the lads' with awareness of a far greater sense of community than is at all conceivable in other aspects of their lives. And it is because the leisure life-world is organised (disorganised) around leisure, pleasure, frivolity and superficiality that this unity of experience is possible (Maffesoli, 1996: 89). In Maffesoli's sense, this is why it is vitalism, not rationality, which best explains the social phenomenon of the leisure life-world of 'the lads'.

This postulated community, as it emerges in the leisure life-world, has two determining features that emphasise the liquid modernity of 'the lads' present condition. The first of these relates to Maffesoli's (1996) crucial point that, today, we live in 'the time of the tribes', and that liquid living is organised around the membership of myriad 'communities' which allow 'the lads' to be simultaneously members of two, three or more culturally distinct groups. Second, and what is perhaps of more significance for 'the lads', is that, in Bauman's (1992a) terms, the leisure life-world provides a DIY shelter from their subjugation and marginality in liquid modernity, which leads to what almost seems to be the permanence of their separation from what is today perceived to be 'normal'. For working-class men today can only look on in vain as their sense of identity is continually being deconstructed, not only economically and politically, but also socially and culturally, in a world where it is not enough to be a 'hard' man. The dominant emotion associated with 'the lads' is their longing for a cure for their homesickness, a sense of liberation from the habitual confines of their autonomous individuality, experienced when 'the lads' make the leisure life-world the centre of their attention. Yet as I have said already this is hardly community in the orthodox sociological sense, which demands a far deeper investment than the highly spectacular and fantastical achievements of 'the lads'.

The discourse of the leisure life-world provides each of 'the lads' with a DIY shelter for bringing out his 'real' sense of self and identity, to gain a sense of the 'truth' about himself, which he would not otherwise have. The leisure life-world is their only constant. Consequently, 'the lads' judge their 'ideal of leisure' by its success in facilitating this redemptive deliverance in their leisure lives. The experience of the spectacular is the positive extreme contrasting with the negative experience of being a working-class man in the late 1990s.

'The lads' inhabit a leisure life-world in which time is malleable, mercurial, in which the past can be the present, in which the clock can stop or run retrospectively. Yet at the same time they are constrained by this chronology, prohibited from really knowing the present by the heavy burden of their history. It becomes clear from the analysis that the leisure situations which 'the lads' are dependent upon to satisfy their 'will to happiness' are also inevitably nascent of their ontological insecurity.

Notes

1 Genosko (1994: 36) defines Baudrillard's code as a 'system of rules for the combination of stable sets of terms into messages'. Baudrillard himself would almost certainly describe this attempt to categorise the code as absurd. Indeed, if there are no more agents (subjects), only objects, how can there be any *system* of rules?
2 Pataphysics is the science of imaginary solutions.

Chapter 7

Felicitation

Still together after all these years: on being together apart

> We cannot help but missing the community, but the community we miss cannot stop being missing.
>
> (Zygmunt Bauman)

The impetus for the discussion in this chapter came about through a chance get-together with Scott and Rachel (Scott's 'new' bird) during the summer of 1997. My family had rented a caravan for a week at Rose Dale Holiday Park on the Yorkshire coast, and on our second day we bumped into Scott and Rachel, who were also holidaying there. What is written in this discussion draws on our mutual holiday experiences and some intimate conversations, particularly between Scott and myself during that week at Rose Dale. However, the discussion is also very much informed by my own interpretation of those events and how they fitted in with my research with 'the lads'. At the time of the holiday I was in the midst of writing up my Ph.D. thesis and was consciously living the double life of the sociologist and 'normal' person. And if what happened at Rose Dale clarified for me a great deal more about the significance of leisure for 'the lads', it also suggested much about working-class leisure experiences, more generally, in the time of 'liquid' modernity.

Building on the last chapter, the following discussion continues with the theme of exploring how leisure is used to play games with time and with reality. How time, that should be linear, becomes structured by another type of rationality, which is not only more reliable but also marvellous. This discussion also shows how these leisure experiences involve affective feeling rather than rational thought: the marvel of remembering what things used to be like and anticipating what things are going to be like through the blur of that nostalgia, where feeling is allowed to outmanoeuvre everything else. In this chapter it is suggested that the grotesque upside-down world of Bakhtin's (1984) carnival has found its way into everyday 'reality', a liquid modern age of purgatory borne of risk, uncertainty and ambivalence, and it is demonstrated that holidays, such as the ones described below, allow 'the lads' and people like them, who share a common culture, to break off from 'liquid' modernity, albeit temporarily, to restore some sense of a 'solid' modernity in their lives.

My arguments suggest that these holidays, in particular, reflect a sense of nostalgia for an order and a pattern which in this case take the form of a quite specific discourse that reflects a working-class modernity of social relations. In relation to 'the lads', we shall see that this discourse manifests itself as a working-class centre myth projected on to everyday reality. Drawing on my and our holiday experiences during that summer of 1997, I shall argue that leisure has increasingly become a means to participate in an orderly world where people can get time off from a prevailing discourse that recognises the right to be 'other' and that identities need not 'solidify'. I want to argue that the holiday in liquid modernity opens up the way for people to choose to reassert previously ascribed social positions, which they can wear as 'light cloaks' rather than 'iron cages' (Bauman, 2000a). As I suggested in Chapter 5, a 'liquid' modern life coupled with a 'solid' modern leisure life. A 'solid' life which has gone but is redeemable as a themed getaway from a 'liquid' existence, now, which has to be endured. In evincing this story, the analysis develops further some concepts associated with Victor Turner and Jean Baudrillard. But in the main the critique draws a parallel between Bauman's sociology of modernity and Derrida's philosophy of discourse and deconstruction. However, in doing so I call the reader's attention to the former's critical project, which gives its attention to 'real' social issues, rather than to the latter's focus on textuality, which gives pre-eminence to signs, signifieds and signifying practices.

To summarise, the analysis developed in this chapter provides the reader with the possibility of glimpsing a further dimension to the sense of togetherness associated with the leisure life-world of 'the lads' and the holiday world beyond it. As such what is written below makes full use of the rhetorical in order to evince the empirical in its continuing dissemination of a very particular story of leisure in liquid modernity. Such theoretical discussion is necessarily somewhat speculative, but it is always supported by concrete empirical evidence. So the author reiterates the request he made to the reader in the second chapter of the book: for the time being take my word and join me in assuming certain things are 'true' and then we can succeed in getting some good work done. Finally, I hope that the reader will countenance the small traces of repetition which this form of analysis produces. Analogous to Fullagar's (2002) work, the discussion begins with a travel narrative to provide the reader with a sense of the feeling of returning to what is 'the lads'' second 'home': Rose Dale. As the reader will see, this is a journey that always anticipates finding happiness through felicitation.

Together together and together apart, or, We do like to be beside the seaside, beside the sea

A warm summer day. The car devoured the road. We were driving towards Rose Dale holiday village, watching the landscape flow past: the same landscape that had flown the other way last summer and the summer before that. The same landscape that had flown the other way back in 1982 when 'the lads' first descended together on this north-east coast of England. A summer landscape that was familiar to us and which always seems to have an enduring and time-less Yorkshire look about it: red-brick cottages, red-tiled roofs, white painted cafés-cum-grocery shops, village pubs, honeys and jams, vegetables and potted plants at the roadside for sale, cows munching complacently in fields of lush green grass.

Small Rydale villages streamed by: Scampston, West Heslerton, East Heslerton, Staxton, Flixton, Folkton, Muston, Flixton. The nearer to Rose Dale we got an increasingly cheery outlook, which was much more than to do with the July sun, and it seemed to suffuse us. At Staxton the car radio selected the Yorkshire Coast station and an old tune sounded through the car, piercing and familiar. It was Gloria Gaynor singing 'I will survive'. In a surprisingly short time the motion-less shapes riding in the car became human and active, all shyness was put on hold and we sang along, ironically, matching Gloria word for word, verse for verse. As Gloria's dulcet tones faded we were even more cheerful and somewhat noisier than we had been four minutes earlier, not only because we felt the glow of satisfaction that comes from a song well sung, but also because we were beginning to recognise that we were now on holiday. By the time we reached the last village on the Ryedale itinerary we were almost in festival mode.

Soon we passed the last house of the village skirting Rose Dale, and over the bridge that runs above the boating lake, and we were within sight of the barricade of caravans enclosing the holiday village, when we saw the sea. It was grey-blue, the sky was another blue, the trees were green and the regimented rows of caravans were white. We crossed the threshold into this magic holiday world through the entrance, which as always at this time of year was straddled with a wall of white roses and creamy pink honeysuckle, looped back either side of the gates like a huge pair of stage curtains. Inside, rows of neat caravans stood just like the terraces back 'home', the different 'streets' of which ran together to form one row, this row that row, any row.

To anybody else this could have been any holiday village on the York-shire coast. Caravans. More caravans. Chalets. Reception. A photo-graph developing booth. A fish and chip shop. A souvenir shop.

A supermarket. An ice-cream kiosk. A newsagent. A pub. A boating lake. A bookmaker's shop. An open-top double-decker bus. And over there a precinct that leads to the 'penny' arcade and the clubhouse. The ubiquitous puffer-train. But to us Rose Dale is not like any other holiday village. Rose Dale is comfortable and comforting; whatever bad goes on in the world goes on outside Rose Dale. Here at Rose Dale we can feel that the furnishings of times gone are still with us – the kiss-me-quick mentality, the familiarity, the sense of belonging, the music; all consolidated by the nitty-gritty of our collective memories. It is a lovely place and it is our holiday place. Rose Dale is our Leeds-on-Sea. But, more than Leeds, it is unchanging. It is clean and orderly, there is no litter on the streets. You can always get a bus or a train. And there are always the same sorts of people here; it is just like 'home' used to be – before the Pakis and all those other underclass types arrived.

Holidaymakers come to Rose Dale, tourists all, in one way or another. But there are those simply coming to the seaside and there are those like us returning to their second 'home' as we know Rose Dale. For us each homecoming feels more like a pilgrimage than a tourist activity. There are others too who, like us, come at intervals, trickling down from the north and up from the south and flooding across from the west in cars and on coaches, their sole destination being 'home', each of them on the brink of exchanging the conformity of their everyday servitude for something else.

On this particular Saturday morning we witnessed the most likely people gathering together, but people at the same time who would otherwise never have acknowledged each other. Here they would be required to acknowledge each other, bound as they were by the rigid conventions of holiday fever. These were some friends, but mostly strangers sharing the same holiday, the same moments in time, the same sights, smells and sounds – the sea shining blue across the bay below the cliff and the windsurfers riding their boards like toys on the choppy water; the waft of honeycomb waffles and pink candy floss; the club 'turns', including Jimmy James and the Vagabonds, Edwin Starr, Black Lace and, for this week only, the 'Original' Drifters. Strangers, maybe, but not unfamiliar people. Season in, season out, there are always the same types of people here. People like us. These are a seemingly permanent and yet transient population of northern, and white, 'working-class' people. Families, boyfriends, girlfriends, grandparents, parents and children always replaced by other families, boyfriends, girlfriends, grandparents, parents and children. Not the same but none too different either.

They come from all over the north of England and there are obviously some key differences that separate them. There is a difference in the football teams they support, just as there is a difference in their manner of speech. Other than that, they all seem to wear their hair the same, dress the same and act the same. Moreover, they are readily prepared to share the comfort of a holiday world with unknown others, whose eyes seem to see what they see, whose leisure interests intersperse with theirs. It is as if they can see their own beliefs, virtues, even memories flickering across each other's eyes. Here at Rose Dale you can witness people who have, in their 'normal' lives, perfected the 'liquid' art of avoidance coming together as one. Even strangers look as if they recognise one another at Rose Dale.

An interlocutory injunction

The kind of happiness about what is Rose Dale is that kind of happiness Agnes Heller (1999) calls felicitation: those 'perfect' moments people are always going back to. Like the Tönnies (1955) type *Gemeinschaft* community, happiness by felicitation is for ever bound to a place: Rose Dale. What Raymond Williams once said of another aspect of community is also true of this kind of happiness. It always 'has been': we are never happy now, only then. Rose Dale happiness is out there, back then, fused with familiar smells, sights and sounds, and to retrieve it is to retrieve them also, to bring them swarming back into our lives: happiness by the way of felicitation.

Finding happiness by felicitation is inseparably bound up with liquid living. Indeed, it is anxiety and uncertainty that are the source of felicitation. What Rose Dale does is eliminate the anxiety and uncertainty of living in liquid modernity by making its guests the architects of their own leisure lives – for a short time, at any rate. The allure of this pursuit of happiness by felicitation, apart from the pleasure it brings, is that it is we who have the power to guarantee the sort of holiday we are going to have; no factors external to it are allowed to impinge on this holiday world. The beauty of happiness at Rose Dale is that it is just like our own leisure life-world, in that it allows you to be part of a 'community' that is central to your pleasures but one which you are not required to confine yourself to. Inherent to the idea of pursuing this kind of happiness is also knowing full well that the 'warmth' of Rose Dale happiness for ever refuses to be completely caught – it always remains partially unfulfilled until the next time; and the time after that.

Another thing that is peculiar about this pursuit of happiness is that Rose Dale has no fixed centre, no one reality, no situation where you can chance upon some sense of definiteness of a time or a place. Rose Dale is working-class, but other than that it does not ask its holidaymakers to believe in or act out any one particular imagination about their own culture; it systematically encourages them to imagine it according to generation. It is generation which locates people here. You see, Rose Dale caters for hearts that are nestled in similar but chronologically different pasts.

At Rose Dale an illusion of a 'solid' working-class culture survives on the edge of a fragmented liquid world: a hassle-free holiday package of old ways of being; reimagined selves underpin this centre-myth. On this type of holiday the self that was once compassionate and companionable, but who since became a person harnessed to work or to consumption, or to both, always doing this and that, paying for this or for that, the slave to some employer or to some debt, present but absent, emerges liberated. What is more, and different from life outside the holiday world of Rose Dale, you don't have to worry about being somebody you are not here. At Rose Dale memories are allowed to unfold, human once again. Happy times are allowed to recur; echoes of what went before. As I've said, Rose Dale is like our own leisure life-world, but in many ways it is better. For if Rose Dale is clean and tidy it is also free of hate and violence; it is about love and affection. Here summer days last long into the evening. Sunsets are brighter than anywhere else, and it only rains of a night just to give the mornings a fresh start. The beaches are clean and tidy and children can be seen happy with bucket and spade in hand. Dad can enjoy a pint and a bet and he also has time to romance Mum. It may sound like a fiction, but really Rose Dale is that sort of place.

A night out

The fourth evening. Already a feeling of rhythm and routine. They came in the clubhouse right on time, already in a customary order: Leeds, Newcastle, Middlesbrough, Northallerton, Leeds, Bradford, York, Leeds, Beverley, Leeds, Leeds, each going straight to the bar. Eight o'clock in the evening. Right on the dot. We stood in the queue for the bar and looked at the early 'early birds', who were already sat regimented on tables with four or six chairs in long rows. We queued patiently for at least fifteen minutes. It was annoying, but a fact of life at this time of night in the clubhouse. But two hours later the clubhouse was even more crowded. By now we were sat with Leeds and Bradford-on-Sea sat tightly packed in the corner, gazing out with our cheery faces at three can-can dancers on the stage. We had teamed up with Ross and Kelly from Bradford. A sound lad, that Ross. They were about our age, with a couple of kids.

After the can-can show the compere told some jokes. Then he asked for some volunteers to take part in an 'adult' game involving the removal of clothing. A queer thing happened. Bashful Scott, sprawled on a lounge chair, jumped up and headed toward the stage.

Twenty minutes later there he was, altogether forgetting why he was supposed to be standing there on the stage with nothing on but his boxer shorts and a 'kiss me quick' hat, flexing his biceps at the amused audience – what a laugh! The game came to an end the other participants slowly dispersed, while Scott emerged as the winner.

Later we talked about holidays gone by. Scott and myself talked about 'the lads', of 'the lads' and then of 'the lads'. And we moved on to our collective memories. Later, we said we loved each other. In the leisure life-world showing emotion is not acceptable – unless you are drunk, of course. And we were drunk by the time the evening was reaching its culmination when we said that we thought that Ross could be 'a lad', too – for tonight, at any rate. We also talked about our grandmas, granddads and nanas visiting on Sundays. It seemed that we'd all have our dinners at two o'clock sharp – whether we were hungry or not: roast beef, mushy peas, mashed potatoes, roasties, carrots, peas and Yorkshire puddings done in a large tin, all served up on a massive plate. How after dinner our mams would wash up and then we'd all go into the living room and watch the Sunday afternoon film: *Chitty Chitty Bang Bang*, *The Sound of Music*, *The Italian Job* at Christmas, John Wayne in some cowboy film, Humphrey Bogart, Clark Gable, Robert Mitchum or somebody like that. We talked about watching John Wayne films in particular. We talked about how John Wayne would ride through our living rooms every other Sunday and that he was our number one hero, because he always came through adversity. It also transpired that we all used to watch *Top of the Pops* on Thursday evenings and *The Sweeney*. We all said we loved the theme from *The Sweeney* and that we could still remember the tune today. *The Sweeney* was about fighting men, hard men, about 'good' versus 'evil', but it was also about something more intimate, about a sense of togetherness and belonging, something else which was like us. We all laughed when somebody said that every week, every Sunday afternoon the grown-ups would drop off to sleep and we'd be told to keep quiet or get out to play. Come five o'clock or thereabouts, though, our mams would be making the tea and we'd get ham sandwiches, jelly and trifle. We all agreed that that world seemed as if it would last for ever. And we all said we were confused as to why we had all let it go.

In this sense Rose Dale is very much like the working-class Hunslet which Hoggart (1957: 39) recalls:

> individual details which give this kind of domestic life a recognizable quality of its own . . . the Sunday smell of the *News of the World* – mingled with roast beef . . . the waste of Sunday afternoon, relieved

by occasional visits of relatives or to the cemetery . . . Like any life with a firm centre, it has a powerful hold: working-class people themselves are often sentimental about it.

(Hoggart, 1957: 39)

Just like Baudrillard's (1989) *America*, our Rose Dale is characterised by the absence of difference. And if, for Baudrillard, Disneyland is authentic America, Rose Dale is our authentic working-class northern England. Being the perfect simulacrum, it is an open door to the continuation of some kind of working-class culture. In his discussion of the East End of London version of this working-class culture acted out at Clacton-on-Sea, Hobbs (1988: 234) argues that holidays, such as the ones at Rose Dale:

> are crucial in the confirmation and reinforcement of a culture constantly besieged by bourgeois society and market trends . . . we [can] return to a golden age of ever-open doors, conversation, and street-life; of Chas and Dave and sing-songs, a place that is safe and predictable, basic yet compatible with the way we were before avocado bathroom suites, Lord Devlin, and containerization.

The point of these holidays is to re-enact a familiar past. At Rose Dale we can magic ourselves into a holiday world in which all we are required to do is reimagine ourselves and our own authentic working-class culture. Everybody else does the same. It is all so easy.

Back to the night out

The DJ started playing Jimmy Ruffin singing 'Farewell is a lonely sound when told to someone you love'. Now Jimmy Ruffin can sing a love song. Human shapes, as if fixed in time, began to move to make fresh patterns in the memory, some different, but for the most part familiar. Scott and Rachel got up to dance. We got up to dance. Everybody seemed to get up to dance. People inches apart, sharing a desire to consume the past. We were happy, at peace with ourselves, safe. The nostalgia expressed in Jimmy's voice impelled us to recreate the world of our past. And we were prevented from spinning out of this fantasy because both the music and the alcohol were incredibly good. You felt that we did not want it to end, this holiday away from ourselves, at our second 'home' together.

An academic interlocutory injunction

As was indicated in the preceding chapter, liminality, communitas and anti-structure are the three most frequently discussed concepts from Victor

Turner's anthropology. However, the concepts of social drama, ritual, symbolic interaction play an equally important role in Turner's work to show that he recognised that social life must always be understood as essentially processual. This aspect of his work shows that Turner's understanding of social life can help us to move his ideas beyond the limited scope of structural functionalism. Turner pre-empted Pierre Bourdieu in his use of Kurt Lewin's (1949) field theory to distinguish between cultural and social fields in his research. And in relation to cultural and social fields another key concept developed by Turner (1967) came from his observations of the ways Ndembu tribesmen and women understood the spirits that haunted them as supernatural rituals of affliction directed at them by deceased relatives whom they had neglected to remember. Turner described these spirits as *shades*.

The fundamental formula for 'the lads'' leisure, our leisure, both together and together apart, can also be understood through this metaphor. But whereas the Ndembu understood their *shades* as an affliction, we perceive ours as a form of happiness by felicitation, because they enable us to create a particular sense of community out of a multiplicity of leisure experiences. Turner's concept of the *shade*, understood as a Derridaean centre myth, enables us to explain these leisure experiences as significant cultural phenomena. It is because the *shade*, in its composition, manifests certain ready-made guidelines, reflecting a temporal but habitual form of cultural resistance, which ensures that through our leisure our lives can take on a meaning they would otherwise lack. In this sense, for us *shades* are an effect of time lost and a phenomenon of collective memory.

End of the evening

Full moonlight now drenched Rose Dale and searched it. So clear, so calm a night. It wasn't late, just after eleven-thirty. Nonetheless the to-and-fro of the cars, coaches and the ubiquitous 'puffer-train' had stopped. The immaculately cleaned main thoroughfare, like the yellow brick road, sent a mirror image up skyward. Below, the shops opposite the taxi rank reflected ethereal black in a transparent shadow. Walking back to our caravan through this temporary 'city' of a night, it looked as if the rows of lit-up caravans glowed incandescent like the old terraces of Hoggart's Hunslet, doubly unreal, detached from both time and place. Cosy 'homes' speaking of once-upon-a-time, another place, where you knew where you stood, certain.

One particular caravan stood out. It was surrounded with plant pots on the flagstones with too many flowers to mention. In front of the caravan stood a hollow pot swan with a plant attached, with long, slim leaves marked by fine yellow veins. If you sat on one of the green plastic chairs adjacent to the swan, you could see the plaque situated proudly above the door. The owners had baptised their caravan without hesitation: Home from Home. Stopping outside our own caravan, we stood and watched Rose Dale people flow by, returning to their own transitory 'homes', a stream of familiar folk – all like each other, all like us, strolling, chatting, touching – which renews itself every evening when the clubhouse empties, every week and every season. Friends, neighbours, families, somebody's grandparents, parents, aunts, uncles, children, mostly strangers, but all together in a particular sort of way. Each side by side, not at all ill at ease with one another, concerned only with the ordinariness of another wonderful holiday evening.

It seemed such a long time since the summer of 1982 when 'the lads' descended here for the first time. It seemed such a long time since those first days at the beginning of the week. It had felt as if it would go on and on. As the week had unfolded we seemed no longer in now time, just as we were no longer in the now world. During the last week Rose Dale had become, as if by magic, time apart from the confusion and ambivalence associated with the now; a different quality of time. The time when the DJ made us think of 1982; that summer had clung to us – Hazy Fantaazy funking to John Wayne is Big Leggy; George Michael and Andrew Ridgley flunking to Club Tropicana; Dexy's Midnight Runners singing 'Come on, Eileen' and 'the lads' going mental; the Jam belting out 'A Town Called Malice'. Recollections, not of ourselves now, but of other similar but unfettered selves re-emerging, prescient, from a summer past. A summer before the world was an uncertain and lonely place.

An interlocutory injunction

The world of the past had taken on a mythical quality. Fragments of a remembered time and place had entered our minds and we had come once again together. They might have been absent, but Stout, Sean, Benno, Colin, D-ranged, Fat Louis, even the Hogan brothers, they were with us in spirit: 'the lads': together apart. It was as if we had discovered, while we were at Rose Dale, that the sense of belonging that some of us had unthinkingly been deconstructing over the years had not, after all, outlived its usefulness. We had been reminded once again that, to keep something, you must take care of it. More, you must understand just what sort of care it requires. We could do that at Rose Dale. We had been doing it all week.

The wider significance of a working-class world lost is also reunited by the presence of people of a shared culture of sorts, which has its roots in all of us at Rose Dale. Our constant curiosity permits us to penetrate these other 'like' worlds, and by meeting 'like-thinking' people from different places in new surroundings – they're a sound pair, that Ross and Kelly. Moreover the presence of 'us who are all the same' kind of characters in more than one world does not constitute merely an abstract link between us: it unites our atmosphere, reminds us of who we are, and our essence. This happens because we share a particular sort of world vision, which has an imagination that surrounds what we are.

But we aren't daft. Deep down inside we know that we are not really one; we know that we are not really a community. Close inspection of this so-called community reveals that it is not a community at all, but a largely stitched-together affair that has no centre to it; it just swirls around in a pleasant-sounding eclectic, scratchy fashion, seemingly like a community. Yet no amount of charm and funky wriggling can compensate for such a fatal dearth of vision and discipline. We may have had the look of a community but we are, as Baudrillard might argue, a postmodern mutation, a revision, a hyperreal version of an old model comprising a neuter body of signs and signifying practices, whose concerns are not to make history, but merely to consume a history that has already been made. This is because we have a fondness for rewriting history to put our marginalised social positions at centre stage. We know that we are but part of a eusociality of holidaymakers, a flock whose god is the god of social fragmentation. We know also that we are but part of a bigger diaspora of white working-class people trying to reforge old meanings of togetherness through their leisure lives. And it is obviously clear that this diaspora does not have among it any real sense of community; the holiday bit hasn't anyway. For we are merely an assembly of *ersatz* intimations who aspire to a sense of a shared identity. The truth is that people here holiday together but holiday very much apart. We know that these are really only holiday encounters. Maybe so. But there is one thing for sure, our leisure life-world is real – we can vouch for that.

The eighth day

The previous evening's power over Rose Dale and the imagination had now declined. The siege of daylight had emerged; the search for 'home' was over for the time being; the yellow brick road still had a look of spotlessness but nothing more. Whatever had glittered there before was now invisible or had gone. Next to the coach stop, in the dreary Saturday morning light, the clubhouse looked nothing like it had the previous seven evenings. It seemed incongruous that last night's mirage had been capable of convincing us that we were one, a sort of community – but it had. Yet in the cold light of this Saturday morning it seemed likely that there would never be such an experience again.

Those who were leaving by coach stood at the coach stop. There was a group of Geordies there standing shoulder to shoulder in the queue, clasping their suitcases, bags and mementoes; their children carrying packets of sweets and bottles of pop they had bought for the journey. They, like the rest of us, had been reminded that they were still 'homeless' on this the last day of their leave. The next few hours would take them to the present. The feeling of homeliness by now was slowly evaporating. For the Geordie group, however, like glass, the illusion shattered as the Newcastle coach emerged from around the corner.

Pretty soon for us too the holiday experience of Rose Dale would end as abruptly as it began, and the return to everyday mundanity would be as disagreeable as the leaving of it had been intoxicating. This glimpse of another, better world would serve also to further de-value the experience of ordinary life. Just the same, to create the feeling of 'home' that we required in one way provided a triumphant culmination to our holiday. Yet in another way it was obvious that this could be no more than a persuasive parody. How could we try to evoke something in which not one of us believed? A 'home' in a nihilistic age is obviously something of a delusion.

In a liquid modern world satiated with difference new selves soon become, for the market, uneconomical and, for individuals themselves, boring. The accoutrements of recently acquired identities – the holidaymaker, the exciting lover, the trendy image – once the catalyst for a splendid metamorphosis, soon become instead prison warders whose mere presence is a constant reminder of our captivity. For this reason – which is one among many – us moderns are continually compelled to begin the process once again, stealing away into new selves, where once again we can experience the possibility of becoming all things. And so this process goes on. For Bauman (1990, 1992a), this process of contingent self-creation is racked with a sense of the ambivalence of existence, and he challenges us to confront the reasons for this ambivalence. This is because Bauman understands what the ambivalence associated with struggle for self and identity in modernity is really about. He realises that it is the struggle, not the end itself, that we really want, what we really get off on.

At Rose Dale we find ourselves engaged in the pursuit of a floating, but essentially diminishing, centre myth, a Baudrillardian lost object; and the holiday itself becomes a sort of temporary centring play, an artistic ruse involving a high degree of self-deception on the part of us, the participants. The well spring of this artistic process is a lack, or the absence, of a 'home', that is, a 'real' working-class culture. This lack, however, does not preclude the pursuit of some sort of fulfilment that can be endlessly perpetuated each time we visit Rose Dale, together or together apart, generating new meanings, or in the Derridaean meaning, an unending intertextuality.

The desire for a centre/presence – in this case a working-class solid modernity – is the motivating force for our leisure, but like Bauman's (1997) 'will to happiness', were it to find its conclusion, it would cease to generate itself, freezing the 'play of meaning' (Derrida, 1970). In Derrida's textual analysis, as in Bauman's ambivalent liquid modernity, liquid modern men and women are hopelessly caught up in the play of a game of *homesickness* where they are striving after something they will never find. And paradoxically it is they who are the ones who prevent themselves from fulfilling their own mission. This is because '[h]omesickness is not just about the absence of home, but – albeit unknowingly – about the impossibility of ever finding one; it is about keeping the hope alive by the expedient of infinite postponement' (Bauman, 1995: 48). Indeed, 'the possibility of the home-dream ever coming true is as horrifying as the possibility of its never becoming real' (Bauman, 1995: 97). This is a holiday

> short-cut to togetherness, and to a kind of togetherness which hardly ever occurs in 'real life': a togetherness of sheer likeness, of 'us who are all the same' kind; a togetherness which for this reason is unproblematic, calling for no effort and no vigilance, truly pre-ordained; a kind of togetherness which is not a task but 'the given', and *given* well before any effort to *make it be* has started.
>
> (Bauman, 2000a: 99–100)

Here at Rose Dale we are pleased, for the duration of the break, at any rate, to be caught in a Derridaean double bind created by our pursuit of a working-class centre myth which runs contrary to the discourse of liquid modernity. First, and betraying our individualistic 'liquid' principles, we place our irresistible desire for fulfilment on things and others outside ourselves. Secondly, we desire – albeit temporarily – an idea of the self in a 'home' that is both secure and solid and which has a structure that limits the amount of change, free play and possibility. If Bauman (2000a) is correct in bringing to our attention the fact that social class in liquid modernity is no longer made of the 'solid' die-cast stuff; he perhaps underestimates the extent to which melted liquids can temporarily be reset. This is what happens at Rose Dale for the duration of the holiday.

Rose Dale is just like our leisure life-world Mark II. Really it is our second 'home'. Here we can search for the stability that we perceive is missing from the wider experience of our everyday lives. Even though in the quotidian we usually, like other 'liquid' men and women, tend to fend off anything or anyone who offers stability to us. This is because stability implies constraint, and constraint is experienced as oppression in liquid modernity. We recognise that 'home' can be as confining and claustrophobic as it can be comforting, and that over-keenness can actually signal drowning. This is because we are guided by the wider discourse of individualism, and we are reflexive individuals who are guided by the will of ourselves rather than by the will of others (Bauman, 1997).

Yet in Derrida's (1970) schema the possibility of order will always remain for those who resist the disorderliness of 'difference' that holds sway in liquid modernity. In order to sustain this situation, what is required of us is the basic acceptance of an internal contradiction. In the chocolate box that is liquid modernity there are no longer any 'solid' centres, only 'liquid' centre myths: those that are created momentarily by the free play of difference. In liquid modernity everyone needs their own inventory of other places to make their actual, lived lives more tolerable. If in our everyday lives we cannot find our 'true' ipse-selves, at least together – and together apart at Rose Dale – we can embrace the bounded universe of a working-class possibility that leisure offers. Even so, the togetherness of the leisure sort is bound to be ephemeral. For, as in the case of many other commodities purchased on sale in liquid modernity, this sense of belonging is more often than not:

> less than fully honoured. Few fabrics stay in one piece for long after leaving the premises; few encounters survive the last-order call or the end of the holiday season. Meta-togetherness is first and foremost a land of endless experiments, of trials and errors – but errors that do not pre-empt further trials, and trials that do not aim at being foolproof.
> (Bauman, 1995: 49)

Meta-togetherness of the Rose Dale sort involves ephemeral experiments, which take on collective forms of *individuals* at play with difference. As Zygmunt Bauman might say, 'individually, together' these 'communities' also include those more enduring forms of togetherness which constitute 'low maintenance' communities, whose members come together only fleetingly in their leisure, for short periods of time. In relation to the emancipatory potential of these forms of community, this chapter has been, to say the least, cautionary. But I would like to suggest that, with the waning of 'solid' modernity it is possible to identify forms of togetherness with the re-enchantment of the social; a world where self-expression and contemporary sociality come together in manifest ways. Contrary to 'solid' modernity, 'liquid' modernity engenders the miraculous and the fantastical; it remystifies and deinstrumentalises life.

Yet this kind of belonging is both immutable and unashamedly malleable; it is both constituted by and constitutive of liquid modernity. This type of community does not reflect logical or rational senses of either time or space; it reflects a community without frontiers, it is outside history. Paradoxically, however, a fundamental aspect of this community is its dependence on historicity: history is a postulate to construct the imagined community. It allows its members to make selective readings of the past; in this sense it is both distorting and undermining and coherent and comprehensible at the same time.

The truth is that Rose Dale, like our own leisure life-world, is suspended in the backdrop of liquid modernity like a time capsule, with its verisimilitudes intact – its caravanning, its beach, its clubhouse, its kiss-me-quick partying, its music. It is also a place familiar and constant in other key ways – with its whiteness, its sense of working-classness, its sense of belonging, its familiarity – but somehow it is not fixed at any one moment in time. It is a holiday world out of linear time – its figures could belong to the bucket-and-spade way of holidaying of the 1950s as much as to one transformed by Billy Butlin in the 1960s, by foreign travel in the 1970s or by Margaret Thatcher in the 1980s. At Rose Dale we can occupy a time and a space that is evidently both real and a seamlessly floating hyperreality. It is a unity unified by its atmosphere. The experience of Rose Dale is an episode in and outside time, a cornucopia of felicitations, when life freeze-frames, when what happens goes on happening, down the summers, again and again, digitally remastered replays of lucid quality, the resonances of which are always the same yet also subtly different, hued with the insights of both the present and other new yesterdays.

It is commonly argued that the enduring feature of the magic of the carnival is its ability to uncover, undermine, even extinguish – albeit temporarily – the hegemony of any ideology which attempts to have a final say about the world. As Bakhtin (1984: 280) argues, carnival creates a world that 'lies beyond existing social forms'. But what role does carnival play in a world where dominant social forms such as social class no longer exist in their 'solid' modern guise? I want to argue that, paradoxically, in liquid modernity it is our everyday reality that is experienced as carnival. (See Bauman's, 2000a, discussion of the almost carnivalistic aestheticism, catastrophe, uncertainty, risk and ambivalence associated with work in our contemporary condition, for example.)

Here I have argued that the Rose Dale sort of holiday offers a means to participate in an orderly world where people can get time off from a prevailing discourse that recognises the right to be 'other', that identities need not 'solidify' and where communities wear 'light cloaks' rather than 'iron cages' (Bauman, 2000a). The narrative not only showed us how 'the lads' maintain a sense of togetherness even when they are apart, but it also gave us some valuable insights into the role of holiday experiences for constructing community as a postulate. Indeed, the discussion evinced not only how 'the lads' maintain their social network, but also how the rudiments of a working-class cultural identity, which seems to be losing its significance in liquid modernity, can be searched for and somehow restored during the holiday experience.

Letting 'the lads' have the last word

The pursuit of the illusory signified described above expresses the force of our desire (Derrida, 1970) or our seduction (Bauman, 1992a), our fetishism for a particular lost object (Baudrillard), a shade (Turner, 1973), which is the major motivational force driving us. But the key reason why we love our holiday here is that it delivers what we perceive veritably to be our 'reality'. A 'reality' somewhat remote from our everyday life experiences. Our leisure life is a sort of life we pretend we would like to live and the sort of people we would like to be – for a week or two, at the very most. The sort of leisure life that we pursue at Rose Dale is best understood as an offshoot of liquid modernity that is surprisingly not too confusing – for those in the know, at any rate. It is a bolthole maintained between a solid past and the immediate, liquid space beyond.

Conclusion

It has been observed in both this and the preceding chapter that the process of rational analysis sets a limit on our understanding of the significance and value of leisure in liquid modernity. My approach to interpretation accordingly extended beyond a purely rational approach to provide a synthesis which elucidated the sense of the non-rational, that is, the emotional and the magical involved during leisure experiences. This was achieved in Chapter 6 through an approach to analytical writing that evinced both 'the affective feel' of the leisure life-world and 'the cognitive "truth" of it' (Rinehart, 1998: 204), in an underlying continuum, a progression from the mundane to the spectacular. Both the mundane and the spectacular were seen to be at times inconsistent with rational thought, and it was shown that it is vitalism that best explains the leisure life-world of 'the lads'. For 'the lads', time and space will always fall into variations of these two basic narratives. The guiding thread running through the mundane and the spectacular is that, for 'the lads', the feeling of fragmentation underlying liquid modernity, which separates them from each other, is bridged during their leisure time and space. In the leisure life-world 'the lads' enjoy what they perceive to be a heightened sense of unity and belonging without having to commit themselves to a community in the orthodox sociological sense. Although these affiliations tend to be short-lived, the narratives inscribed during the mundane and the spectacular come to seem to be longer in memory, because of the significance that they hold for 'the lads'. This is because the leisure life-world gives 'the lads' their 'truth' about the world, and this is what motivates their efforts to achieve a sense of the spectacular: the 'ideal' leisure experience. Both historicity and the imaginary play crucial roles in this form of praxis, which is always fused by lyricism and aura.

In this chapter this way of writing also provided a feel for the affective sort of belonging associated with Rose Dale as a 'dream of belonging'; as Zygmunt Bauman might say, of having a 'home' rather than a place merely in one. It told a story about 'the lads'' and others' observations of history and how they are put into motion in the present. We saw that at their leisure these people experience something that is fantastical, magical and sublime; the 'ideal' manifestation of a narrative that underpins their 'dream of belonging'. The discussion showed how holidays play games with time and with reality and what the point of these holidays is: to re-enact a familiar past. To this end, the analysis showed how people can magic themselves into a holiday world in which they hope to re-imagine themselves.

As Bauman's sociology shows us, liquid modernity is best viewed processually rather than entelechically; it has no one fixed centre and it is constantly shifting and fragmenting. Like Giddens's (1990) juggernaut, Bauman's liquid modernity is incessantly mutable and like Derrida's text it always signals a process of perpetual postponement. This is because liquid modernity is:

> by definition forever on the run, always (and incurably) *noch nicht geworden*. What is modern about any project is precisely its being a step, or two, or a hundred steps ahead of reality; what is modern about modernity is its inbuilt capacity to self-transcend, to push the finishing line further on in the course of running, and so to bar itself from ever reaching it.
>
> (Bauman, 2000b: 229)

A holiday of the Rose Dale kind is one where people temporarily stop running and can choose to holiday alongside versions of themselves of the kind that in their everyday lives they have let pass them by. At Rose Dale what they perceive to be their 'real' world comes into focus on holiday, along with other truths concerning their inner lives and their joint visions of who and what they are, and would like to be.

We also saw that if it is confirmed by the material reality of Rose Dale the particular 'dream of belonging' that is my, our version of 'home' on holiday – like the leisure life-world – is also contingent upon its own 'solid' modernist discourse. Yet this should not surprise us. This version of 'home' on holiday could not be any other place than in the past: when the present makes us anxious and the future is uncertain, it is inevitable that we will look to the past to alleviate our anxieties, to find some certainties. In that sense, this holiday version of reality may be described as imagined, but it is not imaginary; it is not outside the 'real' world. For sure, the type of leisure experienced during the episodes described was always manifestly 'real' in a material sense. Yet, in addition to the competences for rational thought and reflexivity, 'the lads' and others possess various other faculties which have 'the opportunity to assume the throne of majesty' (Natoli, 1997: 46) in their lives, particularly in their leisure. Indeed, it is the faculties of the imagination, the imagined, of touch, of memory, of intuition and heightened awareness – brought on

by leisure experiences – which give them their sense of 'reality in itself and the truths that lie within'. Like the leisure life-world Mark II, Rose Dale offers a leisure life by felicitation always ten, fifteen, twenty years ago, but always now. But, more than that, and what is really special about Rose Dale, is that the leisure life it offers can be experienced both together and together apart.

Chapter 8

Emancipation

Fractured lives, certain leisure?

We picture Stout as a man of hardness, of extraordinary physical prowess, and we cannot see him in any other way. We still remember the night he finally arrived. It is an image of Stout that lingers in memory, that bang and smack, and the punch in the face. And it remains with us, as an inexplicable feeling of euphoria. To this day it is still talked about, its effects are still felt. We never tire of the story. And time and again we have played out this scene, as if quoting directly from the unpublished discourse of our leisure life-world, as if narrating our leisure experiences in 'real' life. Every stupid cunt that has ever dreamt of fuckin' with the Stout man has tasted some of what the Miggy flid got on that night out.

Although it is ostensibly about Stout, the above quotation by me confers a good interpretation of the leisure life-world of 'the lads'. It sums up completely what 'the lads' are about: modern, white, working-class, heterosexual, 'perfect' and superior 'manliness'. It also depicts very well what the 'world' looks like when 'the lads' turn outside themselves; at that moment they passionately and creatively encounter and experience the Other, when they produce absolute centredness. In their leisure, 'the lads' know they are 'perfect' and know how Others should respond to them: as if a cerebral modern centre myth were stimulated by their mere presence. 'The lads' believe that the discourse of the leisure life-world can and should delineate the whole complex 'reality' of men, women, subjects, objects and ideas which constitute the 'world' of their leisure experiences. In this sense, 'the lads' have their own 'resident ways of bringing to presence what is absent' (Natoli, 1997: 196). As I have said already, in the absence of a more certain world 'the lads' have created their very own 'solidly' modernist centre myth, which is a celebration of a 'solid' modern discourse born well before their time – a discourse born of modern values and which represents a fulfilment of Enlightenment suppositions.

'The lads' believe and practise the supremacy of passion over modern rationality, although they respect the truth of modern rationality, which informs them how to construct the Other. This rationality is based on the fixity of a myth involving both images and words, which allows them to attach 'solidly' modernist-inspired visions of the Other to people around them, like resplendent images more real than the actual bodies they obscure. In the fluidity of the quotidian of liquid modernity 'the lads' have to watch powerless as these characters self-righteously crowd around them, invading uninvited their physical and material realm: women controlling their bedrooms, women telling them what to do, women and black people taking their jobs, buying their houses, taking over their shops and their schools. But in the leisure life-world 'the lads' are in control. Here the features of the Other begin to elongate and liquefy, swell and then re-solidify, transformed into 'the lads'' own DIY custom-made creations: 'Pakis', 'flids', 'spastics', 'slags' and 'fanny' living 'solidly' modern lives, excluded from the leisure world that has created them. These characterisations of the Other become symbols of subjugation, power and knowledge, the luscious fruit of a 'solid' leisure life lived in a 'solid' version of truth. The 'universal' truth of the rationality which divides 'the lads' and Others into two categories: us and them, same and Other.

The way of reasoning just described provides a sense of the problems, contradictions, conflicts and quandaries I have had to encounter and resolve while 'doing' the research and writing this book. This study has not just been about a group of 'lads' in Weston, it has been about me and some of my lifelong friends, with whom I have shared so much. The study has been about their leisure life-world, my leisure life-world, our leisure life-world. I can still enter this magic world any time I feel disposed. But today I'm apprehensive of 'moving' with 'the lads', although I don't think of it as a fear. It feels more like a disinclination. My excitement at being with them has not diminished, but sometimes I feel childish or ashamed, because I feel it is wrong to be enthralled by something that can be so iniquitous. It also seems that what is happening now when I am with them is somehow contrived on my part. The very atmosphere of the leisure life-world seems too different, the behaviour of 'the lads' too inflexible, clawing into my visceral realm and leaving no space for my 'new' self.

In this sense, the book has also conveyed a fracture between my life now, within the academy, and my past life, without the academy. In so doing, it has revealed a sense of the extent of my distance from my past self. My 'old' self admires, if it does not accept, 'the lads'' efforts to shut out and change, with such a huge effort, the outside world. But my 'new' self sees that striving as wasted, pathetic and useless. Yet another part of this 'new' self dimly appreciates these exertions of 'the lads', who have nowhere else to go. Liquid modernity does not need 'the lads'' version of what constitutes proper working-class men.

I don't really believe in the fantasy any more. But I feel ambivalent towards it: I abhor some of it, but respect most of it. This ambivalence reveals a sense of my distance from the academy, too. For I also appreciate 'the lads'' culture, which is also part of my culture. And I appreciate what 'the lads' attempt to sustain in such uncertain times as these. This book has not really been overly critical of 'the lads', then, it has merely attempted to put some flesh on the complex forces that both shape and constrain the leisure lives of working-class men in the late 1990s.

With regard to academia, I hadn't thought it would be like my previous life. Yet there is that horrible sameness under its deceptive facade. And just as 'the lads' depreciate those in the world they create, academia, typically in the guise of masculinity or feminist theory, censures or ridicules them, and their like, in terms of their obdurateness. But just as 'the lads' know 'fuck-all' about the discourses played out in the universities, the reality is that academia in the main knows little about men like 'the lads'. At a face-to-face level most academics are like as not scared the shit of 'the lads' and their sort. They despise them for that, among other things. But in the world that really matters it is 'the lads' who will always be overwhelmed by how small and insignificant they are. The academic careerists know this and typically defile working-class men and use them as straw targets in their third-rate sociologies. They know that 'the lads' are incapable of fighting back on what is an unlevel playing field. That is what I call hypocritical. I should like to acknowledge 'the lads' in another sense, too. Making the historicity and theory of the leisure life-world, I have had to rely on their stories and have called upon the memories of witnesses as sharp, if not sharper, than my own. That said, I am responsible for everything written in this book.

It is beyond question that another researcher would have seen different things, seen the same things differently, or inquired into testimonies of a distinctly different kind with 'the lads'. This research could not be replicated. For a hermeneutic approach to sociological inquiry is a way of 'making' culture which is contingent upon personal frames of reference, recognising the performative aspects of 'doing' research. In the end, this book represents nothing more than my own fixed centre myth, established in my own inimitable way, which is unique to me. In this sense, the centre myth of the leisure life-world is my own personal narrative, my own form of discourse; that is, a 'true' fiction, which seeks to reveal verisimilitude, but which ultimately remains an imperfect story that is never completed. Like all good cultural studies, the book recognises that implicit in the arguments it has made are manifold limitations. These were discussed in Chapter 2 and it is unnecessary now, in concluding, to deliberate over them again in any detail. However, it should be asserted at this point that the book, in developing in its own particular way, has not always been entirely consistent. Nevertheless, this should come as no surprise, because the contingency of 'doing' social inquiry has continually refocused the orientation of the theoretical framework. The final written text reflects the ambivalences effected by this process.[1]

The thesis underpinning the book also, like any other, invites further elaboration, as many important themes have been neglected. For instance, although Chapter 4 discussed and elaborated on the issue of gender, it did not attempt to explore women's positions in the leisure life-world in any depth. In that chapter the concern was with masculine discourses, practices and institutions, focusing in particular on the concepts of *différance* and polysemic selfhood, and the thesis would have undoubtedly taken a very different tack had it explored these from the position of women. To an even greater extent, the book marginalised 'race' and ethnicity. Given that the thesis has been concerned with a 'solid' modernity of institutional leisure practices this neglect is perhaps not too surprising. For black people, as for women, in any modernity of lived experience, remain marginal and peripheral as the insignificant Other. However, I did use Derrida's idea of the 'trace' to develop an analysis of 'the lads'' leisure time–space activities in relation to black people, suggesting that the racialised black Other fulfils this role impeccably in the time–space of 'the lads'' leisure activities. Much more work needs to be done in this area, but the concept of the 'trace' could prove to be a valuable starting point for exploring the issue of institutionalised racism in leisure and beyond. Although this thesis has been concerned with the lived condition of working-class men in the late 1990s, it has not discussed the issue of social class specifically. This again is a criticism. However, the significance of the debate about social class in liquid modernity seems to be misconceived more generally in leisure studies, as many commentators tend to ignore, marginalise or try, wrongly in my view, to disengage from the class question (see, for example, Rojek, 1995).

These self-reflexive criticisms notwithstanding, what 'appears' in this book is a distillation of a tremendous amount of research time and research material. The initiatory ethnographic research process involved extensive observation, participant observation and unstructured interviews with a range of people, including men *and* women and black 'respondents' without the leisure life-world. This ethnographic work does not appear here in the form of empirical 'data'; however, it has contributed in no uncertain terms to what has been articulated in the book.

In engaging with extant theories the book has developed three themes of particular importance: myth, masculinity and modernity. These three main strands of the book were interwoven in a wider discussion of the postulated community of the leisure life-world of 'the lads'. It could be argued that, in formulating these advances, the thesis has ignored the historicity of the divisiveness inherent to the leisure life-world of 'the lads'. Yet this is not surprising, given that conflicts within the leisure life-world are soon disregarded by 'the lads'. This postulated community is concerned with unloading the burdens of liquid living, not creating internal strife. The book did, however, marginalise the role of the market meta-narrative in constituting the discourse of the leisure life-world. More attention to this area would undoubtedly have proved fruitful. Though the question of consumer culture could be the topic of a whole book in itself.

Summarising the research process: from methodology to hermeneutic cultural inquiry

It perhaps seemed incongruous to encounter in a sociological analysis such a clear disavowal of a 'methodological' approach to social inquiry. However, this book has shown very clearly that it is not necessary to accept the orthodox sociological hypothesis that, beyond our own individual subjective understandings of the social world, a superior methodological approach exists which enables us to solve the puzzle of 'doing' social inquiry. Culture is not given by reality and recorded detached by the empirically minded sociologist; it is created by the sociologist.

To enter into an approach to social inquiry that 'changed the conversation' (Rorty, 1986) was to take a risk and to live dangerously. But the gain was worth the risk involved. Drawing out and criticising explicitly the central tenets of the 'scientific' method of social inquiry was also a dangerous strategy. This was especially true, of course, given the establishment of a methodological conformity, which since the inception of sociology[2] has worked to conceal and prevent the self-evidential 'realities' of 'the voices from the far off' from inspiring the sociological imagination. As I argued in Chapter 2, today this state of affairs is for the most part still the case. For despite a newly emerging sociological heterodoxy, with an increasingly diffuse organisation, a hierarchy still persists. My own struggle to operate within the confines of the standard *modus operandi* of 'doing' social inquiry inevitably brought me into conflict with the worn-out 'methods' of sociology. My alternative was to resist having to resort to dubious and vague rules of a 'methodology' to arrive at the 'truth' about what I was doing and to refuse all participation with an orthodox sociological legacy that gives precedence to empirical work and systematic 'data' collection.

The persuasiveness of this book – originality is hardly an appropriate description for a thesis underpinned by poststructuralism and cultural theory – lies in its ability to elucidate the sense of realism, or 'cultural imaginary' (Castoriadis, 1987), identified with the leisure life-world of 'the lads'. Resulting in the type of cultural inquiry intimated but never fully developed in the works of Michel Foucault as genealogist. In this sense, the book complements the undoubted theoretical advances of poststructuralism and cultural theory offered to sociology with its emphasis on intuition and pragmatism and rhetorical strategies, rather than on rationalism and empiricism, empirical 'evidence' and empirical 'validation', triangulation and the writing up of 'fieldwork'. This book has demanded more enchantment at the expense of 'science' in sociology, having more in common with the writing of novels than most other sociologies. Contrasted with bland 'scientific' writing, which 'systematically' wastes its time validating *the* 'reality' encountered by the researcher, the rhetorical strategies utilised in this thesis have provided the reader with access to the very wellsprings of the leisure life-world itself, bringing the reader to what Stout likes to call 't' crack wit' lads'.

This book has insisted also that sociology should always relate to what Michel Maffesoli calls the actual and the quotidian – people and everyday life – rather than to asocial theorising and the depthless promulgations of ambitious academic careerists, who always appear to be, like Premiership coaches, searching for that unknown with all the answers, or ready to buy into the 'next big thing' – which is invariably the prevailing French superstar.

Finally, there may be a massive gulf between the culture of the academy and the culture of the leisure life-world of 'the lads' but, for myself, the significant point of this book is that for each it has brought a sense of presence to what is radically absent in the other. The presence of a third culture, in which the voices of the academy and the voices of 'the lads' can sit equally side by side, if not with commensurate ease. This thesis attests that, yes, Foucault, Bauman *et al.* are remarkable theoreticians. It attests also that Sean, Stout *et al.* can individually move a performance of equal merit under their own terms of reference. Just so.

Summarising the theoretical framework: from systematic rational analyses to cultural theories, poststructuralism and beyond

The arguments I have advanced in this book grew and evolved over a period of roughly five years, emerging initially from systematic rational analyses of modernity (e.g. Weber and Simmel), late modernity (e.g. Giddens) and post-modernity (e.g. Maffesoli), changing substantially in the last couple of years as my familiarity with the work of the 'poststructuralists' (e.g. Derrida) and cultural theorists more generally, and the poststructuralist-inspired neo-pragmatic philosophy of Richard Rorty, deepened. Most of the ideas formulated in the book were, however, shaped through a dialogue between Foucault and Bauman. From this conversation I learned that the latter understands precisely the former's *Critical History of Thought*, with which the intellectual is challenged to think beyond the conceptual schemas which have become normative of orthodox sociological theorising. Bauman makes a leap of radical sociological importance in recognising that many of the concepts, themes and practices associated with orthodox sociology do not work as well as they once did, and his sociology confirms what we have encountered in this book time and again: that his idea of liquid modernity enables us to see the social world in ways which remain unopened to most orthodox sociological approaches. Bauman teaches us, too, that the challenges of sociology today are subtle ones. He grasps the sociological imagination and adapts it to serve as an alternative way of understanding the social world and he offers us a way to reinterpret and assimilate the most useful of orthodox sociological postulations with 'new' theoretical insights to make sense of contemporary times. Linked together under Bauman's heading of 'liquid' modernity, these aspects of contemporary social life emerged in this book as an intimately interrelated means of interpreting the leisure life-world of 'the lads'.

Bauman also establishes hermeneutics as the central concern of sociology and reconstructs social theory as an affirmation of Rorty's 'never ending conversation' which seeks to secure social theorising as infinite interpretation. This is why Bauman (1992a: 114–48) can bracket together theorists as diverse as Hans Gadamer and Richard Rorty as interpreters. Because each of these theorists grasps what is required of an adequate mode of intellectual inquiry for liquid modern times. The fact that Gadamer organises his hermeneutical intellectual work in a *deep* sense, while Rorty, in company with Foucault, subordinates *deep* hermeneutics to *surface* hermeneutics, is neither here nor there. For Bauman both positions are commensurable in the sense that each inhabits a kind of post-scientific cultural world that has established superiority over its legislative modern rival. I should like to suggest that this book, which has made this paradigmatic leap, could be considered in a similar vein.

Yet if my own sociology is clearly shaped by this post-scientific hermeneutics it emerged in this book in a way that was always dedicated to empirical research. Consequently the theory developed in this book, integrated with the cultural study of the leisure life-world, synthesised a distinctive, if not always coherent, theoretical framework which established the opposition between the leisure life-world of 'the lads' and its 'solidly' modernist, ludic culture, on the one hand, and the wider 'liquid' world of change and history on the other; the synchronic versus the diachronic. In synthesising in this way, the book established a locally inspired theoretical framework, or a 'new' discourse, for theorising about the leisure life-world of a group of men that I have called 'the lads'. A number of interrelated themes were central to this theoretical framework which explored a 'modernity' of leisure experience. In this conclusion, I shall elaborate on this theoretical framework to combine and further elucidate these themes. However, it is most important, first of all, to put into context briefly the metaphysical assumptions underlying the central arguments evinced in the book.

As I have said already, as the thesis advanced it was constantly being complemented and augmented by subsequent analyses, many of which emphasised the 'solid' and 'liquid' modern distinction. I argued that this juxtaposing was central to theorising about modernity, because it is difficult to conceive a clear sense of the 'liquid' modern 'disorder of things' without a concomitant understanding of the 'solid' modern 'order of things'. The work of Rojek (1995) is relevant in this context, not since he focuses on this dichotomy, but because it is the relevance of the epistemology of decentredness for leisure that Rojek is interested in. As Rojek shows, modern epistemological thinking no longer holds good – if it ever did – and there is much import in thinking about leisure in ways that decentre the 'neatness' of modern theories, which tend to allude to centred, foundationalist and essentialist interpretations of the social world. Whereas actions and meanings tend to be 'centred' and taken for granted in modern accounts, a 'liquid' hermeneutic approach offers an interpretation that recognises their fragmentary grounds.

However, Rojek, in common with Scott Lash (1994: 215), mistakenly, in my view, thinks that rational analysis – drawing selectively on concepts derived from poststructuralism – can do a better job in understanding our contemporary social condition than can poststructuralism. Analogous to Lash, Rojek wants his poststructuralist cake and he wants to eat it. But what both Rojek and Lash fail to recognise is that, if you remove the 'centre' from social analysis, universal and absolute rules of judgement no longer hold good and no one interpretation can be trusted to dependably represent, understand or interpret the social world. From the point when we begin to think in terms of 'decentring' the social world, then, as Derrida (1978: 411) remarks, 'everything becomes discourse'.

For Derrida, as for Wittgenstein (1968) and Lyotard (1979), the world is no-thing beyond our language and it reveals itself through 'language games' which 'are embedded within the broader cultural conventions or forms of life. It is not the world as it is that necessitates our callings but the relationships in which we participate' (Gergen, 1991). Gergen is alluding to a Foucauldian perspective, which recognises that cultural conventions, verily all forms of praxis, must be recognised, understood and described, not in terms that 'centre' on individual choices and actions, but in terms which give primary importance to discursive practices and institutional achievements. That is, attention should focus on 'what we know and what we say, what we do and how we do it and what institutions we establish to carry out what we know and do what we have to do' (Natoli, 1997: 6). This is because individual choices and actions are always inscribed into and shaped by discourse. In 'liquid' modernity, we might believe in the sanctity of the individual, but as Harland (1987: 9) suggests, according to poststructuralist thinking, 'the individual self is only a relatively recent *cultural construct* added on to human reality by the seventeenth-century rise of the bourgeois ethic of individualism'. From a poststructuralist perspective, the individual is ineluctably subsequent to discourse. Yet in precluding a Foucauldian anti-realism that sees the world only through the lenses of textuality the research approach developed in this book showed that the discursive is best read as a 'social' affair, always implicating 'the lads' at once as speaking and acting 'subjects', texturing the genealogy of the leisure life-world as an adventure in discourse and action.

My own ontological perspective was also conceived in explicit opposition to interpretations that would imagine the 'reality' of the leisure life-world merely in terms of a liminal experience. In a brief and rather conservative discussion of liminality in relation to leisure spaces, leisure practices, configurations of association and identity formation, Rojek suggests that liminal conventions and practices are ultimately so appealing because individuals recognise in them the promise of freedom and the opportunity to 'be oneself'. Liminoids and liminal identities offer this 'because they appear to be 'free spaces' beyond the control of civilized order' (Rojek, 1995: 88). For Rojek, however, these thresholds of spontaneity and manumission cannot at any time be of any real facility, because:

> as Shields points out, liminal zones can never be areas of either genuine freedom or genuine control. In them . . . 'rather than complete suspension of morality one finds the lifting of the curtain of morals followed by embarrassed or guilty returns to moral codes' (1992: 8). And so the attempt to escape perishes because it depends upon the very conventions that make everyday life possible. By searching for the total sexual encounter, the orgy of freedom and self-expression, the unbridled carnivalesque and the other 'real' experiences which lie beyond civil society, we collide with the antinomies of our desire.
>
> (Rojek, 1995: 88)

Rojek's analysis is alive to the dominant discourse of individualism and the individualisation processes inherent in liquid modernity, thus recognising Beck's (1998:49) quintessential point that, although the liquid imagination relies on the principle of self-determination and a 'duty to oneself', it understands that this orientation towards self-liberation as process does not preclude the fact that today men and women are always actively engaged in the search for new forms of solidarity and ways of belonging and togetherness (Maffesoli, 1996).

However, he misses the point that leisure experiences can be made sense of only from the narrative, story or sense of realism which produces them. Contrary to what Rojek's discussion presumes, in liquid modernity there is no master narrative that provides the 'universal' truth about what constitutes either genuine freedom or genuine control. And in the reality frame, or 'world as it is seen' by 'the lads', it is liquid change that is perceived as not 'real'; and, contrary to conventional wisdom, their leisure time and leisure space provide them with the means by which they can challenge and undermine the 'irrationalities' of their present condition. 'The lads' today live in a changing landscape. They feel that they grew up in a different world from the one in which they currently live. If liquid modernity in which 'the lads' live represents a refusal of fixity, then the leisure life-world Mark II impersonates a solid modernity revamped in the form of a reflexive masculinist working-class centre myth. For above else it is certainty that their collective past contains. The leisure life-world allows 'the lads' to become self-indulgent, so rich and particular as to submerge and liquefy the categories which normally govern their everyday reality. Contrary to the so-called 'real' world, in their leisure time–space, life appears to them to be still of a more certain and 'solid' modern world, which they perceive *is* their 'really existing reality'.

As Bauman shows us, liquid modern living is fundamentally incoherent and is experienced as episodic:

> The overall result is a *fragmentation* of time into *episodes*, each one cut from its past and its future, each one self-enclosed and self-contained. Time is no longer a river but a collection of ponds and pools.
>
> (Bauman, 1995: 91)

Contrary to 'solid' modernity, 'liquid' modernity engenders the miraculous and the fantastical; it remystifies and de-instrumentalises life. This means that anybody has the *potential* to be anything they 'choose' to be. Indeed, reflexive modernisation (Beck, 1994) presents the actor with a variety of emancipatory choices, both new and old, which have infinite ontological possibilities. What this means is that, in liquid modernity, social actors can be embedded in multiple 'realities'.

After Baudrillard, how we understand and theorise 'reality' can never be the same. Yet this should not mask the important point that, as with Rojek's discussion of liminality, Baudrillard himself makes no move to develop his own thinking in this direction. Compounding the difficulty of relating the 'real' to the hyperreal is Baudrillard's refusal to acknowledge that 'reality' can any longer be perceived. This book has throughout attempted to address this weakness in Baudrillard's work.

Baudrillard (1983) never develops the theory of hyperreality articulated in the book *Simulations*. And this line of thought remains an eccentricity, because of Baudrillard's dogmatic faith in Nietzschean nihilism being the ultimate consequence of rationality. And once Baudrillard banishes rationality from the 'business of life' there can no longer be any single objective reality, or any observation that is not merely postulation; what we have is nothing more than 'the play of signifiers . . . in which the code no longer refers back to any subjective or objective "reality", but to its own logic' (Baudrillard, 1975: 127).

This expiring of the social and 'reality' from Baudrillard's schema weakens his theory of hyperreality almost to the point of disappearance. For Baudrillard (1983: 11), even if it is admitted that the hyperreal enters the realm of human existence, in terms of actual human experience this accomplishment is of little importance, because: the hyperreal is the reflection of a basic reality; the hyperreal masks and perverts a basic reality; the hyperreal masks the absence of a basic reality; and last, but not least, the hyperreal bears no relation to any reality whatever: it is its own pure simulacrum. The only conclusion to be drawn from Baudrillard's concept is that, whatever the material conditions in which it emerges or arises, simulation has replaced reality and reality can no longer be realised, not even as an adjunct or a contingent side effect of the hyperreal.

This book has shown that my use of the hyperreality chooses to ground the important aspects of this concept in an analysis of the concrete and reflexively motivated sociality associated with the leisure life-world. The thesis assigns to leisure a crucial role in this process, showing that the hyperreality of the leisure life-world is 'real' in both its experiences and its consequences; it is not pantomime for 'the lads' with a night off from 'reality' to relive the excesses of the 1970s and 1980s. When this 'solidly' modern leisure experience is current it is experienced as very real and pleasurable for 'the lads'. For those who do not fit the 'solid' modern mould, particularly women, black people and non-heterosexuals, this leisure experience is encountered as equally real, but anything but pleasurable. When this leisure experience has passed the refinement and extension of this discourse remain subsequently as an enduring addition. It must, for it is essential to 'the lads'' sense of ontological security (Giddens, 1991). Moreover, successive leisure experiences of this kind serve to consolidate the intensity of the 'solid' modernity of the leisure of the life-world.

Finally, this book has also confirmed Rojek's (1995) point that, in liquid modernity, if nostalgia lies at the heart of everyday life it often lies at the very heart of people's leisure experiences. The conceptual framework of the leisure life-world as an exemplar of what Moore (1996) describes as 'restoring paradise' provides a more general theory of socio-cultural processes that permeate liquid modernity. As both Zygmunt Bauman and Dean MacCannell argue, homelessness is today with all men and women. The synergism of the leisure life-world is perceived as just right, because it is a special nostalgic place that 'restores paradise' (home) by combining Eden (Moore, 1996) and adolescence: it re-enchants their leisure lives and allows 'the lads' to be 'lads'.

The ambivalence and contingency of the leisure life-world

The central problem of postmodernity [liquid modernity] will be to create ersatz 'communities' to manufacture . . . a 'sense' of community . . . The complexity of this feat of social engineering – that is, the construction of a believable symbol of community where no community exists – should not be underestimated, nor should the drive to accomplish this feat be underestimated.

(Dean MacCannell, 1992: 138)

The gap between what, on the one hand, Dean MacCannell is saying about the spurious meaning of community in liquid modernity and what, on the other hand, I have articulated in this book about the leisure life-world being a form of collective interpretive practice, which is reflexively inspired and self-constituted, appears, on the face of it, altogether chasmic. However, I should like to argue that this purported gap covers a thoroughly ambivalent territory, meaning that community in liquid modernity is paradoxically *both* spurious and depthless *and* substantial and deep. The analysis also placed a premium on the contextuality and contingency of the local and historically specific social practices. As we have seen with the leisure life-world of 'the lads', their community is characterised by contingency rather than by fixity.

We have seen too that the leisure life-world both constrains and determines the ways 'the lads' act, the way they talk, the beer they drink, and so forth, leaning unrelentingly in the direction of a 'solid' modernity of leisure experience. Nevertheless this seemingly rigid and simplistic social structure they adhere to has no deeper means located beneath the surface. The leisure life-world has no code to crack, it is uncomplicatedly 'solidly' modern. 'Outside' the leisure life-world 'the lads'' behaviours are markedly different. These ambivalences are illustrative of the relativism inherent to all liquid social relations.

Yet, if this postulated community is, in once sense, insubstantial, it is also, and paradoxically, tremendously meaningful. Indeed, the warmth and pleasure caught inside the protective cocoon of this world has a real formidability. Unlike in their work and other encumbrances, 'the lads' do not feel either seclusion or exposure when they leisure together. They feel as though they occupy a protective cocoon where they are 'naturally' safeguarded, and out of which they can gaze at Others with both unqualified impunity and total disdain. 'The lads' talk of the leisure life-world as though it is symbolic of all human activity, as though they are enacting an intermittent drama of all that's right against all that's wrong, of good against bad, of the fantastic achievements that make 'the lads' the sure vanquishers in an imaginary and uneven game of contingency.

If it is understood that a normative 'solid' modernity of experience is fundamental to 'the lads'' knowing of the social world, it should be appreciated also that the leisure life-world does not rest on a fixed, modern discourse. It depends on a *version* of a 'solid' modern centre myth through which the world of 'the lads' is made and experienced and which reveals the ironic signalling of the difference of the narrative of the leisure life-world at the very heart of its similarity to the modern meta-narrative (Hutcheon, in Natoli, 1997: 106). Discourses never stand still. The discourse of the leisure life-world 'progresses', in the 'solid' modern sense, to instigate discursive change in the world of 'the lads'. These are changes informed by 'the lads' love of the history of the leisure life-world, but also informed by the inter-textuality of additional discourses from their wider social milieu. This inter-penetration of additional discourses within an ostensibly closed leisure life-world not only challenges and defers truth of any kind but provides the trace of the Other in which 'the lads' 'play with difference' to construct 'coherent and meaningful . . . circumstantially compelling life courses' (Gubrium and Holstein, 1994: 697).

We have seen also that, most particularly in its consummate form as the spectacular, the leisure life-world is both irreconcilable and reconcilable with rational thought at the same time. This ambivalence lies in the hybridity of the seemingly inarticulate and puissant discourse connecting 'the lads' magically and passionately with their leisure life-world, which is also, and paradoxically, a thoroughly modern discourse. In the words of Zygmunt Bauman, this 'solid'/'liquid' modern hybridisation represents the 'irreparable and irredeemable ambivalence' of the leisure life-world. In their leisure 'the lads' sense they have a 'choice' between the hyperreal leisure life-world, which they perceive to be 'normal', and a more egalitarian liquid modern world of leisure; with 'solidly' modern confidence they 'choose' the hyperreal. Quite simply 'the lads' just want the contemporary world to fuck off. In marked contrast to their everyday lives, the leisure life-world is rational, pure and logical, in the 'solidly' modern sense, sealed off and growing ever more remote, the world as it is outside this protective cocoon gazing at them antagonistically as they drift further away from normalcy.

'The lads' are perpetually concerned with the search for a 'solidly' modern absolute judiciously interwoven into their experience of the leisure life-world. As we saw in Chapter 3, they love the Stout fantasy. For it was when that Stout demolished the flid that a miracle occurred, making a reality perma-nently etched in the collective memory of 'the lads'. A picture that has become static and frozen in time, which makes them feel something for absent friends, a surreal connection more intimate than any 'new' friendship can offer. It makes them and their leisure lives feel vindicated and worth-while. Such fantasies bring a presence to what is absent. Today they clutch such fantasies with an ever growing sense of purpose. This is why the 'death' of 'a lad' called Tony Blackshaw is today a loss less relevant than the 'birth' of 'a lad' called Stout in 1978.

This story of the leisure life-world captured perfectly a local version of a working-class masculinity in transition. The leisure life-world is based upon a distinct period of 'the lads'' history, and is also from a distinct period of working-class history – though its edicts appear illusory and arti-ficial. 'The lads' seem as if they have retreated into a parody of a distinctly modern working-class community of leisure. They haven't. 'The lads' have simply frozen a 1970s moment rather ingeniously. So ingeniously in fact that the leisure life-world is experienced as as 'solidly modern' as that which preceded it, representing 'the lads'' escape route to 'solid' modernity. The leisure life-world always involves a journey into the past: ontologically and ideologically 'the lads' are still leisuring in the late 1970s and early 1980s.

Yet the passage from the leisure life-world Mark I to its current discursive formation was hardly a total break: the change that took place some time in the late 1980s may have eclipsed what went before but it did not supersede it. If the leisure life-world Mark II was to remain relevant in a wider world which had turned into a consumer culture it had to resemble its predecessor. What occurred was merely the reflexive transformation of the leisure life-world as 'the lads', fearing they were about to lose something really precious, began to preserve something they knew was really theirs. Post-1980s 'the lads' chose the path of contemplation.

On the face of it the leisure life-world today seems to be nothing more than a paean to a worn-out hegemony, to a masculinist idyll of a ritualised dream symbol, lifted straight from the pages of 'the lads'' very own discourse. But beneath the froth resonates something altogether more significant, centring on the ways in which this dream symbol is made real at the weekend when they are together. 'The lads' may never have heard of Soren Kierkegaard, but like him they claim that life – meaning their leisure life – can be recollected only by looking to the past. Be that as it may, if they feel nostalgia for a particular kind of past, this never lapses into elegiac melancholy. Indeed, in the leisure life-world 'the lads' constantly relive episodes from their collective past rather than inertly recollecting them, because in this process what they are nostalgic for is recollected forwards, not backwards, and it remains alive rather than dead. The leisure life-world Mark II always has a familiar 1970s feel. To that extent, it is not a rebirth but a continuity of, if sometimes exposed, set of superannuated talents. 'The lads' may be figures carved in the past, but their identities are maintained in the present.

However, the pursuit of ultimate happiness is an idea 'the lads' have essentially given up on. They know it exists, that it can be found, but they feel they have been made to sacrifice it at the hand of other commitments and responsibilities. They've been made to trade happiness for something else, the diligent stage reproduction of another time and another place, but with the same actors, which instead gives them the feeling of happiness through felicitation. At 'home' in the leisure life-world, 'the lads' have their own centre myth and are able to relativise it: that 'original' and all-absorbing sense of belonging associated with this 'community' may have been lost, but 'the lads' today perceive that they have the best of both worlds, because they have found the key that enables them to restore paradise in their leisure lives. It is only because of the impossibility of the leisure life-world that the leisure life-world Mark II is possible at all. In the leisure life-world Mark II the hyper-real subverts and displaces the real. It could be argued, however, that, even if 'the lads' are deadly serious about this project of institutional reflexivity, they themselves serve only to subvert the seriousness of this collective mission with their own absurd inappropriateness and self-parody. But as this book has shown very clearly, if the discourse of the leisure life-world does represent an image of a 'solidly' modern masculinity that is absurd and out of step with the present 'norm', it also personifies a reflexive liquid modernism.

Concluding remarks: the leisure life-world of 'the lads' – a shield against ambivalence and contingency

There is no tidy novelistic completeness to the story of the leisure life-world of 'the lads'. But if I were to summarise the book I would say it has been about a group of 'solid' modern resisters in a war against a changing liquid modern world, who in creating an imaginary leisure life-world around them can abandon, for a short time at least, a world inhospitable to 'lads'. In that sense, this leisure life-world can be understood as a quest for truth – as well as a string of drunken binges. Spitting in the face of 'progress' and harking back to an unproblematic past, 'the lads' have concluded that there must be some form of closure in their leisure lives. Our course of access to this cultural imaginary was by the way of rhetorical strategies, elucidating the mythology of the leisure life-world. A mythology which itself is based on images and memories rather than words, because 'the lads' do not explicate themselves in that way.

Whenever I think of the leisure life-world, I think of this mythology and its all-pervading sense of mutuality and belonging. I say that is how it is, but I am sure that is probably just the way it seems. For each memory of the leisure life-world constitutes a hefty, rose-tinted blur that tinges every thought undertaken to explain it. Every image and memory of the lives and times of 'the lads' may have been remade in this book, but each is very 'real'. Moreover, each is discursively interconnected. And every fantasy and emotion belonging to those images and memories is clearly understood by 'the lads', becoming more and more meaningful as time goes on, because these get moulded closer to their 'solidly' modern ideal. There are, of course, horrible fantasies associated with the leisure life-world, but they are not really fantasies at all, because these 'the lads' choose to forget.

Both the normalcy and the passion and fervour that constitute the discourse of the leisure life-world are communicated through institutions and practices for which there is no definitive grammatical structure, but which still reflect a 'solidly' modern form. As we saw, this discourse is punctuated with a succession of practices which are articulated with regular consistency. We saw also that this most rigid pattern is imposed by a 'solid' modern discourse. A pattern of leisure made of a modernity of experience, a modern centre myth that brings 'the lads' ludic delight, which they protect by putting all possible space between themselves and other people. We saw how the 'presence' of this leisure life-world keeps them protected from the outside world. We saw also how they can always replay this ritual with great alacrity, because they have repeated it so accurately and consistently for so long.

We also observed how the boundaries of their inner world do not expand out, but in, so that there is a massive ludic gap between the gruff exteriority of the leisure life-world distending inward until it gets to the 'solid' modern centre myth that it safeguards. In this sense, for 'the lads', the leisure life-world must always triumph: you either join it and leisure by its ways or you succumb to the hauntings of the liquid present. 'The lads' are haunted by their present predicament. They understand that in a life fragmented and uncentred they must get back to their own centre and get back to 'real' life and 'real' leisure. The quotidian of liquid modernity is not their 'real' life; the leisure life-world is. The story of the leisure life-world of 'the lads' is a story of a not too distant past which still stubbornly resonates today. When 'the lads' leisure together it is like watching a film unfold which you know the end of.

But in their leisure 'the lads' experience only intimations of a return to a deeper, more certain world that has in reality disappeared: modernity 'has come to be known to us mainly through its disappearance. What we think the past had is what we know we do not have' (Bauman, 1997: 87). This observation alerts us to the anxieties 'the lads' feel about the hauntings of their present condition, and which are rooted in their anxieties about themselves. The present is insecure and the past exists only as their mutual nostalgia; the future is a dull threat, untrustworthy and uncertain. The causes of these anxieties are manifold and relate to the profound social, cultural, economic and political changes which have foreordained that today white working-class men are merely equal members in an uncertain world where it is no longer enough to be a 'man's man'.

'The lads' understand this and are resigned to their fate; they know that the weekend experience of the mundane and the spectacular is just a leisure break. These days on their nights out together 'the lads' essentially end up chronicling a very particular but essentially vanishing masculinist culture. The leisure life-world is a world that is there only in fragments now. There 'the lads'' own private universe remains complete and infinitely appropriate, even if in 'real life' it has all but been obliterated. None the less, they still rehearse their parts, biding their time, until 'real' life resumes as normal on a Friday or Saturday night. The evenings out are times when 'the lads' can be together, when once more they can go back 'home' to the postulated community of the leisure life-world. Being part of the leisure life-world, it seems to be without a history, in a vacuum. This leisure life is something special and symbolic; it happens in a warm and cosy place where only 'the lads' can feel at 'home'. They also know that here the quotidian of the mundane and the spectacular is always a potential and beguiling possibility. The leisure life-world never loses its potency because with it there is never any form of culmination or ending and it is *the* pivotal point in a fragmented life, which allows them to fashion a sense of order out of the disorder of the everyday. Meanwhile each of 'the lads' is merely enduring his necessary, though unfortunate, pretender's role as a present-day pariah.

These days 'the lads' live to leisure. If the leisure life-world Mark II is characterised by intimations of its previous incarnation, the performativity this shield against ambivalence and contingency vitalises seems, on one level at least, an act of defiance, of resistance to a liquid present; an assertion, not of 'the lads'' relevance to anything as such, but of their undiminished stamina in the face of encroaching middle age. 'The lads' are trapped in a cycle of performance and display and the leisure life-world is full of images, language and gestures which used to serve as a construct of a notion of a particular kind of working-class masculinity. 'The lads' do not question these; they have no ambivalence to them as such, and the leisure life-world can be read as a celebration of that way of life. Much like their fathers before them, they see themselves simply as working-class men. Their fathers, though, lived in solid modernity, they merely leisure in the time of liquid modernity.

In one sense the postulated community might be an existential experience only in the sense that it is no more than a temporal image; as Baudrillard might say, a simulacrum of the 'real' thing. We observed this throughout the book, from the initial introduction to 'the lads' in Chapter 1 to the explication of the mundane and the spectacular in Chapter 6. We saw how this 'solidly' modern discourse imposes strict limitations on the leisure practices of 'the lads' and others', too. This being because the leisure life-world demands a vision that places 'the lads', and those whom they encounter, at 'home', at the 'centre' of a 'solidly' modern discourse. In this centre myth Weston lads are lads, Miggy men are cunts, women are for fucking and black people remain peripheral. And what 'the lads' mean by 'home' is 'that small and cosy plot inside which our moral impulse, and the moral impulses of all the others inside, are alert and lively, eager to tell us where the line between good and evil lies and warn us against trespassing' (Bauman in Bauman and Tester, 2001: 130). In the leisure life-world Mark II 'the lads' have the best of both worlds: they have their myth and are able to relativise it as a contingent leisure experience which has its own monologic. Indeed, the *modus operandi* of 'the lads'' leisure together always presumes this form of closure: the conformation of hegemonic masculinity and the restoration of disrupted stability, which provide intimations of a past world of communal bliss in a protected time–space in which the leisure life-world attempts to impose the fixity of a masculinist, working-class myth on to the fluidity of everyday life. However, it was also seen, particularly in Chapter 7, that another basic axis of the postulated community is provided by the material reality of the 'outside' world that surrounds it. Indeed, the majority of holidaymakers at Rose Dale *are* white and working-class, the club house *is* decorated *circa* a mid-1970s theme, the open-top double-decker buses run as a viable commercial concern, the local radio station plays only retro music. On the level of experience, it is that between two different realities – one involving the material world as it is experienced with 'real' human relationships, the other, as we saw, tending to exclude them – by which the leisure life-world can be achieved.

The leisure life-world is then a fantasy, a construct of 'the lads'' collective consciousness. It has no bricks and mortar – it is on one level purely discursive. The events which constitute this leisure life are the myths 'the lads' leisure by, but they are distortions and elaborations of things that for sure have happened in one way or another; the 'liquid' survivors of some 'solid' bygone moments in time. In the leisure life-world these myths are always here and now, with everything that implies. You can look at them, see them in each of 'the lads'' faces, in their actions, in the ways in which they are with each other, and most particularly with others. They cannot be denied, and therefore they suggest a reality – as well as fantasy. The leisure life-world, then, suggests that the imagination is neither irreal nor hyperreal but rather it *is* 'the lads'' deeper reality.

If 'the lads' do not share the *natural* unity of a community, where their sense of 'belonging comes about as if of itself, like other "facts of nature"' (Bauman, 1990: 72), they do have a longing, which manifests itself as a desire to be supported and made to feel secure. It is in their leisure that they can enjoy this sense of a 'special' and 'superior' belonging, without having to commit themselves to a community in the orthodox sociological sense. The main conclusion to be drawn from this study is therefore that the postulated community of the leisure life-world of 'the lads', whether it is at 'home' in Weston or at its second 'home' in Rose Dale, offers its incumbents something rather bizarre: an image of a 'solid' working-class modernity that is alive and yet lifeless, there and not there, real but illusory. A leisure life always ten, fifteen, twenty years ago but always now. A phenomenon Jacques Derrida would describe as an 'undecidable' zombie category of social life.

I have enjoyed writing this book to reconstruct the changes that have transported me from the carefree ludic universe of my youth to the careful sobriety of the academy, with all my paper qualifications intact. It concludes hereafter with both an end and a new beginning: the death of a 'lad' and the birth of a new self. The narrative itself concludes with many contentious issues and much to discuss – no ending, but a starting point for further discussion and more research.

Epilogue: implosion

[We] shall implode, as if this centripetal plunge might save [us] from doubt and error, from the time of ephemeral change, from the slippery descent before and after, bring [us] to a time of stability, still and smooth, enable [us] to achieve the one condition that is homogeneous and compact and definitive. You explode, if that's more to your taste, shoot yourselves all around in endless darts, be prodigal, spendthrift, reckless: [We] shall implode, collapse inside the abyss of [ourselves], towards [our] buried centre, infinitely.

(Italo Calvino)

It was 23 December. End of the year, end of the week, end of the evening. 'The lads' were walking through the newly refurbished Leeds City Station at the end of a night of consummate exuberance. The concourse was teeming with people. Outside, adjacent to the taxi rank, most were either pissed, necking somebody, singing or fighting – or all of these – or begging, or catatonic with fear, wishing that they were somewhere else. Six men moved towards the end of the taxi queue. It was 4.00 a.m. on Sunday morning, and these men had spent the last eight hours being younger versions of themselves.

Some of them had known each other for thirty years. They had all suffered adolescence together. They had gone on many adventures together: drinking, gambling, singing, fucking and fighting. Time and again in the Farmer's Arms they had vowed never, ever, to lose touch with one another. And, though there were at times long lapses, they never had. The eldest would be thirty-eight in two weeks' time. But if you stepped back and didn't look too closely, you could easily mistake these for younger men. They had appearances younger than they usually wore, and their faces seemed to belong somewhere else. Another time. Another place.

As they neared the front of the taxi rank each of them knew that very soon the leisure life-world would begin to recede into unreality – it would lose its climacteric edge of immediacy and it would become merely a series of dim stories in the head, almost as if it were a fiction, a disturbing performance of the imagination. Indeed, the next hour would take them back to the present, to an age of purgatory borne of uncertainty and ambivalence, veritably an unrelenting spinning wheel. But last night they broke off from that wheel, so they were not sad. And with their long-standing attachment to each other, they each knew that they would have to wait only a short while for that call, that infinite pang of nostalgia, to 'restore paradise' in their leisure lives once again.

This is the last of the leisure life-world and the end of the book.

Notes

1 This occurs, most notably, in my use of poststructuralism, which smacks too much of Anglo-Saxon thinking.
2 I recognise that sociology is a 'solidly' modernist discipline.

Bibliography

Abrams, P. (1982) *Historical Sociology*. Shepton Mallet: Open Books.
Anderson, B. (1991) *Imagined Communities: Reflections on the Origin and Spread of Nationalism*, 2nd edn. London: Verso.
Bakhtin, M. (1981) 'Discourse in the Novel' in Holquist, M. (ed.) *The Dialogic Imagination*. Austin TX: University of Texas Press.
Bakhtin, M. (1984) *Rabelais and his World*. Bloomington IN: University of Indiana Press.
Baudrillard, J. (1975) *The Mirror of Production*. St Louis MO: Telos Press.
Baudrillard, J. (1981) *For a Critique of the Political Economy of the Sign*. St Louis MO:Telos Press.
Baudrillard, J. (1983) *Simulations*. New York: Semiotext(e).
Baudrillard, J. (1988) in Poster, M. *Selected Writings*. Stanford CA: Stanford University Press.
Baudrillard, J. (1989a) *America*. London: Verso.
Baudrillard, J. (1989b) 'The Anorexic Ruins' in Kampar, D. and Wulf, C. (eds) *Looking Back on the End of the World*. New York: Semiotext(e).
Baudrillard, J. (1990) *Fatal Strategies*. New York: Semiotext(e).
Baudrillard, J. (1993) *Symbolic Exchange and Death*. London: Sage.
Baudrillard, J. (1998) 'The End of the Millennium, or, The Count Down', *Theory, Culture and Society* 15 (1) 1–9.
Bauman, Z. (1987) *Legislators and Interpreters: On Modernity, Postmodernity and Intellectuals*. Cambridge: Polity Press.
Bauman, Z. (1990) *Thinking Sociologically*. Oxford: Blackwell.
Bauman, Z. (1991) *Modernity and Ambivalence*. Cambridge: Polity Press.
Bauman, Z. (1992a) *Intimations of Postmodernity*. London: Routledge.
Bauman, Z. (1992b) 'The Telos Interview' in Beilharz, P. (ed.) (2001) *The Bauman Reader*. London: Blackwell.
Bauman, Z. (1994) 'Desert Spectacular' in Tester, K. (ed.) *The Flâneur*. London: Routledge.
Bauman, Z. (1995) *Life in Fragments: Essays in Postmodern Morality*. Oxford: Blackwell.
Bauman, Z. (1997) *Postmodernity and its Discontents*. Cambridge: Polity Press in association with Blackwell.
Bauman, Z. (1998) *Globalization: The Human Consequences*. Cambridge: Polity Press in association with Blackwell.

Bauman, Z. (1999) *In Search of Politics*. Cambridge: Polity Press.
Bauman, Z. (2000a) *Liquid Modernity*. Cambridge: Polity Press.
Bauman, Z. (2000b) 'The Duty to Remember – But What? Afterword to the 2000 Edition' in Bauman, Z. (1989) *Modernity and the Holocaust*. Cambridge: Polity Press.
Bauman, Z. (2001a) *The Individualized Society*. Cambridge: Polity Press in association with Blackwell.
Bauman, Z. (2001b) *Community: Seeking Safety in an Insecure World*. Cambridge: Polity Press.
Bauman, Z. (2002) 'Violence: Old and New'. Seminar at the University of Leeds, 7 February.
Bauman, Z. and Tester, K. (2001) *Conversations with Zygmunt Bauman*. Cambridge: Polity Press.
Bech, H. (1997) *When Men Meet: Homosexuality and Modernity*. Cambridge: Polity Press.
Beck, U. (1992) *Risk Society: Towards a New Modernity*. London: Sage.
Beck, U. (1994) 'The Re-invention of Politics: towards a Theory of Reflexive Modernization' in Beck, U., Giddens, A. and Lash, S. *Reflexive Modernization: Politics, Tradition and Aesthetics in the Modern Social Order*. Cambridge: Polity Press.
Beck, U. (1998) *Democracy without Enemies*. Cambridge: Polity Press.
Beck, U., Giddens, A. and Lash, S. (1994) *Reflexive Modernization: Politics, Tradition and Aesthetics in the Modern Social Order*. Cambridge: Polity Press.
Beilharz, P. (2000) *Zygmunt Bauman: Dialectic of Modernity*. London: Sage.
Bhabha, H. (1994) *Location of Culture*. London: Routledge.
Bourdieu, P. (1984) *Distinction: a Social Critique of the Judgement of Taste*. London: Routledge.
Butler, J. (1991) 'Contingent Foundations: Feminism and the Question of "Postmodernism"' in Butler, J. and Scott, J. (eds) *Feminists Theorize the Political*. London: Routledge.
Castoriadis, C. (1987) *The Imaginary Institution of Society*. Cambridge: Polity Press.
Cixous, H. (1975) 'Sorties' in Marks, E. and de Courtivron, I. (eds) (1980) *New French Feminisms: an Anthology*. Amherst MA: University of Massachusetts Press.
Clifford, J. and Marcus, G. (eds) (1986) *Writing Culture: the Poetics and Politics of Ethnography*. Berkeley CA: University of California Press.
Cohen, A. (1985) *The Symbolic Construction of Community*. London: Tavistock.
Cohen, S. and Taylor, L. (1992) *Escape Attempts: the Theory and Practice of Resistance to Everyday Life*, 2nd edn. London: Routledge.
Connell, R. W. (1995) *Masculinities*. London: Polity Press.
Connell, R. W. et al. (1982) *Making the Difference: Schools, Families and Social Division*. Sydney: Allen & Unwin.
Connor, S. (1989) *Postmodernist Culture*. Oxford: Blackwell.
Cuff, E. C. and Payne, G. C. F. (eds) (1979) *Perspectives in Sociology*. London: Allen & Unwin.
Debord, G. (1995 1967) *The Society of the Spectacle*. New York: Zone Books.
Debord, G. and Wolman, G. J. (1956) 'Methods of détournement', *Les Lèvres nues* 8 (May).

Delanty, G. (2000) 'Postmodernism and the Possibility of Community' in *Modernity and Postmodernity*. London: Sage.

Deleuze, G. (1988) *Bergsonism*. New York: Zone Books.

Deleuze, G. and Guattari, F. (1983) *Anti-Oedipus: Capitalism and Schizophrenia*. Minneapolis MN: University of Minnesota Press.

Demetriou, D. Z. (2001) 'Connell's Concept of Hegemonic Masculinity: a Critique', *Theory and Society* 30 (3) 337–61.

Dennis, N., Henriques, F. and Slaughter, C. (1969) *Coal is our Life: an Analysis of a Yorkshire Mining Community*. London: Tavistock.

Denzin, N. K. (1989) *The Research Act*. London: McGraw-Hill.

Derrida, J. (1970) 'Structure, Sign and Play in the Discourse of the Human Sciences' in Macksey, R. and Donato, E. (eds) *The Structuralist Controversy*. Baltimore MD: Johns Hopkins University Press.

Derrida, J. (1973) *Speech and Phenomena, and other Essays on Husserl's Theory of Signs*. Evanston IL: Northwestern University Press.

Derrida, J. (1974a) *Of Grammatology*. Baltimore MD: Johns Hopkins University Press.

Derrida, J. (1974b) *Glas*. Lincoln NE: University of Nebraska Press.

Derrida, J. (1978) *Writing and Difference*. London: Routledge.

Derrida, J. (1990) 'Some Statements' in Carroll, D. (ed.) *The States of Theory*. Stanford CA: Stanford University Press.

Derrida, J. (1998) *Monolingualism of the Other, or, The Prosthesis of Origin*. Stanford CA: Stanford University Press.

Douglas, J. (1976) *Investigative Social Research: Individual and Team Field Research*. Beverley Hills CA: Sage.

Dreyfus, H. L. (1991) *Being-in-the-World: a Commentary on Heidegger's 'Being and Time', Division 1*. Cambridge MA: MIT Press.

Durkheim, E. (1933) *The Division of Labour in Society*. New York: Macmillan.

Durkheim, E. (1951) *Suicide: a Study in Sociology*. London: Routledge.

Elias, N. (1987) *Involvement and Detachment*. Oxford: Blackwell.

Erlandson, D. A., Harris, E. L., Skipper, B. L. and Allen, S. D. (1993) *Doing Naturalistic Inquiry: a Guide to Methods*. Newbury Park CA: Sage.

Featherstone, M. (1991) *Consumer Culture and Postmodernism*. London: Sage.

Featherstone, M. (1995) *Undoing Culture: Globalisation, Postmodernism and Identity*. London: Sage.

Foucault, M. (1972) *The Archaeology of Knowledge*. London: Tavistock.

Foucault, M. (1973) *The Order of Things: the Archaeology of the Human Sciences*. New York: Vintage.

Foucault, M. (1979) *Discipline and Punish: the Birth of the Prison*. Harmondsworth: Penguin.

Foucault, M. (1980a) 'Two Lectures' in Gordon, C. (ed.) *Michel Foucault: Power/Knowledge*. Hemel Hempstead: Harvester.

Foucault, M. (1980b) 'Truth and Power' in Gordon, C. (ed.) *Michel Foucault: Power/Knowledge*. Hemel Hempstead: Harvester.

Foucault, M. (1981) *The History of Sexuality* I *An Introduction*. Harmondsworth: Pelican.

Foucault, M. (1983) 'Preface' in Deleuze, G. and Guattari, F. *Anti-Oedipus: Capitalism and Schizophrenia*. Minneapolis MN: University of Minnesota Press.

Foucault, M. (1986) *The History of Sexuality* III *The Care of the Self*. New York: Pantheon.

Foucault, M. (1987) *The History of Sexuality* II *The Use of Pleasure*. London: Peregrine.

Foucault, M. (1988) 'Power and Sex' in Kritzman, L. D. (ed.) *Politics, Philosophy, Culture: Interviews and other Writings 1977–1984*. London: Routledge.

Foucault, M. (1998) 'Different Spaces' in Faubion, J. (ed.) *Michel Foucault: Aesthetics, Method and Epistemology*. London: Penguin.

Fulgham, R. (1995) *From Beginning to End*. New York: Ballantine Books.

Fullagar, S. (2002) 'Narratives of Travel', *Leisure Studies* 21 (1) 57–74.

Geertz, C. (1973) 'Thick Description: Towards an Interpretive Theory of Culture' in *The Interpretation of Cultures*. London: Hutchinson.

Geertz, C. (1995) *After the Fact*. Cambridge MA: Harvard University Press.

Genosko, G. (1994) *Baudrillard and Signs: Signification Ablaze*. London: Routledge.

Gergen, K. (1991) *The Saturated Self: Dilemmas of Identity in Contemporary Life*. New York: Basic Books.

Giddens, A. (1990) *The Consequences of Modernity*. Cambridge: Polity Press.

Giddens, A. (1991) *Modernity and Self-identity: Self and Society in the Late Modern Age*. Cambridge: Polity Press.

Giddens, A. (1992) *The Transformation of Intimacy: Sexuality, Love and Eroticism in Modern Societies*. Cambridge: Polity Press.

Gitlin, T. (1995) *The Twilight of Common Dreams*. New York: Metropolitan Books.

Glaser, B. and Strauss, A. (1968) *The Discovery of Grounded Theory*. London: Weidenfeld & Nicolson.

Goffman, E. (1969) *The Presentation of the Self in Everyday Life*. Harmondsworth: Penguin.

Guba, E. G. and Lincoln, Y. S. (1994) 'Competing Paradigms in Qualitative Research' in Denzin, N. K. and Lincoln, Y. S. (eds) *Handbook of Qualitative Research*. Thousand Oaks CA: Sage.

Gubrium, J. F. and Holstein, J. A. (1994) 'Grounding the Postmodern Self', *Sociological Quarterly* 35 (4) 685–703.

Habermas, J. (1976) *Legitimation Crisis*. London: Heinemann.

Habermas, J. (1979) *Communication and the Evolution of Society*. Boston MA: Beacon Press.

Habermas, J. (1981) 'Modernity versus Postmodernity', *New German Critique* 22 3–14.

Hall, S. (1992) 'The West and the Rest: Discourse and Power', in Hall, S. and Gieben, B. (eds) *Formations of Modernity*. Cambridge: Polity Press in association with Blackwell and the Open University.

Hammersley, M. and Atkinson, P. (1995) *Ethnography: Principles in Practice*, 2nd edn. London: Routledge.

Harland, R. (1987) *Superstructuralism: the Philosophy of Structuralism and Poststructuralism*. London: Routledge.

Hearn, J. (1996) 'Is Masculinity Dead? A Critique of the Concept of Masculinity/Masculinities' in Mac An Ghaill, M. (ed.) *Understanding Masculinities*. Buckingham: Open University Press.

Hebdidge, D. (1979) *Subculture: the Meaning of Style*. London: Methuen.

Heidegger, M. (1962) *Being and Time*. Oxford: Blackwell.

Heller, A. (1999) *A Theory of Modernity*. London: Blackwell.

Hobbs, D. (1988) *Doing the Business: Entrepreneurship, the Working Class, and Detectives in the East End of London*. Oxford: Oxford University Press.

Hoggart, R. (1957) *The Uses of Literacy*. London: Chatto & Windus.

Horrocks, R. (1994) *Masculinity in Crisis: Myths, Fantasies and Realities*. Basingstoke: Macmillan.

Horrocks, R. (1995) *Male Myths and Icons: Masculinity in Popular Culture*. Basingstoke: Macmillan.

Hughes, J. (1990) *The Philosophy of Social Research*. London: Longman.

Internationale Situationale I (1958) 'Definitions'. Paris: Central Bulletin of Situationalist International.

Irigaray, L. (1985a) 'Any Theory of the Subject has Already been Appropriateen ny the Masculine' in *Speculum of the Other Woman*. Ithaca: Cornell University Press.

Irigaray, L. (1985b) *This Sex Which is Not One*. Ithaca NY: Cornell University Press.

Jenkins, K. (1995) *'What is History?': From Carr and Elton to Rorty and White*. London: Routledge.

Jenks, C. (1993) *Culture*. London: Routledge.

Jenks, C. (1995) 'Watching your Step: the History and Practice of the Flâneur' in Jenks, C. (ed.) *Visual Culture*. London: Routledge.

Krell, D. F. (1989) 'On Jacques Derrida' in Urmson, J. O. and Rée, J. (eds) *The Concise Encyclopædia of Western Philosophy and Philosophers*, 2nd edn. London: Routledge.

Kristeva, J. (1986) *The Kristeva Reader* ed. Toril Moi. New York: Columbia University Press.

Lash, S. (1994) 'Reflexivity and its Doubles: Structure, Aesthetics, Community' in Beck, U., Giddens, A. and Lash, S. *Reflexive Modernization: Politics, Tradition and Aesthetics in the Modern Social Order*. Cambridge: Polity Press.

Layder, D. (1986) 'Social Reality as Figuration: a Critique of Elias's Conception of Sociological Analysis', *Sociology* 20 (3) 367–86.

Layder, D. (1994) *Understanding Social Theory*. London: Sage.

Lewin, K. (1949) *Field Theory and Social Science*. London: Tavistock.

Lincoln, Y. S. and Guba, E. G. (1985) *Naturalistic Inquiry*. Beverley Hills CA: Sage.

Lyotard, J-F. (1979) *The Postmodern Condition: a Report on Knowledge*. Minneapolis MN: University of Minesota Press.

Lyotard, J-F. (1988) *Peregrinations: Law, Form, Event*. New York: Columbia University Press.

Mac An Ghaill, M. (ed.) (1996) *Understanding Masculinities*. Buckingham: Open University Press.

MacCannell, D. (1992) *Empty Meeting Grounds: the Tourist Papers*. London: Routledge.

Maffesoli, M. (1996) *The Time of the Tribes: the Decline of Individualism in a Mass Society*. London: Sage.

Marcuse, H. (1970) *Eros and Civilisation*. London: Allen Lane.

Marcuse, H. (1972) *One Dimensional Man*. London: Allen Lane.

McRobbie, A. (1994) *Postmodernism and Popular Culture*. London: Routledge.

Merton, R. (1973) *The Sociology of Science: Theoretical and Empirical Investigations*. Chicago: University of Chicago Press.

Mestrovic, S. (1998) *Anthony Giddens: the Last Modernist*. London: Routledge.

Mills, C. W. (1959) *The Sociological Imagination*. Harmondsworth: Penguin.

Moore, D. (1994) *The Lads in Action: Social Processes in an Urban Youth Subculture*. Aldershot: Arena.

Moore, T. (1996) *The Re-enchantment of Everyday Life*. London: Hodder & Stoughton.

Mullarkey, J. (1999) *Bergson and Philosophy*. Edinburgh: Edinburgh University Press.

Natoli, J. (1997) *A Primer to Postmodernity*. Oxford: Blackwell.

Parsons, T. (1951) *The Social System*. Glencoe IL: Free Press.

Pike, K. (1967) *Language in Relation to a Unified Theory of the Structure of Human Behaviour*, pt 1, Preliminary Edition, Glendale Summer Institute of Linguistics.

Poster, M. (1994) 'Critical Theory and Technoculture: Habermas and Baudrillard' in Kellner, D. (ed.) *Baudrillard: a Critical Reader*. Oxford: Blackwell.

Rée, J. (1998) *Heidegger: History and Truth in Being and Time*. London: Phoenix.

Ricoeur, P. (1991) *From Text to Action: Essays in Hermeneutics* II. Evanston IL: Northwestern University Press.

Ricoeur, P. (1992) *Oneself as Another*. Chicago: University of Chicago Press.

Rinehart, R. (1998) 'Fictional Methods in Ethnography: Believability, Specks of Glass and Chekhov', *Qualitative Inquiry* 4 (2) 200–24.

Ritzer, G. (1997) *Postmodern Social Theory*. London: McGraw-Hill.

Roberts, K. (1999) *Leisure in Contemporary Society*. Wallingford: CABI.

Rojek, C. (1985) *Capitalism and Leisure Theory*. London: Tavistock.

Rojek, C. (1986) 'The Problems of Involvement and Detachment in the Writings of Norbert Elias', *British Journal of Sociology* 37 (4) 584–96.

Rojek, C. (1992) 'The Field of Play in Sport and Leisure Studies' in Dunning, E. and Rojek, C. (eds) *Sport and Leisure in the Civilizing Process: Critique and Counter-critique*. London: Macmillan.

Rojek, C. (1995) *Decentring Leisure: Rethinking Leisure Theory*. London: Sage.

Rojek, C. (2000) *Leisure and Culture*. Basingstoke: Macmillan.

Rojek, C. and Turner, B. S. (2000) 'Decorative Sociology: Towards a Critique of the Cultural Turn', *Sociological Review* 48 (4) 629–48.

Rorty, R. (1979) *Philosophy and the Mirror of Nature*. Princeton NJ: Princeton University Press.

Rorty, R. (1982) *Consequences of Pragmatism*. Minneapolis MN: University of Minnesota Press.

Rorty, R. (1985a) 'Solidarity or Objectivity' in Rajchman, J. and West, C. (eds) *Post-analytic Philosophy*. New York: Columbia University Press.

Rorty, R. (1985b) 'Habermas and Lyotard on Postmodernity' in Bernstein, R. J. (ed.) *Habermas and Modernity*. Cambridge MA: MIT Press.

Rorty, R. (1986) 'The Contingency of Community', *London Review of Books*, 24 July.

Rorty, R. (1989) *Contingency, Irony and Solidarity*, Cambridge: Cambridge University Press.

Rorty, R. (1991a) *Philosophical Papers* II *Objectivity, Relativism and Truth*. Cambridge: Cambridge University Press.

Rorty, R. (1991b) *Philosophical Papers* II *Essays on Heidegger and Others*. Cambridge: Cambridge University Press.

Rorty, R. (1993) 'Feminism, Ideology, and Deconstruction: a Pragmatist View', *Hypatia* 8 (2) spring (special issue: Feminism and Pragmatism).

Rorty, R. (1998) 'Against Unity', *Wilson Quarterly*, winter edition.

Ryan, L. (1996) 'The Trouble with Men', *Marxist Review of Books*: *Living Marxism* 90 43–6.

Sacks, H. (1974) 'On the Analysability of Stories in Children' in Turner, R. (ed.) *Ethnomethodology*. Harmondsworth: Penguin.

Scatzman, L. and Strauss, A. (1973) *Field Research: Strategies for a Natural Sociology*. Englewood Cliffs NJ: Prentice-Hall.

Scheff, T. J. (1997) 'Unpacking the Civilizing Process: Shame and Integration in Elias's Work' at http://shop.usyd.ed.au/su/social/elias/confpap/scheff2.htm 17 February 2000.

Schwandt, T. A. (1994) 'Constructivist, Interpretivist Approaches to Human Inquiry' in Denzin, N. K. and Lincoln, Y. S. (eds) *Handbook of Qualitative Research*. Thousand Oaks CA: Sage.

Schutz, A. and Luckman, T. (1973) *Structures of the Life World*. Evanston IL: Northwestern University Press.

Seabrook, J. (1982) *Working Class Childhood: an Oral History*. Southampton: Camelot Press.

Seidler, V. J. (1994) *Unreasonable Men: Masculinity and Social Theory*. London: Routledge.

Shields, R. (1991) *Places on the Margin*. London: Routledge.

Shields, R. (ed.) (1992) *Lifestyle Shopping*. London: Routledge.

Shields, R. (1996) 'Foreword: Masses or Tribes?' in Maffesoli, M. (ed.) *The Time of the Tribes*: *the Decline of Individualism in a Mass Society*. London: Sage.

Smith, D. (1999) *Zygmunt Bauman: Prophet of Postmodernity*. Cambridge: Polity Press.

Spivak, G. (1974) 'Preface' in Derrida, J. *Of Grammatology*. Baltimore MD: Johns Hopkins University Press.

Stallybrass, P. and White, A. (1986) *The Politics and Poetics of Transgression*. London: Methuen.

Sugden, J. and Tomlinson, A. (1999) 'Digging the Dirt and Staying Clean: Retrieving the Investigative Tradition for a Critical Sociology of Sport', *International Review for the Sociology of Sport* 34 (4) 385–97.

Tawney, R. H. (1958) 'Foreword' in Weber, M. (1930) *The Protestant Ethic and the Spirit of Capitalism*. New York: Scribner.

Thomas, J. (1992) *On Doing Critical Ethnography*. Newbury Park CA: Sage.

Thompson, G. (1981) 'Holidays' in *Popular Culture and Everyday Life*. Milton Keynes: Open University Press.

Tönnies, F. (1955 *1887*) *Gemeinschaft und Gesellschaft*, trans. as *Community and Society*. London: Routledge.

Turner, V. W. (1967) *The Forest of Symbols: Aspects of Ndembu Ritual*. Ithaca NY: Cornell University Press.

Turner, V. W. (1973) 'The Center Out There: Pilgrim's Goal', *History of Religions* 12 (3) 191–230.

Turner, V. W. (1974) *Drama, Fields and Metaphors: Symbolic Action in Human Society*. Ithaca NY: Cornell University Press.

Turner, V. and Turner, E. (1978) *Image and Pilgrimage in Christian Culture: Anthropological Perspectives*. London: Blackwell.

Weber, M. (1930) *The Protestant Ethic and the Spirit of Capitalism*. London: Unwin Hyman.

Weedon, C. (1987) *Feminist Practice and Poststructuralist Theory*. Oxford: Blackwell.

Whannel, G. (1998) 'Reading the Sports Media Discourse' in Wenner, L. A. (ed.) *Mediasport*. London: Routledge.

White, H. (1978) *Tropics of Discourse*. Baltimore MD: Johns Hopkins University Press.

Whyte, W. F. (1943) *Street Corner Society: the Social Structure of an Italian Slum*. Chicago: University of Chicago Press.

Williams, R. (1970) *The English Novel*. Harmondsworth: Penguin.

Williams, R. (1976) *Keywords*. London: Fontana.

Willis, P. (1977) *Learning to Labour: How Working Class Kids get Working Class Jobs*. Farnborough: Saxon House.

Wittgenstein, L. (1968) *Philosophical Investigations*. London: Blackwell.

Woodward, K. (1997) 'Concepts of Identity and Difference' in Woodward, K. (ed.) *Identity and Difference*. London: Sage in association with the Open University.

Žižek, S. (2002) 'Are we in a War? Do we Have an Enemy?, *London Review of Books* 24 (10) 3–6.

Index